ISLAMIC BANKING AND FINANCE: A GLOBAL STATE OF ART

Edited By

ABDULLAH MOHAMMED AYEDH
ABDELGHANI ECHCHABI

About the Editors

Abdelghani Echchabi is currently an Assistant Professor of Finance at the College of Business, Effat University, Jeddah, Saudi Arabia. He is holding a PhD in Business Administration (Finance) from the International Islamic University Malaysia. He is also an ex-banker, having worked for Banque Marocaine du Commerce Extérieur (BMCE) in Morocco. His areas of interest include a wide range of banking and finance aspects.

Abdullah Mohammed Ayedh is a lecturer at the Faculty of Economics and Muamalat, Universiti Sains Islam Malaysia (USIM). His areas of specialization are auditing and corporate governance Islamic Banking and accounting (shari'ah audit and waqf). His teaching and research have been focused on accounting and Islamic banking. He participated in several International conferences in accounting and Islamic banking. He is also actively conducting research in the area of waqf and Islamic banking.

About the Contributors

Abu Umar Faruq is a Senior Researcher at the International Sharī'ah Research Academy for Islamic Finance (ISRA), and an Associate Professor of Islamic Finance at INCEIF, the Global University of Islamic Finance;, Kuala Lumpur, Malaysia. He also chairs the Sharī'ah Supervisory Board of Islamic Cooperative Finance Australia Ltd. (ICFAL). Drawing from his unique expertise in both the theory and practice of Islamic banking and finance, Dr. Faruq has published 4 books and monographs, 3 chapters in books, 25 peer reviewed refereed journal articles, and 6 conference proceedings on different areas of the subject of his specialisation. He is a regular speaker at international conferences held in Asia, Europe, Australia, America and Africa. He has a particular interest in Sukuk, Takaful and Retakaful, banking regulations, Sharī'ah compliance as well as case studies of Islamic banks and financial services providers from legal and regulatory perspectives and promoting Sharī'ah-compliant products in global financial market. Dr. Faruq has championed Islamic finance in Australia. His research on the subject is the first landmark contribution to Australian Islamic finance in terms of its regulation and the Sharī'ah compliance of its current practice. He is the Founding Editor of *International Journal of Excellence in Islamic Banking and Finance* (UAE), Co-editor *of ISRA International Journal of Islamic Finance* (Malaysia), Senior Editor of *Australian Journal of Basic and Applied Sciences* (Jordan), and a Member of the International Editorial Board of 3 UK based Emerald published journals namely the *International Journal of Islamic and Middle Eastern Finance and Management, Humanomics: The International Journal of Systems and Ethics,* and *Journal of Islamic Accounting and Business Research*

Abul Kalam Muhammed Shahed is an Associate Professor of Islamic Studies at the International Islamic University Chittagong (IIUC). He obtained his Ph.D. (2001) in Islamic Theology and Philosophy at the Department of Islamic Studies, Universiti Kebansaan Malaysia (UKM). He also earned his MA in Islamic Revealed Knowledge and Heritage from the International Islamic University Malaysia (IIUM) in 1997. He earned both his BA (Honors) and MA in Arabic Language and Literature from the University of Chittagong (CU), Bangladesh in 1981. Dr. Shahed initiated his academic career 1997 as an adjunct faculty in the Department of Qur'an and *Sunnah* Studies, International Islamic University Malaysia and continued till 1998. He joined as Lecturer at Manarat International University (MIU), Dhaka and served there for about 5 years (2001-2005). Dr. Shahed has participated in many international seminars and symposiums and presented a number of papers on various topics on his field of specialization at these academic forums. He has published over 10 articles in numerous peer reviewed refereed journals.

Adel Mohammed Sarea received his PhD from Islamic Science University of Malaysia in 2011. Dr Adel joined Ahlia University in January, 2012 as Assistant Professor, Accounting and Economics Department, College of Business and Finance. He Conducted research in the area of Accounting for Islamic Financial Institutions and published in the journals of repute. He is appointed as a recognized supervisor by Brunel University (UK). He also serves as a member of the editorial boards in a number of international journals. Currently he is the Director of Ahlia MBA program.

Ahmad Bello Dogarawa is a Senior Lecturer (Assistant Professor) at the Department of Accounting, Ahmadu Bello University, Zaria, Nigeria. He received his B.Sc. in Business Administration from Ahmadu Bello University, Zaria; Master of Banking and Finance (MBF) from Bayero University, Kano, Nigeria; and M.Sc. Accounting and Finance; and Ph.D. Accounting and Finance from Ahmadu Bello University, Zaria, Nigeria. In addition, he obtained Professional Diploma in Education (PDE) from Institute of Education, Ahmadu Bello University, Zaria, and belong to several professional bodies. His area of interest is banking, entrepreneurship, human resource management and Islamic finance. Dr. Dogarawa has travelled throughout Nigeria and some neighbouring countries to present papers and give sensitisation lectures on various topical issues particularly Islamic banking and finance, and Islamic perspective of economic empowerment, investment and poverty eradication. He is the Assistant Coordinator of the Institute of Administration's Certificate course in Islamic Banking and Finance; Coordinator of IRTI-ABU Distance Learning Programme on Islamic Banking and Finance; and Training Director of the Green Oasis's Islamic Banking and Finance programmes. He is also a resource person to Islamic Banking and Finance Institute, Nigeria (IBFIN), and a Visiting Senior Lecturer at the postgraduate programme of the International Institute of Islamic Banking and Finance (IIIBF), Bayero University, Kano. He has published in refereed academic journals (local and international) and has presented many papers at local and international conferences. He is currently the Head, Department of Accounting; Chairman of Institute of Administration's Standing Committee on Diploma student's O' Level result Verification; Chairman of Faculty of Administration's Alumni Contact Committee; Senate Representative on Budget Estimates Committee; and Member, ABU Teaching Hospital Health Research Ethics Committee.

Allam Hamdan joined Ahlia University in 2009 as Assistant Professor, Accounting and Economics Department, College of Business and Finance. He Conducted research in the area of Accounting and published in the journals of repute. Currently he is the Head of accounting department and economics.

Ameen Al-Nahari is a senior lecturer at the Department of Fiqh and Usul, Academy of Islamic Studies, University of Malaya. He has written and published numerous research articles in international journals in both Arabic and English language. He has also presented papers in international conferences and seminar in both Arabic and English. Dr. Ameen has also supervised numerous research students at both graduate and undergraduate levels. His areas of interest are centred on Fiqh and Usul Fiqh.

Ashurov Sharofiddin is a PhD Candidate specialising in Islamic banking and Finance. His main areas of interest include *sukuk* valuation, *takaful* and *waqf* oeprations.

Bilal Ahmad Malik is a research scholar at the Centre of Central Asian Studies. He holds an M.A in Islamic studies from the Islamic University of Science and Technology. His main area of study is Islamic banking and finance in the Post-Soviet Central Asia.

Chaabane Oussama Houssem Eddine is a PhD candidate in accounting at the Faculty of Economics and Management Sciences, International Islamic University Malaysia. His areas on interest include earnings management, Islamic endowment, and Islamic banking operations.

Dhekra Azouzi is a PhD candidate in Finance at the Faculty of Management Sciences and Economics, El-Manar University Tunisia. She has recently completed her PhD thesis focused on the forward premium puzzle in emerging countries. Her areas of interest include a wide range of

Fatiha Echchabi is an independent researcher mostly active in research related to the regulatory and legal aspects of the Islamic banking industry. She has been greatly involved in international projects intended to solve legal and regulatory issues in the Islamic Finance industry.

Fayaz Ahmad Lone is a well-known scholar in the field of Islamic Finance. He is working as Assistant professor in College of Business Administration in Salman Bin Abdulaziz University, Al-Kharj Saudi Arabia. Before joining this university, he was teaching at Post Graduate Department of Commerce and Management Studies at Government Degree College Bemina, Srinagar. Dr Fayaz has completed Bachelors' degree in Business Administration and Master's Degree in Commerce from University of Kashmir (India). He has completed PhD from Aligarh Muslim University (India) on the topic "Islamic Finance: An Analysis of Compatibility of its Objectives and Achievements". His PhD thesis was sponsored by Indian Council of Social Science Research, New Delhi and he has visited Malaysia and United Arab Emirates for data collection for his PhD work. World Database for Islamic Banking and Finance is his personal website related to Islamic Finance. Dr Fayaz Ahmad has published more than a dozen research papers on Islamic finance in International and National Journals and has presented many papers in international conferences.

G.N. Khaki is the director of the Centre of Central Asian Studies, University of Kashmir. He holds a PhD and M. Phil in Islamic studies. He has published over 30 papers in international refereed journals and presented over 40 papers in international conferences and seminars.

Habibullah Khan is a Professor of Economics and Academic Registrar at GlobalNxt University, Malaysia. He has a distinguished academic career, having taught at the National University of Singapore (NUS) during 1982-2004 and U21Global, Singapore during 2004-2012. His research areas include development economics, the economies of ASEAN and NIEs, economics of tourism, and Islamic economics. He has consulted widely with international organisations such as the World Bank, UN-ESCAP, UNCRD, and the ASEAN Secretariat. Prof Khan has published widely, including a book on *Socioeconomic Development of ASEAN*, and three other books that he co-authored. He has also contributed chapters to a number of books and his articles appeared in international refereed journals such as *Social and Economic studies*, *Social Indicators Research*, *Singapore Economic Review, Journal of Travel Research,* and *Journal of Islamic Banking & Finance*. He has written more than 50 journal articles and presented numerous international conferences and is widely recognised as an authority on Singapore and ASEAN economies. He holds a PhD in Economics from the University of New South Wales, Australia and is a Singapore citizen.

Hassanuddeen Abd. Aziz is a Finance/Islamic Finance Professor at the Faculty of Economics and Management Sciences, International Islamic University Malaysia. He is currently holding an Islamic Finance Scientific Chair at Effat University, Jeddah, Saudi Arabia. He has authored many articles and books on both conventional and Islamic Banking. His areas of interest include behavioral finance, Islamic finance and international finance.

Mamunur Rashid holds a PhD in Behavioural Finance, and currently is Assistant Professor of Finance and Deputy Director, Centre for Islamic Business and Finance Research, at the University of Nottingham Malaysia Campus.He has been teaching international finance,

Islamic finance and corporate finance for last ten years in different countries. An active researcher, hepublishes widely in Islamic economics, investor behaviour and corporate social responsibility, and has presented papers at the Harvard University Islamic Finance Forum, IslamicDevelopment Bank conference in India, Asian Finance Association in Macao, British Academy of Management in London and Malaysian Finance Association in Malaysia, among others.

Mohamed Sharif Bashir is an associate professor of Economic and Islamic Finance at Al-Imam Muhammad Ibn Saud Islamic University, Kingdom of Saudi Arabia. His research and writings cover a variety of topics ranging from international trade, development economics, macroeconomics and Islamic economics and finance. He has published numerous articles and technical reports in several renowned journals, government documents.

Mosab I. Tabash is Assistant Professor of Finance in the Faculty of Management Studies (FMS), University of Delhi. He is B. tech, MBA, and PH. D in Management. He specialized in the field of Islamic banking and finance. He has participated in several national and international Conferences/ seminars and also having several publications in many referred national and international journals. His research interests include Islamic banking and finance, monetary policies and risk management.

Mustafa Mohd Hanefah is Professor of Accounting and Taxation, Faculty of Economics and Muamalat, Universiti Sains Islam Malaysia. He is currently the Dean for Research and Innovation, USIM, and was the former Dean of the Faculty of Economics and Muamalat. Mustafa was a visiting professor at Economic Research Centre, Nagoya University, Japan from April 15, 2011 to June 15, 2011. He has published many papers in international journals in the areas of Islamic financial reporting and accounting, taxation, zakat and awqaf. He also serves as a member of the editorial boards in a number of international journals.

Neila Boulila Taktak is a Professor of Accounting at ISG, University of Gabes, Tunisia. She is an Interdisciplinary Finance Researcher whose initial contributions to the finance literature were in the corporate governance, accounting manipulations, financial stability and Islamic finance fields. She is the author of several scientific publications dealing with the Tunisian and international context. She is a member of the editorial team for Journal of Islamic Accounting and Business Research.

Nor Hafiizah Haji Mail is Holder of Bachelor of Science in Islamic Finance for Sultan Sharif Ali Islamic University, Brunei Darussalam in 2011 and holder of Master of Art in Islamic Finance from University of Brunei Darussalam in 2013. Currently working as Finance Officer in Ministry of Finance, Brunei Darussalam.

Omar K M R Bashar is a Lecturer in Accounting and Finance in Swinburne Business School, Swinburne University of Technology, Australia. His research interests include open economy macroeconomics, economic growth and development, international finance, and Islamic finance. Omar published peer-reviewed articles in the *Journal of Developing Areas, Studies in Economics and Finance, Journal of Islamic Banking and Finance, The Bangladesh Development Studies, Malaysian Journal of Economic Studies, International Journal of Trade and Global Markets, Bank Parikkrama, and The AIUB Journal of Business and Economics.*

Osman Sayid Hassan Musse is a PhD candidate in Islamic Finance, at the Faculty of Economics and Mualamalat, Islamic Science University of Malaysia. His areas of interest include a wide range of themes: Islamic Banking and Finance, International Finance, Monetary Economics and Finance, etc.

Paolo Pietro Biancone, ITP at London Business School, is professor of Islamic Finance at the University of Turin and Director of the Center for Research on Islamic Finance in the same

University. His main field of research, teaching and writing concerns Islamic Finance and Financial Institutions. Moreover, he practices these disciplines by supporting companies as a public certified accountant and as an independent auditor. He is the Director of the PhD Degree Program in Business & Management in Department of Management of University of Turin. Also, he is the Editor in Chief of the European Journal of Islamic Finance (EJIF) that is published by the University of Turin and sponsored by the Center for Research on Islamic Finance with the aim of providing scientific researches and studies that provides prospective solutions for all related arising issues and challenges in the Islamic finance field.

Raj S. Dhankar, is the Dean and Professor of Finance in the Faculty of Management Studies, University of Delhi. He has held several responsible administrative positions in the past, including the Vice Chancellor of Maharshi Dayanand University, Rohtak, Chairman, Finance Area, Faculty of Management Studies and Professor-in-Charge, SP Jain Centre of Advanced Management Research, University of Delhi, South Campus. Prof. Dhankar, a recipient of commonwealth scholarship and post doc scholarship to his credit, has published widely in area of finance in leading national and international journals. He did post-doctoral work at Anderson School, UCLA, USA, and has taught at several universities abroad. With a Ph. D. and PDS in Finance, he is actively involved in teaching, research, training, and consultancy since 1977.

Renat Bekkin (b. 1979). D.Sc. in Economics, Ph.D. in Law. One of the leading Russian experts in Islamic law, Islamic economy and finance. The pioneer of studying Islamic economy in Russia. The author of monographs: 'Insurance in Islamic Law: Theory and Practice' (2001), 'Islamic Economy: Short course' (2008), 'Islamic Economic Model Nowadays' (2009 – 1st edition, 2010 – 2nd edition), 'Islamic Insurance (*Takaful*)' (2012 – 1st edition, 2014 – 2nd edition) and more than 100 articles on Islamic economy, finance and Islamic law. In 2012 he provided Islamic insurance products for "Evro-Polis" insurance company firstly launched *takaful* at the Russian market. Permanent member of Shariah board at Mutual insurance society "Takaful" (Kazakhstan) – since 2010; Shariah advisor at "Evro-Polis" insurance company (2012–2013). The head of Oriental and Islamic studies department at the Kazan Federal University (Kazan, Russia); Senior research fellow at the Institute for African studies, Russian Academy of Sciences (Moscow, Russia).

S. M. Imamul Haque is working as professor in the Department of Commerce, Aligarh Muslim University, Aligarh. His academic career has been meritorious. He is M. Com (Gold Medalist) from Aligarh Muslim University. He also holds M.Phil. & Ph.D. degrees in Commerce from the same University. His academic areas of interest are Human Resource Management, Information Technology applied to Business and Finance. He is a prolific writer and has published more than fifty research papers in the leading journals, namely Indian Journal of Commerce, Indian Management, Management Insight, Yojana, Parbandh, BJIMR, Treasury Management, Johar etc. Prof. Haque has also authored and published books in the areas of Railway Management and Computer Application in Business. His recent book published on Dynamics of Management. He has so far successfully produced 10 Ph.Ds. Currently a number of researchers are engaged and pursuing research work under his exclusive guidance and supervision in the areas of HRM, Finance and Marketing. He has teaching and research experience of over twenty-four years.

Sarra Ben Slama Zouari is an Associate Professor of finance at the Higher Institute of Management and High Institute of Accounting and Business Administration (ISCAE), Tunis. She conducts research on financial systems stability, the informational efficiency of financial markets and Islamic finance. Her research has been published in journals such as Journal of Islamic Accounting and Business Research, International Journal of Business and Finance Research and International Journal of Islamic and Middle Eastern Finance and Management. She is also reviewer in International Journal of Islamic and Middle Eastern Finance and Management and the Journal of Islamic Accounting and Business Research.

Preface

Islamic finance has gone a long way from it start, back in the early sixties where Dr. Ahmad El-Naggar made many attempts to establish Islamic finance and implement it in Egypt and several other countries. Today, Islamic finance is being implemented in more than 70 countries at different levels and scales.

As the implementation of Islamic finance is being across countries with different religious and cultural backgrounds, there were slightly different models of Islamic finance implemented as well. This has resulted in a positive diversity of Islamic finance instruments, but has also caused contradicting reactions and controversies regarding a number of Islamic banking instruments. For instance, *Bay' Al 'inah* is commonly applied in Malaysia and other South East Asian countries, while it is undesired in the Middle East and in North Africa, and the same thing applies to *Bay' Bithaman Ajil*. This diversity was also influenced by the geo-political particularities of each of the countries where it was implemented.

This edited book is an attempt to have some exposure on the status of Islamic finance practices across a number of countries. Initially, more than sixty countries were planned to be included in the book. Nevertheless, due to scarcity of researches and resources, the number of cases and chapters was limited to nineteen. Nevertheless, the totality of the chapters still covers most of the world's regions i.e. the Middle East, South East Asia, South Asia, Central Asia, Europe and Africa.

Editor's note

Islamic finance in its wide scope has been currently introduced in more than 70 countries. Nevertheless, until today, little is known and documented abut Islamic finance in many settings. This book is a first attempt to uncover the status of Islamic finance in various countries. The Chapters in this book have been carefully selected and merged to provide the reader with a comprehensive view on the practices of Islamic finance across jurisdictions. The book covers most of the regions, reflecting the diversity of Islamic finance and its numerous instruments. This book has six parts. three chapters are in the first part related to Islamic Banking and Finance in Middle East, two chapters in second part related to Islamic Banking and Finance in South East Asia, two chapters in third part related to Islamic Banking and Finance in South Asia, two chapters in fourth part related to Islamic Banking and Finance in Central Asia, three chapters in fifth part related to Islamic Banking and Finance in Europe and three chapters in the last part of this book related to Islamic Banking and Finance in Africa.

The first chapter by Adel Mohammed Sarea, Mustapha Mohd Hanefah and Allam Hamdan investigates the extent of compliance with the AAOIFI standards by the Bahraini Islamic banks. The findings revealed that Islamic banks in Bahrain are in full compliance with the AAOIFI standards. The authors employed the diffusion of innovations theory which is a highly applied theory for individual perception purposes. This finding provides great insights to the policy makers and regulators on parameters to consider while formulating accounting standards for Islamic financial institutions in Bahrain and similar countries.

The second chapter by Mosab Tabash and Raj Dhankar analyses the relationship between the Islamic financial system development and economic growth in the United Arab Emirates (UAE) during the period spanning 1990 through 2010. Their findings indicated that there is a strong positive association between Islamic banking system development and economic growth in the UAE, and that the causal relationship happens only in one direction, i.e., from Islamic finance development to economic growth. Furthermore, the results show that Islamic finance contributed to the increase of investment and in attracting Foreign Direct Investment inflow (FDI) in the long term and in a positive way in UAE. The results also indicate that there is a bidirectional relationship between Islamic finance and FDI. It means that FDI reinforces Islamic finance and Islamic finance attracts foreign direct investment.

The third chapter by Abdullah Ayedh, Abdelghani Echchabi and Ameen Al-Nahari examines the factors that influence the adoption of Islamic banking services in Yemen, through a survey covering 300 respondents from most of the Yemeni regions. The findings revealed that generally the Yemeni customers are willing to adopt Islamic banking services, while the main factors that influence this decision are the environmental influence as well as the decision-making control.

The fourth chapter by Mohamed Sharif Bashir and Nor Hafizah Mail investigates the consumer perceptions of *takaful* companies in Brunei Darussalam. The findings showed that the most common problem encountered by *takaful* policyholders involves the claiming process. Accordingly, some suggestions have been offered for improving the *takaful* industry performance in Brunei such as upgrading technology to foster delivery of services and upgrading staff skills by more training.

The fifth chapter by Habibullah Khan and Omar Bashar emphasises the growth and potential prospects of Islamic finance in Singapore. The paper argues that despite having a relatively small domestic market and ferocious competition from Malaysia, Singapore can still position itself in a niche market for Islamic finance in the region. Through its strategy of integrated financial and economic development, Singapore can create new opportunities for Islamic finance and related financial products in the region.

The sixth chapter by Abdu Umar Faruq Ahmad, Mamunur Rashid and Abul Kalam Muhammad Shahed examines the Shari'ah principles for operation of Islamic banking in Bangladesh, the genesis of Islamic banking in Bangladesh, the factors which have led to the emergence of Islamic banking as well as the growth, development and future of Islamic banking in Bangladesh, and the deposit and investment mechanisms of Islamic and conventional banking in Bangladesh. Their findings indicated that although Islamic banks in Bangladesh are competing successfully with their conventional counterparts in an environment where no independent guidelines or acts exist for them, the products and services they use often resemble those used by conventional banking.

The seventh chapter by Fayaz Ahmad Lone and Imamul Haque demonstrates the role Islamic banking can play in the development of the Indian economy as a whole, using SWOT analysis and Michael Porter's five forces model. The chapter also provides recommendations for the commencement and development of the Islamic banking industry in India.

The eighth chapter by G.N. Khaki and Bilal Ahmad Malik provides an overview on the practice of Islamic banking in Kazakhstan and the current status of its implementation. In this regard, the author argues that the Islamic banking industry in Kazakhstan has been gradually evolving from the early years in terms of regulation, infrastructure, and the number of market participants. Hence, the author foresees that the industry will have a prosperous future, especially with the continuous support from international Islamic banking institutions.

The ninth chapter by Ashurov Sharofiddin examines the challenges and issues surrounding the practice of conventional banking in Tajikistan, and the possibility of introducing an Islamic financial system to the country and its acceptance by the Tajik public. The author's findings reveal that awareness and relative advantage are important factors in influencing the Tajik customers to subscribe to Islamic banking services.

The tenth chapter by Abdelghani Echchabi and Fatiha Echchabi investigates the perception of the French Muslims regarding Islamic insurance services. The authors covered a sample of 100 respondents from various regions of the country, and used structural equation modelling (SEM) for data analysis. The authors found that subjective norms have a positive influence on the attitude of French Muslims towards Islamic insurance services. Furthermore, attitude and perceived behavioural control were found to have a positive influence on the intention to adopt these services. Finally, the French Muslims have shown willingness to adopt Islamic insurance services as an alternative to the existing conventional insurance services depending on the above dimensions.

The eleventh chapter by Paolo Pietro Biancone outlines and discusses the prospects of Islamic finance in Italy. The author argues that Islamic finance is an opportunity for the integration of a portion of the immigrant population in Italy. Furthermore, he argues that the ethical aspect arising from the religious principles is a very important component in the comparison between the "doubtful" conventional finance, and the Islamic finance alternative.

The twelfth chapter by Renat Bekkin provides an overview on Islamic finance in Russia. The author covered a wide range of areas including takaful, waqf, zakat, and Islamic investment funds. The author concludes that Islamic finance will continue growing in Russia, through a number of Islamic finance institutions entering the market. However, their contribution might be relatively small to make an immediate major impact on the overall finance arena in Russia.

The thirteenth chapter by Hassanuddeen Abd. Aziz, Abdelghani Echchabi, Abdullah Ayedh, Dhekra Azouzi, Osman Sayid Hassan Musse, and Chaabane Oussama Houssem Eddine presents an overview on Islamic banking in Morocco, and investigates some of the factors that might improve Islamic banking practices in Morocco. The authors used extensive review of literatures as well as questionnaire surveys to achieve their objective. The authors found that there are legal and regulatory challenges facing the progress of Islamic banking in Morocco. Furthermore, relative advantage, compatibility, and social influence are found to have significant influence on the adoption of Islamic banking services by Moroccan customers.

The fourteenth chapter by Ahmad Bello Dogarawa explores the viability of Islamic banking in Nigeria and its opportunities. The paper is both descriptive and exploratory, based on review of theoretical and empirical literature in this area. The author argues that Islamic banking would provide a lot of economic benefits to the Nigerian economy, through serving as a vehicle for fund mobilisation, a means of achieving financial inclusion, employment generation, and exchange of expertise, etc. However, the author suggests that this achievement requires major steps to be undertaken by the central bank and bank operators, especially regarding the regulatory and operational aspects.

The fifteenth chapter by Neila Boulila Taktak and Sarra Ben Slama Zouari provides an overview on the history, current state as well as the future prospects of Islamic finance in Tunisia. The authors argue that there is a need to establish a specific regulatory framework, supervisory standards and rules of accounting for the Islamic financial institutions. Furthermore, they suggest the development of Islamic financial education to strengthen the role played by the Islamic financing Ecosystem and to help Tunisia promote local and exportable expertise to other countries. Finally, the authors recommend the authorities to focus more on promoting market Sukuk, Takaful and microcredit to fund SME.

TABLE OF CONTENT

PART 1:

ISLAMIC BANKING AND FINANCE IN MIDDLE EAST

Chapter 1

Adoption of AAOIFI Accounting Standards by Islamic Banks of Bahrain

Adel Mohammed Sarea

College of Business and Finance, Ahlia University, Kingdom of Bahrain and

Mustafa Mohd Hanefah

Faculty of Economics and Muamalat, Universiti Sains Islam Malaysia

Allam Hamdan

College of Business and Finance, Ahlia University, Kingdom of Bahrain and

Introduction

Financial statements for Islamic financial Institutions are now considered more important to *Shari'ah* scholars, writers and internal and external users of financial statements. However, the first study that addressed the need of accounting for Islamic financial institutions conducted by Abdel Magid (1981) he documented that the need of accounting for Islamic financial institutions are become highly increasing demand among writers to ensuring the accounting practice based on *Shari'ah principles*. Thus, it is proposed here a framework to prepare financial statements based on a unique model of accounting standards for Islamic financial institutions that makes financial statements more comparable, transparent and reliable accounting information for users. According to Hameed (2001) conventional accounting is inappropriate for Muslim users and Islamic organizations. In another related study conducted by Karim (1987) he indicates that, it is inappropriate to impose unmodified Western accounting practices on developing countries. In addition, International Accounting Standards (IASs) based on such techniques would create difficulties for Muslims around the world (Shadia Rahman, 2007). Therefore, it is vital for Muslim accountants to develop accounting standards which are specially adapted to Islamic needs and for Muslim countries (Shadia Rahman, 2007). Thus, this chapter highlights and focuses on the adoption of AAOIFI accounting standards by Islamic banks in Bahrain.

Developments of Islamic banking in Bahrain

Cooperation Council for the Arab States of the Gulf region (GCC) has a rich history of banking sector, going back to 1918 when the British first opened a bank in Bahrain (Olson and Zoubi,

2008). Islamic banking began in Bahrain in 1979 with the establishment of the Bahrain Islamic bank (Hussein, 2004).

The Islamic banks operating in the kingdom of Bahrain are diversified globally in which the GCC, EU, and North America constitute their main markets over the last ten years. According to Central Bank of Bahrain (CCB), "*The growth of Islamic banking in particular has been remarkable, with total assets in this segment jumping from US$1.9 billion in 2000 to US$26.3 billion by June 2009, an increase of over 12 times. The market share of Islamic banks correspondingly increased from 1.8% of total banking assets in 2000 to 11.1% in June 2009. Islamic banks provide a variety of products and services*" (CBB, Islamic Finance Report, 2012).

The importance of the AAOIFI accounting standards

Due to rise in globalization, increased competition, communication revolution, new regulations and the revolution in the Islamic financial institutions system, this chapter seeks answers to the question: To what extent Islamic banks of Bahrain comply with the AAOIFI accounting standards?

The Accounting and Auditing Organization for Islamic Financial Institutions (AAOIFI) formulates and issues accounting, auditing, and corporate governance standards, as well as ethics and *Shari'ah* standards for Islamic financial institutions (IFIs). AAOIFI as an independent international organization, is supported by institutional members (200 members from 45 countries, so far) including central banks, Islamic financial institutions, and other participants from the international Islamic banking and finance industry, worldwide (AAOIFI, 2010). Currently, AAOIFI has published 85 standards that comprises of 26 accounting standards, 5 auditing standards, 7 governance standards, 2 ethics standards, and 45 *shari'ah* standards (AAOIFI, 2010).

AAOIFI has been recognized and mandated to develop accounting, auditing, governance and ethics standards that are in line with *Shari'ah* principles in order to promote comparable, transparent and reliable accounting information for users. Thus, the main objective of AAOIFI is to prepare and develop accounting, auditing, governance and ethical standards relating to the activities of Islamic financial institutions. In line with the objective of this study, this chapter attempts to contribute to the current framework and serve as a guide for Islamic financial institutions.

Financial Reporting Framework

The conceptual framework for financial reporting contains objectives that are aimed at providing meaningful information (1) for creditors and investors to aid in making an informed decisions, (2) for the assessment of future cash flows, and (3) regarding the enterprises resources (assets) and changes in them, i.e., the users of financial statements (Lovet,2002).

There are many studies that related with diffusion and innovation theory, have discussed the adoption of International accounting standards by companies and banks as mandatory or as guidelines for instance, Lovet (2002) and Hussein (1981), but no previous studies had discussed the adoption of accounting standards for Islamic financial institutions in terms of diffusion and innovation theory. Therefore, as previously mentioned, the proposed chapter is acknowledged as one of the first attempts to analyze the adoption of AAOIFI accounting standards in terms of diffusion and innovation theory. Thus, this chapter aims to examine to what extent Islamic banks of Bahrain are complying with the AAOIFI accounting standards? The chapter, however, chose the diffusion and innovation theory as its main underlying theory because it is able to explain the problem and the extent of compliance with accounting standards by Islamic Banks of Bahrain. Furthermore, diffusion and innovation theory may be used to investigate the process of adopting accounting standards and the need for further study before the theory can either be accepted or dismissed as inappropriate for inquiry into the nature of the accounting standards setting process (Hussein, 1981). This is because it has been found in prior study that, the acceptance of accounting standards appears to follow the pattern of the diffusion of innovation process (Hussein, 1981). The purpose of this chapter is also to determine if the attributes of the variables, as specified by (Rogers, 2003) influence the adoption of AAOIFI standards by Islamic banks of Bahrain.

Rogers's theory states that the perceived attributes of an innovation, relative advantage, compatibility, complexity, trialability, and observability influence the rate of adoption of accounting standards. It is depicted in figure 1 below.

Figure 1
Stages of adoption/ compliance

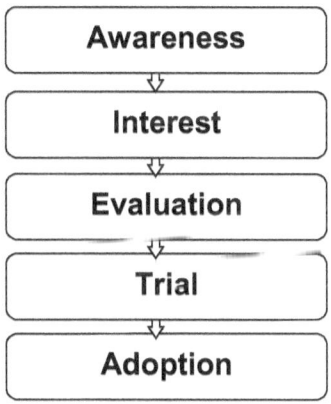

According to Rogers (2003), the innovation diffusion theory interprets the process through which an individual passes from initial knowledge of an innovation to forming an attitude toward the innovation, to a decision to adopt or reject, to implementation and use of the new idea and the confirmation of this decision and how a new invention will be successfully spread among members of a social system within the context of the diffusion elements.

The identification of a theory is needed to serve as a basis of interpretation of the variables influencing the adoption of the AAOIFI accounting standards. Quite a number of writers in the field of accounting have adopted the diffusion theory in their studies. For instance, Hussein (1981) applied diffusion theory to the adoption of domestic accounting standards, and measured the attitude towards the adoption of accounting standards based on book statements pertaining to specific US Generally Accepted Accounting Standards, this therefore resulted in empirical evidence that diffusion can be applied in measuring adoption of accounting standards.

Rogers's theory suggests that innovation diffusion can be applied in adopting or rejecting any idea, which involves relative advantage, compatibility, complexity, trialability, and observability influencing the rate of adoption of accounting standards. Thus, Rogers model consist of five stages namely: knowledge, persuasion, decision, implementation and confirmation. Among these five stages, the second stage which perceives characteristics of innovation had been studied more frequently and is generally considered the most significant in explaining the rate of adoption (Kendall, et al. 2001). Rogers (2003) identified that the rate of adoption of an innovation is influenced by five variables namely; the perceived attributes of the innovation, the type of innovation-decision, the communication channels, the nature of the social system, and the extent of influence of the change agent. See (Figure 2).

Figure 2

A Paradigm of Variables Determining the Rate of Adoption of Innovations

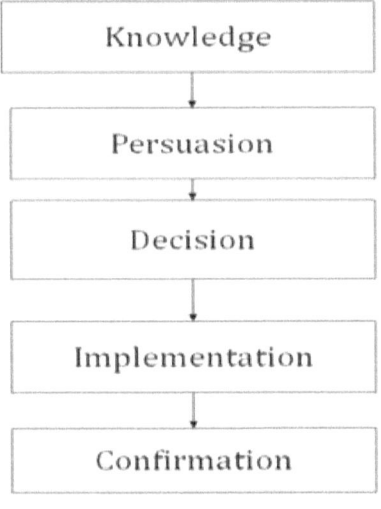

Source: Rogers, 2003

In this chapter, relative advantage is described as the benefits perceived by Islamic banks in adopting the AAOIFI accounting standards. Compatibility deals with how well AAOIFI accounting standards will suit the current business process. Complexity is how Islamic banks perceive AAOIFI accounting standards to be. If they are too complex then the standards may not be adopted, and vice versa. Trialability as applied in the current study explains the ability to engage in the AAOIFI accounting standards without incurring cost (cost of compliance). Observability is the degree to which the results of AAOIFI are visible to others such as users of the financial statements. See figure 3.

Figure 3

Roger's variables to determining the rate of adoption

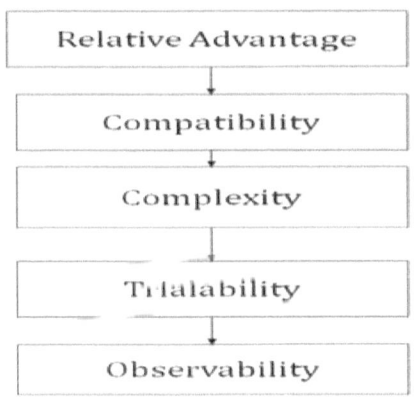

Source: Rogers, 2003

Rogers modeling has been applied to study the adoption of innovations in many disciplines. It has been applied in marketing to determine the acceptance of new products, in education to determine the acceptance of new teaching techniques, in medicine to determine the acceptance of new procedures, and in agriculture to determine the acceptance of hybrid crops (Lovett, 2002).

The use of Roger's model in studying compliance with the AAOIFI accounting standards by Islamic banks is rather new, especially in the case of Islamic banks of Bahrain in the field of accounting discipline. Lovett (2002) for instance indicates that, the acceptance of accounting standards appears to follow the pattern of the diffusion of innovation process. As a result, he found that, there is a positive relationship between the relative advantage, compatibility, trialability and observability and adoption of general accepted accounting standards by American companies in the State of Florida. On the other hand, the complexity indicated negative influence on the adoption of international accounting standards, which means that the more complex the international accounting standards the less likely they will be adopted.

In Study

The population of the study consists of accountants working in Islamic banks in Bahrain. The rule-of-thumb sample size in social science according to Sekaran (2000) is between 30 and 500 for effective analysis based on the questions investigated. Therefore, a study sample rather than the entire population is more likely to produce reliable results, which could reduce cost and time (Cooper and Schindler, 2006). A total of 312 questionnaires were distributed to the accountants of Islamic banks of Bahrain. Only 129 copies were returned to the writers, approximately 41% which is sufficient for statistics reliability. The sample was drawn from the total population of accountants in Islamic banks of Bahrain.

Table 1: Methods of questionnaires distribution

Islamic banks	workplace	Total
Bahrain	312	312

Table 2 Responses to the survey questionnaire

Islamic Banks in Bahrain		
Total distributed	Total received	Respondent rate
312	129	41 percent

5.2 Study Hypothesis:

The following hypotheses explain the relationship between independent variables as stated by Rogers (2003) and adoption of AAOIFI accounting standards in terms of the relative advantage, compatibility, complexity, trialability, and observability.

H1: The more relative advantage of the AAOIFI accounting standards, the more likely AAOIFI accounting standards will be adopted.

H2: The more compatibility of the AAOIFI accounting standards, the more likely AAOIFI accounting standards will be adopted

H3: The more complex AAOIFI accounting standards, the less likely they will be adopted.

H4: The more trialability of the AAOIFI accounting standards, the more likely AAOIFI accounting standards will be adopted.

H5: The more observability of the AAOIFI accounting standards, the more likely AAOIFI accounting standards will be adopted.

Table 3: The labels and measurement of the study variables:

Variable	Label	Definition and Measurement
Independent variables:		
Relative advantage	ADVANT	Relative Advantage is the benefits associated with the compliance of AAOIFI accounting standards by Islamic banks. This was measured through a number of items (9 questions)
Compatibility	COMPAT	Compatibility is the degree to which an adoption is perceived as being consistent with AAOIFI requirements. This variable was measured through (8 questions)
Complexity	COMPLEX	Complexity has been explained in term of the degree to which an AAOIFI is perceived as difficult to understand and use. This variable was measured through some items (6 questions)
Trialability	TRIAL	Trialability involves the ability to engage in AAOIFI standards without gaining cost (cost of compliance). This was measured through a number of items (3 questions)
Observability	OBSER	The more disclose of information to adopt AAOIFI the more likely the organizations will adopt that. This variable was measured through some items (4 questions)
Dependent variable: Adoption of AAOIFI	AAOIFI	Adoption of AAOIFI Accounting Standards by Islamic Banks of Bahrain. This variable was measured through AAOIFI accounting standards (17standard)

5.3 Study Model Development

The study model is based on Rogers (2003) which represent the relationship between independent variables and adoption of AAOIFI accounting standards in terms of the relative advantage, compatibility, complexity, trialability, and observability

Model as follows:

$$AAOIFI = \beta_0 + \beta_1 ADVANT + \beta_2 COMPAT + \beta_3 COMPLEX + \beta_4 TRIAL + \beta_5 OBSER + \varepsilon$$

Where:

AAOIFI = AAOIFI accounting standards Adoption.

ADVANT = Relative advantage

COMPAT = Compatibility

COMPLEX = Complexity

TRIAL = Trialability

OBSERV = Observability

$\beta 0$: is the constant.

$\beta 1.5$: is the slope of the independent variables.

ε: random error.

Empirical investigation

Descriptive statistics

Table 4 shows the descriptive statistics of the independent variables. The variables reflect the level of compliance with AAOIFI accounting standards. The variables also refer to the level of understanding and acceptability of AAOIFI accounting standards to be adopted by Islamic banks in Bahrain. Overall, the mean of the variables is positive and that reflects the high level of compliance with AAOIFI accounting standards. This result is in line with prior studies to reflect higher level of compliance with AAOIFI accounting standards.

Table 4: Descriptive statistics for Independent and Dependent variables

Independent variables			
Variable	Minimum	Maximum	Mean
ADVANT	1.000	5.000	3.72
COMPAT	1.000	5.000	3.60
OBSERV	1.000	5.000	3.40
TRIAL	1.000	5.000	3.14
COMPLEX	1.000	5.000	3.06

Dependent variable	
Variable	Mean
AAOIFI	4.01

Testing of Hypotheses and Discussion of Findings

The hypothesis aims to test the level of compliance with AAOIFI accounting standards and the acceptability of these standards to be adopted by Islamic banks of Bahrain. We hypothesis that, the more relative advantage, compatibility, trialability and observability of the AAOIFI accounting standards, the more likely AAOIFI accounting standards will be adopted. On the other hand, the more complex the AAOIFI accounting standards, the less likely AAOIFI accounting standards will be adopted.

The multiple regression results are shown in tables 5, 6 and 7.

Table 5: Regression Model

Model	R	R Square	Std. Error of the Estimate
1	.621(a)	.386	9.72708

Table 5 presents the results of regression model that examine the change in the level of compliance with the AAOIFI accounting standards in terms of independent variables. The model is significant with R^2 of 0.38. This means, R^2 of 0.38 changes in the levels of compliance with the AAOIFI accounting standards by variables identified by Rogers', which are five independent variables (e.g. the relative advantage, compatibility, complexity, trialability and observability).

Table 6: ANOVA (b)

Model		Sum of Squares	Df	Mean Square	F	Sig.
1	Regression	7319.903	5	1463.981	15.473	.000(a)
	Residual	11637.787	123	94.616		
	Total	18957.690	128			

Table 6 shows that the independent variables in the study are significantly related to the levels of compliance with the AAOIFI accounting standards, F-value (5, 123) = 15.4, P<.000. These results show that the accountant's perceptions on the level of compliance with the AAOIFI accounting standards influence their decision to comply with the AAOIFI accounting standards.

9

Table 7: Predictors Coefficients (a)

Model	Unstandardized Coefficients		Standardized Coefficients	T	Sig.	Collinearity Statistics	
	B	Std. Error	Beta			B	Std. Error
(Constant)	9.993	13.637		.733	.465	9.993	13.637
Relative advantage	1.645	.239	.519	6.872	.000	1.645	.239
Compatibility	1.360	.520	.203	2.615	.010	1.360	.520
Complexity	-1.105	.389	-.227	-2.843	.005	-1.105	.389
Trialability	-1.403	.552	-.200	-2.539	.012	-1.403	.552
Observability	.506	.275	.139	1.838	.069	.506	.275

Dependent Variable: adoption of the AAOIFI accounting standards

The results reveal that, the level of compliance with the AAOIFI accounting standards are affected by factors identified by Rogers' diffusion innovation theory. The results support the study which state that, the more relative advantage, compatibility and observability of the AAOIFI accounting standards, the more likely of the AAOIFI accounting standards will be adopted. On the other hand, complexity variable is negatively related to the level of compliance with the AAOIFI accounting standards, which means, the less complex the AAOIFI accounting standards, the more likely AAOIFI accounting standards will be adopted. Meanwhile, the trialability variable is negatively significant, which means that *shari'ah* principles are not for trial but must be fully adopted by all parties. Furthermore, the AAOIFI accounting standards need to be mandated by the government in order to be fully adopted by Islamic banks and other institutions. Bahrain has mandated that AAOIFI accounting standards must be fully complied by all banks and financial institutions.

Summary, Conclusion and Recommendations

This chapter examined the impact of relative advantage, compatibility, complexity, trialability, and observability on the level of compliance with accounting standards. It is found that, relative advantage, compatibility and observability have positive influence and significant on the compliance with the AAOIFI accounting standards. The more relative advantage, compatibility and observability of the AAOIFI accounting standards, the more likely the AAOIFI accounting standards will be adopted. On the other hand, the complexity and trialability variables were found to have negative influence on the compliance with AAOIFI accounting standards which means that, the less complex the accounting standards, the more likely the AAOIFI accounting

10

standards will be adopted. In addition, the trialability was negatively related due to the fact that, the AAOIFI accounting standards needs to be made mandatory in order to be adopted. The findings indicate that, Islamic banks in Bahrain comply fully with the AAOIFI accounting standards.

Implication of the study

To the best knowledge of the writer, this chapter is first of its kind that investigated the compliance with the AAOIFI accounting standards in terms of diffusion and innovation theory as well as exploring the accountant's perceptions. Lovett (2002) investigated the adoption of international accounting standards by American companies in Florida State in terms of diffusion and innovation theory. The writers used diffusion and innovation theory as underlining theory to write this chapter and to achieve objectives. Therefore, the findings may have some theoretical implication and policy implication. The theoretical framework is concerned with the accountant's perceptions on the level of compliance with the AAOIFI accounting standards in terms of diffusion and innovation theory, which is the most well-known model and most appropriate perception studies (Lovett, 2002). From this model, a design for questionnaire that reduces the gap in theoretical framework in accounting studies and achieving a desired outcome was made. The variables were important in explaining differences in the perception of compliance with the AAOIFI accounting standards.

Based on that discussion, this chapter may be considered as a first attempts to contributes to the accounting literature in terms of the impact of the relative advantage, compatibility, complexity, trialability, and observability on the efforts of adoption or compliance with the AAOIFI accounting standards as well as this chapter is expected to provide some benefits to regulators and policy makers to understand the AAOIFI accounting standards.

Implications for Theory and Practice

The findings show significant support for the current debate regarding the level of compliance with the AAOIFI accounting standards. However, Islamic financial institutions comply with *Shari'ah* requirements due to religious necessities in Muslim Community. Thus, the results are expected to serve as guide to the regulatory bodies such as Central Bank of Bahrain (CBB) and regulators of accounting standards for Islamic financial institutions.

The results indicate that Islamic banks in Bahrain have high level of compliance with the AAOIFI accounting standards. These findings imply that the standards are fully complied and could also be useful to the investors and professional bodies.

Due to limited study in the area of financial reporting for Islamic financial institutions, this study contributes to the literature that will be useful to other studies. The AAOIFI accounting standards for disclosure standards and measurement standards were selected for the purpose of the writing. In this regard, this chapter contains the following limitation:

Methodology and data limitations

This chapter, just like many others studies, faces data limitations. Sample size employed contains only the accountants in Islamic banks of Bahrain. In addition, the data analysis measures the compliance with the AAOIFI accounting standards in terms of respondent's perceptions and firm characteristics in terms of the descriptive statistics and multiple regressions instead of using banks' actual implementation of the AAOIFI accounting standards according to bank's listing status. However, this study focuses only on Islamic banks, and did not include other Islamic financial institutions such as Takaful companies.

Finally, the limitation associated with the employment of questionnaire whereby most of the respondents are from the mainstream accounting rather than Islamic accounting background. This might constitute a bias in the data analysis and findings.

Future of the book

Based on the conclusions, suggestion for future of the chapter could be in the following areas:

1. Design and extended sample size: in term of the sample size, the study focuses on numbers of accountants in the Islamic banks. Thus, different groups of sampling size such as Shari'ah advisory and firm auditors could be gathered on the issues related to compliance with the AAOIFI accounting standards. Future of this chapter may consider auditing, governance, ethics and other Shari'ah standards issued by other regulators, such as IFSB.

2. Population of the study: this study only studied Bahrain, but future could include Islamic banks in OIC in order to elicit international evidence.

3. Due to the lack of prior study in this area, future studies can be extended by looking at AAOIFI standards adoption by Islamic banks in other countries where AAOIFI standards are mandatory or voluntary.

References

AAOIFI (2008), *Financial Accounting Standards*, Accounting and Auditing Organization for Islamic Financial Institutions, Manama, Bahrain.

AAOIFI (2010), *Financial Accounting Standards*, Accounting and Auditing Organization for Islamic Financial Institutions, Manama, Bahrain.

Abdel-Magid, M.F. (1981), "The Theory of Islamic Banking: Accounting Implications", *The International Journal of Accounting*, Vol, 17 No.1, pp.79-102.

Cooper, D.R. and Schindler, P.S. (2006), *Business Research methods,* (International edition), Mcgraw-Hill, Singapore.

CBB (2012), *Islamic Finance Report*, Central bank of Bahrain, Available at http://cbb.complinet.com/cbb/display /display.html?rbid=1821&element_id=2509 (Accessed: 1 Feb 2012).

Hameed, S. (2001), "Islamic Accounting - Accounting for the New Millennium?". *Asia Pacific Conference 1- Accounting in the New Millennium*, October 10-12 Reinassance Hotel Kota Bharu. Malaysia.

Hussein, K. (2004), "Banking efficiency in Bahrain; Islamic vs. Conventional banks", *Islamic research and training institutes*, Vol. 68, pp. 1-76.

Hussein, M.E. (1981), "The innovative process in financial accounting standards setting", *Accounting, Organizations and Society*, Vol. 6, No. 1, pp. 27-37

Karim, R.A.A. and Tomkins, C. (1987), "The Shari'ah and its implications for Islamic financial analysis: An opportunity to study interactions among society, organization, and accounting", *The American Journal of Islamic Social Sciences*, Vol.4 No. 1, pp. 101-115.

Kendall, J.D., Tung, L.L., Chua, K.H., Hong, C., Dennis, N. and Tan, S.M. (2001), "Receptivity of Singapore's SMEs to electronic commerce adoption", *Journal of Strategic information managements*, Vol. 10, pp. 223-242. Retrieved April 6, 2003 from Science Direct Database.

Lovett, R. (2002), "*The adoption of international accounting standards: A diffusion of an innovation*", (PhD thesis), Nova Southeastern University, USA.

Olson, D. and Zoubi, T. A. (2008), "Using accounting ratios to distinguish between Islamic and conventional bank in the GCC region", *The International Journal of Accounting*, Vol. 43 No. 1, pp. 45-65.

Rogers, E. M. (2003), *Diffusion of Innovations* (3rd Ed.), The Free Press, New York.

Sekran, U. (2000), *Research Methods for Business: A Skill-Building Approach, 3rd Edition*, John Willey & Sons, Inc. New York.

Shadia, R. (2007), "Islamic accounting standards", Available at: http://islamic-finance.net/islamic-accounting/acctg5.html. pp. 1-9 (Accessed: 7 May 2011).

Chapter 2

Islamic Finance and Economic Growth: Empirical Evidence from United Arab Emirates (UAE)

Mosab I. Tabash

Raj S. Dhankar

University of Delhi

Introduction

During the past years, one of the rising stars in the world of finance has been Islamic finance. Islamic finance is growing as a source of finance for Islamic and other investors around the world. Islamic finance involves structuring financial instruments and financial transactions to satisfy traditional Muslim strictures against the payment of interest and engaging in gambling. It is a field of growing importance for conservative Muslims, especially in the Middle East and large Muslim population in South-Eastern Asia countries, who are uncomfortable with Western-style of financial system and banking, which involve explicit payments of interest. Lately, the Vatican (2009) noted that banks should look at the rules of Islamic finance to restore confidence amongst their clients at a time of global economic crisis. According to Financial Insights, Islamic finance has been growing at 20-30% per year over the past decade, while Kuwait Finance House Group KFH-Group is even more optimistic in its forecast suggesting that Islamic financial assets will reach U.S $ 2.1 trillion by the end 2014. This rapid growth has been fuelled by surging demand for Shari'ah[1]-compliant products not only from financiers in the Middle East and other Muslim countries, but also by investors globally, thus making it a global phenomenon. Global Shari'ah-compliant financial assets have increased significantly over the past three decades, reaching about US$1 trillion in 2011 (Figure 1), up from about U.S. $ 5 billion in the late 1980s (Deutsche Bank, 2011).

---

[1]"The Path", term of Islamic law consists of Islamic instructions based on the Holy Quran and Sunnah.

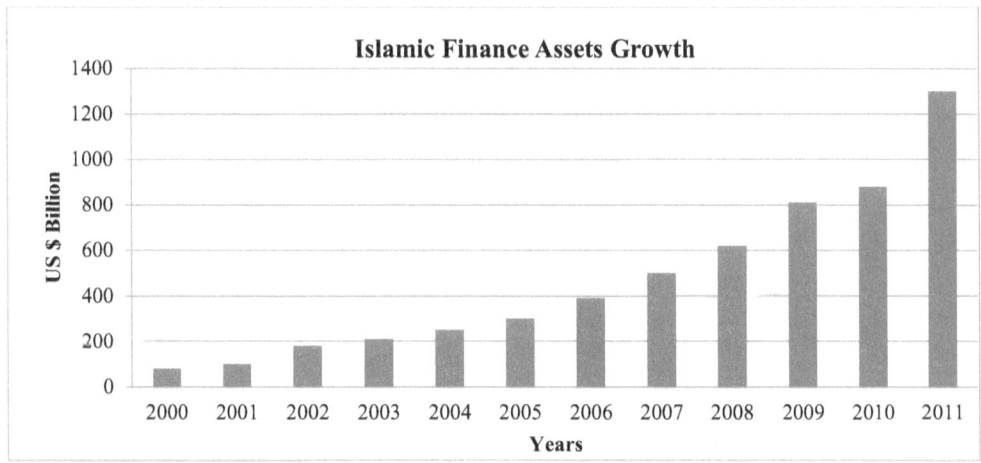

Fig.1: Islamic Finance Assets (2000-2011)

Source: Deutsche Bank, 2011

Islamic Banking assets have been growing rapidly for several decades. They rose from about U.S. $ 386 billion in 2006 to U.S. $ 1.1 trillion in 2011 (Deutsche Bank, 2011). In recent years, growth in Islamic financial assets has generally outperformed conventional financial instruments, particularly following the onset of the financial crisis that has been gripping the world since 2008. The performance and relative stability of Islamic financial institutions during the financial crisis that hit the world in 2008 stems from the distinctive features of the instruments they offer. There is no doubt that Islamic financial sector development plays an important role in the overall development of an economy. Although, there are many empirical studies that examined the relationship between finance and economic growth, but specific empirical studies on the relationship between Islamic finance and economic growth, are not too many. So, this study tries to examine empirically the relationship between Islamic finance and economic growth, and its direction in the UAE.

Islamic Finance and UAE Economic Growth:

The financial sector plays a growth promoting role, if it is able to direct financial resources towards the sectors that demand those the most. When the financial sector is more developed, more financial resources can be allocated into productive use, and more physical capital gets formed, which will lead to economic growth. Global as well as local banks have flourished in recent years in this relatively progressive and vibrant economy. Figure 2 shows the growth of the UAE economy from 1990-2010.

A well-developed Islamic financial system and a high economic growth at the same time draw our attention, to examine whether or not the Islamic banking system that currently applied in the UAE, has really contributed in the long-term to economic growth of the UAE. To know this, we looked at the dynamic interactions between finance and growth by applying models where the financial system influences economic growth, and economic growth transforms the operation of the financial system.

Islamic banking in the United Arab Emirates

The UAE Islamic banking sector's performance continues to benefit from the buoyant economic environment. Combined assets of Islamic banks in UAE have grown with a CAGR of 98.12 % for the period 1990 to 2010. Islamic banks assets' share in total bank assets increased to 17% during 2010 only. Total assets of Islamic Banks in the UAE have increased by 30.5% to $73.1 billion from 50.8 billion during 2010.

Presently, there are 23 national banks and 22 foreign banks operating in the UAE. Out of the 23 national banks, 8 are fully operating under Shari'ah principles (5 of which are public companies) and the remaining banks have both conventional and Islamic banking operations. The UAE banking sector, the largest in the Gulf Cooperation Council (GCC) by total assets, continued its positive trend in 2007. Benefiting from a benign operating environment and a strong demand for credit; operating profits for most banks grew in double digits.

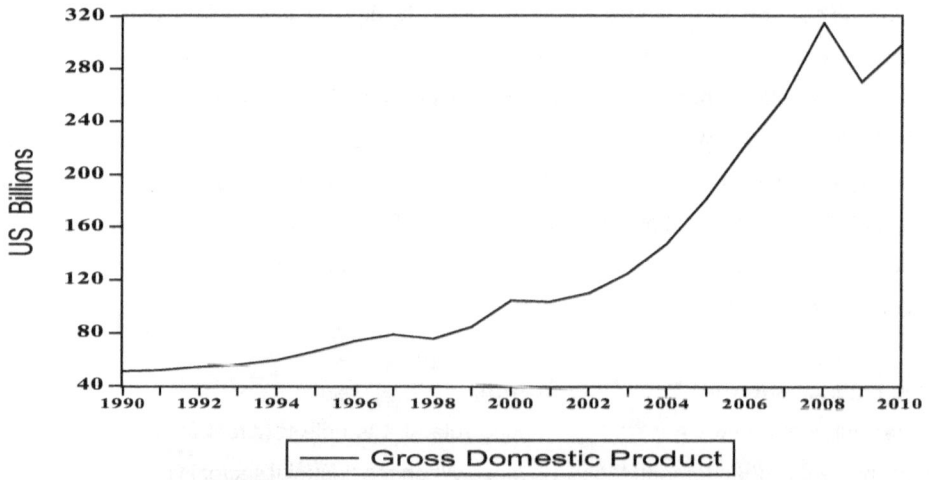

Fig.2: **GDP Growth of the United Arab Emirates (1990-2010)**

Banking penetration in the country continued to grow in 2007. The ratio of credit deployment to GDP stood at 95.4% in 2007 up from 80.5% in 2006, while deposits to GDP ratio was 98.1% in 2007 as compared to 83.1% in 2006. During 2007, total banking assets represented 2.9 times the GDP as compared to Islamic banking assets that recorded a value of 37% of GDP. Given the high penetration in the banking sector, Islamic banks have to compete with the conventional banks for market share (Deutsche Bank, 2011).

Further analysis of the financing component of assets shows that while a variety of Islamic financing modes are used by the banks and the composition of their use vary across countries, Murabahah financing is the dominant mode used by Islamic banks in all countries of Middle East and North Africa region (MENA). In some countries Murabahah constitutes more than 95 percent of financing, like in the UAE; in others it is just below 50 percent. On an average, for overall MENA region, the proportion of Murabahah in total financing is 75 percent. Leasing (or hire-purchase) is the second most used mode in Bahrain, Jordan, Kuwait, Lebanon, and Qatar. Mudharabah financing is the second largest mode in Saudi Arabia, but of lesser importance in other countries. Istisna is third most used mode in MENA region countries (Ali, 2011). Qard Hassan (or zero returns benevolent loan), in any significant amount, is used only in Jordan. Figure (3) shows the incremental increase of Islamic banks' financing in the UAE in the period 1990 to 2010, while figure (4) shows the increase of fixed investments in the period 2001 to 2010 in the UAE, and figure (5) shows the increase of foreign Direct Investment inflow (FDI) in the period 1990 to 2010.

Fig.3: **Islamic Banks' Financing (1990-2010)**

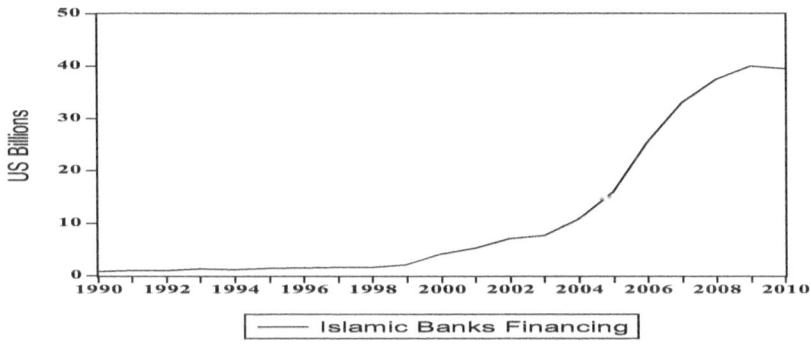

Fig. 4: **Gross Fixed Capital Formation (2001-2010)**

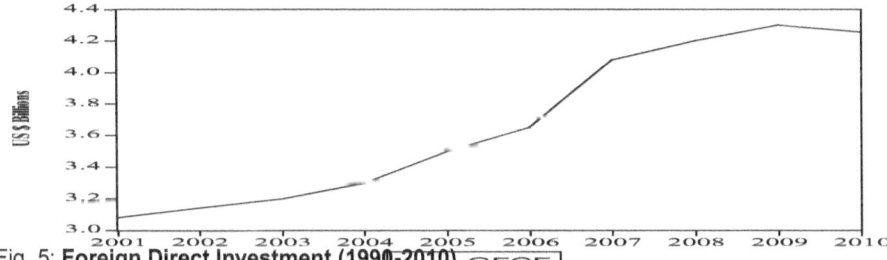

Fig. 5: **Foreign Direct Investment (1990-2010)**

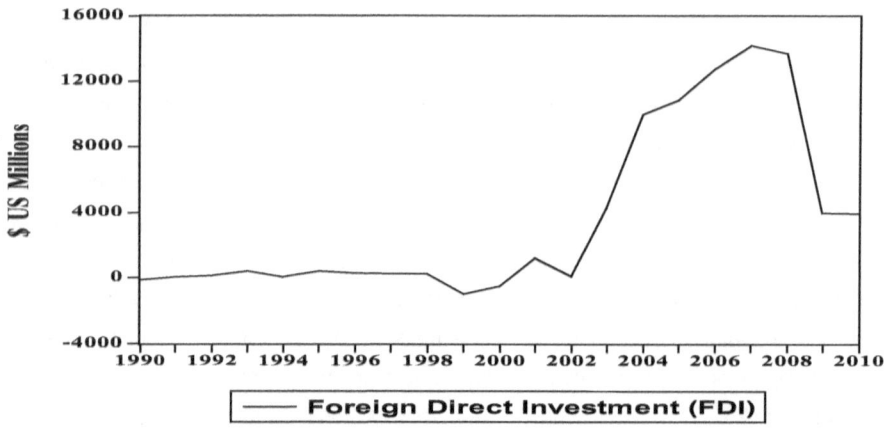

Foreign Direct Investment (FDI)

Literature Review

The relationship between financial development and economic growth has been extensively analysed in the literature. The relationship between financial development and economic growth is a controversial issue. Some authors consider finance an important element of growth (Schumpeter, 1934; Goldsmith, 1969; McKinnon, 1973, Shaw, 1973; King and Levine (1993), whilst for others it is only a minor growth factor (Robinson, 1952; Lucas, 1988). Schumpeter (1934) sees the banking sector as an engine of economic growth through its funding of productive investment. On the contrary, Lucas (1988) argues that the role of finance has been overstressed.

According to the theory, the development of the banking industry is favourable to the economic growth because the activity of the banks increases the mobilization of the saving, improves the efficiency of the resources allowance, and stimulates the technological innovation. Most studies (including recent ones) argue, in accordance with the theoretical predictions that, there is a positive relationship between the financial development and the economic growth. Beck et al (2000), Bekaert et al (2001) and Levine (2005) strongly supported the idea that there is a positive relationship between financial development and economic growth.

Explicitly or implicitly, in all studies, we note that an efficient financial system accelerates the economic development. The main contribution of financial system to materialize growth as it assures the functioning of an efficient and evolutionary payment system, and mobilizes the saving and improves its affectation to the investment. So, the existence of a reliable and sound financial exchange system is a necessary for growth.

Recently, several studies have attempted to deepen this analysis empirically by exploring specific indicators to explain the causal relationship between finance and growth.

18

Three possibilities come to fore, (1) financial development is a determinant of economic growth, supply-leading; (2) financial development follows economic growth, demand-following; and (3) bidirectional causality between finance and growth.

Odedokun (1992) favoured bidirectional causality between finance and growth. Both financial and economic developments are causally related where financial development causes economy to grow, and economic growth triggers financial sector to develop further. Masih (1996) supported demand following hypothesis where economic growth causes financial sectors to develop. As per this view, the more rapid the growth of real national Income, the greater will be the demand by enterprises for external funds (the saving of others), and therefore, financial intermediation, as in most situations' firms will be less able to finance expansion from internally generated depreciation allowance and retained profits. The financial system can thus support and sustain the leading sectors in the process of growth. In this case an expansion of the financial system is induced as a consequence of real economic growth or demand following. Levine and Zervos (1998) studied the empirical relationship between stock market development, banking development, and long-run economic growth. Their research showed that stock market liquidity and banking development are both positively and robustly correlated with contemporaneous and future rates of economic growth, capital accumulation and productivity growth.

Arestis et al. (2001) focused their study on only five developed countries with quarterly data. They confirmed a robust effect of banking sector development and stock markets development on growth in these countries. Fase and Abma (2003) argued that expansion of the financial system could have a positive repercussion on economic growth. The financial sectors in this case act as supply-leading to transfer resources from the traditional, low-growth sectors to the modern high-growth sectors and to promote and stimulate an entrepreneurial response in these modern sectors. Abu-Bader and Abu-Qarn (2005) examined the causal relationship between financial development and economic growth in Egypt for 1960-2001. They used Granger causality tests. They concluded that financial development promotes economic growth either through increasing investment efficiency or capital accumulation.

Tang (2006) used a modified growth model investigated whether financial development would have facilitated economic growth among the APEC countries from 1981 to 2000. Tang did this by specifically focusing on the effects of three aspects of financial development on economic growth: stock market, banking sector, and capital flow. Tang found that the level of stock market development would have no impact on the growth effect of capital flow increase among the APEC countries. In the banking sector his study shows that a well-functioning banking sector would only boost the growth effect of capital flow on the APEC developing countries. Hondroyiannis et al. (2005) and Van Nieuwerburgh et al. (2006) used VAR models to assess long term relationship between financial development and growth.

Hondroyiannis et al. (2005) studied the case of Greece for the period 1986-1999. They found a strong link between financial development and economic growth in the long-run. Van Nieuwerburgh et al. (2006) confirmed the same results in the case of Belgium where both banks and stock markets financing affect economic growth in the long run.

Romeo-Avila (2007) also confirmed the positive impact of finance on growth. He investigated the relationship between finance and growth, with emphasis on the effect of financial deregulation and banking law harmonisation on economic growth in the European Union. The study establishes that financial intermediation impacts positively the economic growth through three channels. Kenourgios and Samitas (2007) examined the long-run relationship between finance and economic growth for Poland, and concluded that credit to the private sector has been one of the main driving forces of long-run growth. Huang et Lin (2009) re-examined the dynamic relationship between financial development and economic growth on the dataset used in Levine et al. (2000). Using a novel threshold regression with the instrumental variables approach, they support a positive linkage between financial development and economic growth, and found that financial development has an important effect on growth in low-income countries.

Hence, there are not too many studies available on the relationship between Islamic finance and economic growth. Abduh and Omar (2012), Furqani and Mulyany (2009) and Majid and Kassim (2008) are among the limited studies in this area. Abduh and Omar (2012) identifies that the relationship between Islamic finance and economic growth is bi-directional. Therefore, the government policies in supporting the development of Islamic finance in Indonesia are strongly needed in order to support the economic development. However, using different time span of quarterly data, findings from Furqani and Mulyany (2009) and Majid and Kassim (2008) are different in terms of the direction of the relationship. Furqani and Mulyany (2009), on the one hand, states that the relationship between Islamic financial development and economic growth is following the view of "demand-following" which means that growth in real sector economy stimulates Islamic banking institutions to change and develop. On the contrary, finding from Majid and Kassim (2008) is in favour of the supply-leading view.

Generally, we find that the empirical studies that have been conducted so far have mainly examined the efficiency, superiority and stability of Islamic banks compared to conventional banks to achieve some intermediate monetary target for the ultimate target which is concentrated towards the achievement of sustaining real economic growth, reducing inflation and lowering unemployment. For example, Darrat (1988) who found that interest-free banking system is more superior to achieve the monetary target.

In the Chapter

The qualitative and quantitative methods have been used. The qualitative approach is used to review the existing literature from all resources such as academic, scholarly journals, newspapers and magazines, documents, workshops, and other related literature of Islamic finance industry. The quantitative approach is used to test the long-term relationship between Islamic finance and growth of economy.

The data set is extracted from Word Trade organization, Global Development Finance and Islamic Banks and Financial Institutions Information (IBIS), database for all Islamic banks' financing in the UAE[2]. To serve our purpose, appropriate variables were established and the long-term relationships between those variables are determined by using econometric estimation methods. We use annually time series data for the variables- Islamic banks' financing through modes of financing as a proxy for financial sector and three variables representing real economic sectors namely Real Gross Domestic Product (GDP) and Gross Fixed Capital Formation (GFCF) and Foreign Direct Investment inflow (FDI) as proxies for economic growth. Based on the availability of data, two time periods are used. From 1990 to 2010 time series to examine the relationship between Islamic banks' financing and GDP, FDI, and from 2001 to 2010 time series to examine the relationship between Islamic banks' financing and GFCF.GDP is a common statistic to represent the income level of a particular country within a certain time range. Study about finance-growth nexus always use GDP as the principal variable reflecting economic growth.

We use gross fixed capital formation (GFCF) as a representation of investment, as it is economic indicators of the level of business activity that measure net new investment by enterprise in the domestic economy in fixed capital assets during an accounting period. Foreign Direct Investment inflow (FDI) is a common measure of the economic growth. FDI promotes economic growth in a capital scarce economy by increasing volume, as well as efficiency of physical investment. In other words, FDI supplies long-term capital with new technologies, managerial skills, and marketing capabilities which, in turn, increase economic growth by creating employment, increasing managerial skills, diffusing technologies and fostering innovations (Asiedu 2002).

The first step of the study is to determine the relationship between financial deepening and economic growth, and whether the series are stationary or not. In a model, for a correct evaluation, time series should be separated from all effects, and the series should be stationary. Thus, logarithms of time series were taken. Augmented Dickey Fuller (1981) and

---

[2]The Islamic Banks and Financial Institutions Information (IBIS) database is built to help researchers and finance professionals working in the area of Islamic economics and finance. It seeks to provide comprehensive data and information on the activities of Islamic finance institutions, up-to-date research and literature. It can be reached through the website http://www.ibisonline.net/IBISHomepage.aspx

Phillips Perron (1988) tests are used. After that, Johansen co-integration test was used to examine the long-term relationship between financial deepening and economic growth. While determining long-term relationship between variables with Johansen cointegration test, established numbers of lag is very important. In this study, Akaike Information Criteria (AIC) is used for selecting the optimal lag. Moreover, in all models, stability test was used and auto correlation tests to residuals were made. Models are generally stable and residuals are not auto correlated. And then, the Granger causality test is used to test the causality between Islamic banks' financing and economic growth. We use Eviews[3]software to test and analyse the results.

Results:

Descriptive Statistics

Table (1) presents summary statistics about the variables used in the econometric analysis for the UAE. Figure 6, 7 and 8 show the relationship between Gross Domestic Product (GDP), Gross Fixed Capital Formation (GFCF), Foreign Direct Investment (FDI), and Islamic banks' financing in the UAE graphically.

Table 1: **Summary Statistics**

Statistics	GDP	GFCF	FDI	IBF
Mean	132,502.4	3,671	3,586.100	11,355.69
Median	103,312.0	3,575	399.9000	4,025.970
Maximum	314,845.0	4,300	14,186.50	39,918.08
Minimum	50,701.00	3,080	-985.3000	0,739.970
Std. Dev.	88057.93	0,495	5,269.399	14,309.46
Observations	21	10	21	21

---

[3]Eviews is a statistical and econometric software package, which provides data analysis, regression, and forecasting tools. It is produced by Quantitative Micro Software (QMS) in Irvine, California, USA.

Fig. 6: **GDP and IBF Growth (1990-2010)**

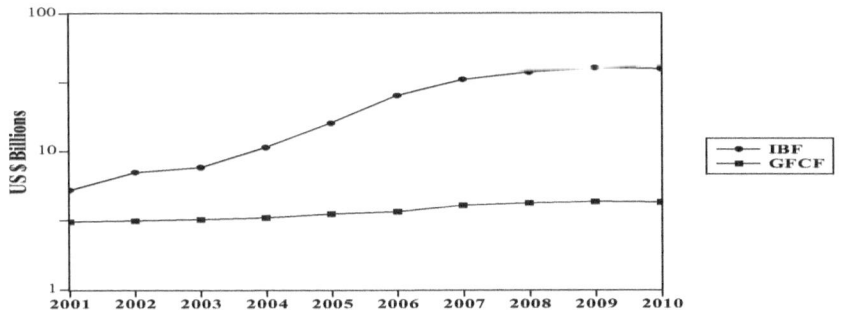

Fig.7: **GFCF and IBF Growth (2001-2010)**

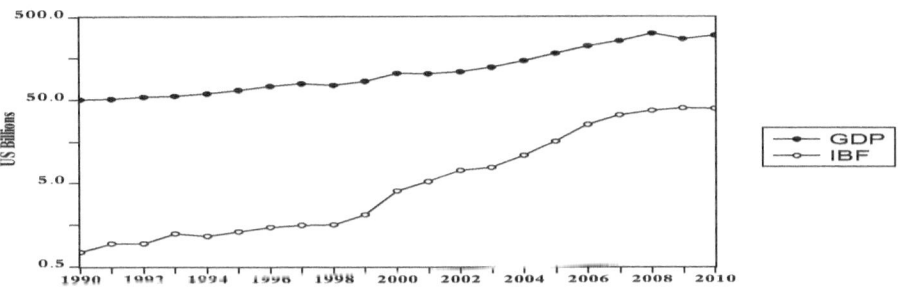

Fig. 8: **FDI and IBF Growth (1990-2010)**

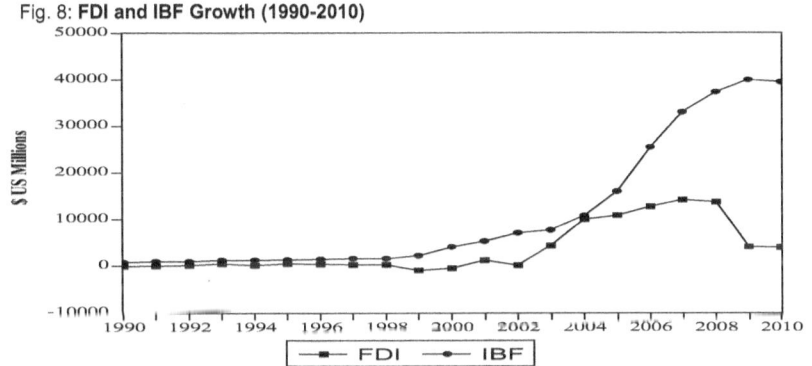

From table 1 and figures 6, 7, 8, we observe that the maximum value for IBFinancing in 2010 reached to (39,918.08) from (0,739.970) in 1990 with standard deviation of (14,309.46). This gives us an indication of high growth of the Islamic finance industry in the recent years. The statistics show that the median for GDP, GFCF, FDI, and IBFinancing is less than the mean, which indicates that the values are positively skewed.

Unit Root Test

Results of ADF and PP tests applied to time series show that all series belonging to economic growth and financial deepening indicators are not stationary at level. To make those series stationary, first differences of series have been taken. Failure to reject the null hypothesis of unit roots implies that the linear combination of the variables is non-stationary; hence we cannot pursue for the cointegation tests.

Table 2: **Unit Root Test**

Variable	ADF Test		Phillip-Person Test	
	Level 1	First difference	Level 1	First difference
Variable	t-statistic P value	t- statistic P value	t- statistic P value	t- statistic P value
GDP	- 2.129647 0.0546	-3.371805** 0.0062	3.912819*** 0.0015	-6.843614** 0.0000
GFCF	- 1.771436 0.5985	- 2.141708 0.4471	-2.141708 0.4471	-11.68149** 0.0010
FDI	- 1.284752 0.6155	-3.382948** 0.0250	-1.399839 0.5615	-3.387761** 0.0248
IBFinancing	- 2.230132 0.0456	-3.491436** 0.0050	3.528265*** 0.0034	-7.164660** 0.0000
*, **, *** Significant at 1%,5%,10% level respectively				

The results of the table 2 indicate that the data at the first difference is stationary at α 1%, 5%, and 10% level of significance respectively. For GDP variable, if p value is less than α, then Ho is rejected, and the series is stationary. The first row in table 2 shows that the p value (0.0062) is less than α (0.05) in ADF test. Similarly, for IBFinancing, the result from the second row shows that the p value (0.005) is less than α (0.05) and for GFCF, the p value (0.0) is less than α (0.05) in PP test and also, for FDI, the p value (0.0250) is less than α (0.05) in ADF test. This suggests that the null hypothesis is rejected for all variables. Hence, the failure to reject the alternative hypothesis indicates that the series are stationary.

Johansen Co-integration Test

Table 3 shows the results of Johansson test for the long relationship between Islamic banks' financing and economic growth. The trace test rejects the null hypothesis if the trace statistics exceeds the critical value. The first row of table 3 shows that the trace statistics (16.52449) exceeds the critical value of (15.41) at 95 percent confidence level for GDP and the trace statistics (16.52449) exceeds the critical value of (15.41) at 95 percent confidence level for GFCF. Similarly, for FDI, the trace statistics (18.46343) exceeds the critical value of (5.41) at 95 percent confidence level. It suggests that the null hypothesis of no cointegrating relationships is rejected. The results confirm that there is a cointegrating relationship among the variables.

Table 3: **Johansen's test (trace statistic)**

			Critical values	
		Trace statistics	5%	1%
Gross Domestic Product (GDP)				
Null hypothesis	Ho: r = 0	16.52449**	15.41	20.04
Alternative hypothesis	H1: r ≥ 1	0.589393	3.76	6.65
Gross Fixed Capital Formation (GFCF)				
Null hypothesis	Ho: r = 0	25.63235**	15.41	20.04
Alternative hypothesis	H1: r ≥ 1	6.931010**	3.76	6.65
Foreign Direct Investment (FDI)				
Null hypothesis	Ho: r = 0	18.46343**	5.41	20.04
Alternative hypothesis	H1: r ≥ 1	3.264960	3.76	6.65
** Significant at 5 % level				

The eigenvalue test tests the null hypothesis of r versus r+1 cointegrating relationships. This test rejects the null hypothesis if the eigenvalue test statistics exceeds the respective critical value. Table4 presents the results from this test. Similarly, the result from the first row of table 4 shows that the eigenvalue test statistics (15.93510) exceeds the critical value (14.07) at 95 percent confidence level for GDP and the eigenvalue test statistics (18.70134) exceeds the critical value of (14.07) at 95 percent confidence level for GFCF. Similarly, for FDI, the eigenvalue test statistics (15.19847) exceeds the critical value of (14.07) at 95 percent confidence level. This suggests that the null hypothesis is rejected. Hence, the failure to reject the alternative hypothesis indicates that there is one cointegrating relationship among the variables.

Table 4: **Johansen's test (Max-Eigenvalue statistic)**

		Max-Eigenvalue	Critical values	
			5%	1%
Gross Domestic Product (GDP)				
Null hypothesis	Ho: r = 0	15.93510**	14.07	18.63
Alternative hypothesis	H1: r = 1	0.589393	3.76	6.65
Gross Fixed Capital Formation (GFCF)				
Null hypothesis	Ho: r = 0	18.70134**	14.07	18.63
Alternative hypothesis	H1: r ≥ 1	6.931010**	3.76	6.65
Foreign Direct Investment (FDI)				
Null hypothesis	Ho: r = 0	15.19847**	14.07	18.63
Alternative hypothesis	H1: r ≥ 1	3.264960	3.76	6.65
** Significant at 5 % level				

The results from table 3 and 4, if read together, show that the null hypotheses of non-cointegation are rejected at 5 percent level of significance. This suggests that in the long run Islamic banks' financing contributes in the growth of GDP and investment of United Arab Emirates (UAE).

Granger Causality Test

Statistics and probability values constructed under the null hypothesis of non-causality are reported in table 5. It can be observed that there is a causal relationship between Islamic banks financing and GDP. However, our results show that one-way causality exists only from Islamic banks financing to GDP, since the probability value (0.01559) less than (0.05). So, the null hypothesis is rejected, and it can be concluded that the higher flow of Islamic finance has led to the growth of the economy. Furthermore, the results show that there is a unidirectional causality between Islamic banks' financing and investment since it is significant at 5percent level, as (0.03207) less than (0.05). Thus, Islamic banks' financing granger causes the development of real economic growth in UAE. The causality between Islamic banks' financing and FDI is bidirectional since it is significant at 5 percent level, as (0.007) and (0.026) less than (0.05) for two variables respectively.

Table 5: **Pair wise Granger Causality Tests**

Null Hypothesis	F statistics	Probability
IBF does not Granger Cause GDP	5.41605	0.01559**
GDP does not Granger Cause IBF	2.02784	0.16842
GFCF does not Granger Cause IBF	7.01785	0.07390
IBF does not Granger Cause GFCF	13.3600	0.03207**
IBF does not Granger Cause FDI	12.8702	0.007**
FDI does not Granger Cause IBF	6.93103	0.026**
** Significant at 5 % level		

Conclusion

Islamic finance theory promotes economic development through its direct link to the real economy and physical transactions, its prohibitions against harmful products and activities, and its promotion of economic growth and social justice. The cointegration results provide evidence of a unique cointegrating vector. In other words, there is a long-term stable relationship between Islamic banks' financing and economic growth in the United Arab Emirates (UAE). That means Islamic banks' financing and economic growth move together in the long-run. It is proved that the UAE has benefited from strong banking system.

This chapter find that the causality relation exists in the Islamic banks' financing to economic growth in a unique direction from the development of financial system to economic growth, but not in the opposite direction. Furthermore, the results show that Islamic finance is a suitable environment for attracting FDI into the country and FDI reinforces Islamic finance. The results also indicate that improvement of the Islamic financial institutions in the UAE will benefit economic development, and it is critical in the long run for the economic welfare, and also for poverty reduction.

The findings of the chapter support strong evidence on supply-leading hypothesis which implies that financial development induces economic growth for GDP and GFCF. This means that Islamic financial system is an efficient financial system that increases the supply of financial services for the growth of the real sector of the economy. In this regard, government of UAE should continue to strengthen Islamic banking industry as it helps the economy to grow in the long-run. For FDI attraction, UAE government should devote attention on Islamic banking by enhancing open markets through trade, investment and financial freedom.

References

Abduh, M. and Omar, M. (2012), "Islamic banking and economic growth: the Indonesian experience", *International Journal of Islamic and Middle Eastern Finance and Management*, Vol. 5 No. 1, pp. 35-47.

Abu Bader, S. and Abu-Qarn, A. (2005), *Financial Development and Economic Growth: Time Series Evidence from Egypt*, Monaster Center for Economic Research Ben-Gueion, University of the Negev.

Ali, S. (2011), *Islamic Banking in the MENA region*. Islamic Development Bank, Islamic Research and Training Institute, Jeddah, KSA.

Arestis, P., Demetriades, P. and Luintel, K.B. (2001), "Financial Development and Economic

Growth: the Role of Stock Markets", *Journal Money Credit Bank*, Vol. 33, pp. 16–41.

Asiedu, E. (2002), "On the determinants of foreign direct investment developing counties: Is Africa different?" *World Development*, Vol. 30 No. 1, pp. 107-119.

Beck, T., Levine, R. and Loayza, N. (2000), "Finance and the Sources of Growth", *Journal of Financial Economics*, Vol. 58, pp. 261–300.

Bekaert, G., Harvey, C. and Lundblad, C. (2001), "Emerging Equity Markets and Economic Development", *Journal of Development Economics*, Vol.66, pp. 465–504.

Darrat, A. F. (1988), "The Islamic Interest-Free Banking System: Some Empirical Evidence", *Applied Economics*, Vol. 20, pp.417-425.

Deutsche Bank (2011), *Global Islamic Banking Report*, November, London, UK.

Dickey, D. and Fuller, W. (1981), "Likelihood Ratio Statistics for Auto- regressive Time Series with a Unit Root", *Econometric journal*, Vol. 49 No. 4, pp. 1057-1072.

Fase, M.M.G. and Abma, R.C.N. (2003), "Financial Environment and Economic Growth in Selected Asian Countries", *Journal of Asian Economics*, Vol.14, pp.11-21.

Furqani, H. and Mulyany, R. (2009), "Islamic Banking and Economic Growth: Empirical Evidence from Malaysia", Journal of Economic Cooperation, Vol. 30 No. 2, pp. 59-74.

Goldsmith, R. (1969), *Financial Structure and Economic Growth in Advanced Countries*, National Bureau Committee for Economic Research, Capital Formation and Economic Growth, Princeton, University Press.

Huang, H. and Shu-Chin, L. (2009), "Non-Linear Finance—Growth Nexus: A threshold with Instrumental Variable Approach", *Economics of Transition*, Vol. 17 No. 3, pp. 439–466.

Kenourgios, D. and Samitas, A. (2007), "Financial Development and Economic Growth in a Transition Economy: Evidence for Poland", *Journal of Financial Decision Making*, Vol.3 No. 1, pp. 35-48.

Kuwait Finance House Group (KFH) (2014), *Islamic finance assets to reach $2.1tr by end-2014*, Saudi Gazette, can be reached through the website http://saudigazette.com.sa/index.cfm?method=home.regcon&contentid=20140209195 199.

Levine, R. (2005), "Finance and Growth: Theory and Evidence", In: Handbook of Economic Growth, ed. by P. Aghion and S. Durlauf, vol.1, pp.865-934, Elsevier.

Levine, R. (1993), "Financial Development and Economic Growth: Views and Agenda", *Journal of Economic Literature*, Vol. 35 No. 2, pp. 688-726.

Lucas R.E., (1988)," On the Mechanics of Economic Development", *Journal of Monetary Economics*, Vol. 22 No. 1, pp. 3-42.

Majid, S.A. and Kassim, S. (2008), *Islamic finance and economic growth: The Malaysian experience*, Kuala Lumpur Islamic Finance Forum, Kuala Lumpur.

Masih, R. and Masih, M. (1996)," Macroeconomic Activity Dynamics and Granger Causality:

New Evidence from a Small Developing Economy Based on a Vector Error Correction Modelling   Analysis", *Economic Modelling journal*, Vol.13, pp. 407-426.

McKinnon, R.I. (1973), *Money and Capital in Economic Development*, the Brookings Institution, Washington, DC.

Odedokun, M. (1992), "Supply-Leading and Demand-Following Relationships between Economic Activity and Development Banking in Developing Countries: An Empirical Analysis", *Singapore Economic Review*, Vol. 37, pp. 46-58.

Osservatore, V. (2009), *Islamic Banking May Help Overcome Crisis* (Press Release).

Philips, P. (1988), "Time Series Regression with a Unit Root", *Econometrical journal*, Vol. 55, pp. 277-301.

Robinson, J. (1952), *The Generalization of the General Theory in the Rate of Interest and Other Essays*, Macmillan, London.

Romeo, A. (2007), "Finance and Growth in the EU: New Evidence from the Harmonization of the Banking Industry", *Journal of Banking and Finance*, Vol. 31, pp.1937-1954.

Ross, L. and Sara, Z. (1998), "Stock Markets, Banks, and Economic Growth", *The American Economic Review*, Vol.88 No. 3, pp.537-558.

Schumpeter, J.A. (1934), The Theory of Economic Development, Harvard University Press, Cambridge, MA.

Shaw, E.S. (1973), *Financial Deepening in Economic Development*, Oxford University Press, New York.

Tang, D. (2006), "The Effect of Financial Development on Economic Growth, Evidence from the APEC Countries", *Applied Economics*, Vol. 38 Vol. 16, pp.1889-1904.

Van Nieuwerburgh, S., Buelens, F. and Cuyvers, L. (2006), "Stock market development and economic growth in Belgium", *Explorations of Economic History*, Vol. 43 No. 1, pp. 3-38.

Chapter 3

Islamic Banking in Yemen in Light of The Arab Uprising: An Empirical Study from Customers' Perspective

Abdullah Mohammed Ayedh
Islamic Science University of Malaysia

Abdelghani Echchabi
Effat University

Ameen Al- Nahari
University of Malaya

Introduction

Islamic banking can be simply defined as "banking in consonance with the ethos and value system of Islam and governed, in addition to the conventional good governance and risk management rules, by the principles laid down by Islamic law S*hari'ah*). Interest free banking is a narrow concept denoting a number of banking instruments or operations, which avoid interest. Islamic banking, the more general term is expected not only to avoid interest-based transactions, prohibited in *Shari'ah*, but also to avoid unethical practices and participate actively in achieving the goals and objectives of an Islamic economy" (Said, Ahmad and Javaid, 2009).

Subsequent to its initial establishment, the Islamic banking industry has witnessed a tremendous growth pattern and has maintained a remarkable growth potential, even compared to its conventional counterpart. This situation has been apparent in a number of countries, especially in the Gulf Cooperation Council (GCC) and Malaysia. However, several other countries, generally with large Muslim populations are still untapped (ATKEARNEY, 2012). This particularly refers to the other MENA countries (non-GCC).

In this respect, Islamic banking emerged in Yemen back in 1996, whereby a first Islamic bank by the name Islamic Bank of Yemen for Finance and Investment (YSC) was established by virtue of the Act number 21 of the Yemeni commercial law, with an initial capital of USD10 million. In the same year, Tadhamon International Islamic Bank (TIIB) was subsequently established with a capital of USD93 million. Currently TIIB is considered one of the largest Islamic banks in Yemen with over 50 branches throughout the country. In 1997, Saba Islamic Bank (SIB) was subsequently established, and grew at a fast pace to reach presently 18 branches in both Yemen and Djibouti. Subsequently, Shamil Bank of Yemen and Bahrain (SBYB) was established in 2002. In addition, there are a few conventional banks that use Islamic banking windows to provide Islamic banking services solely (Central Bank of Yemen announcement , 2009).

This growth trend has been accompanied by a considerable amount of empirical studies to examine the customers' sentiments regarding Islamic banking and its major instruments. Most of these studies applied the common attitudinal theories such as theory of reasoned action (TRA), theory of planned behaviour (TPB), and theory of innovations diffusion (TID). These studies covered countries like Malaysia (Lada, Tanakinjal and Amin, 2009; Abdul-Razak and Abduh, 2012; Amin and Chong, 2011; Echchabi and Olaniyi, 2012; Alam, Janor, Zanariah, Che Wel and Ahsan, 2012; Amin, Abdul-Rahman and Abdul-Razak, 2013; Khalek, 2014), Indonesia (Abduh and Omar, 2010), Morocco (Echchabi and Abd. Aziz, 2012), Nigeria (Gumel and Othman, 2013), Tunisia (Echchabi, Ayinde and Azouzi, 2014), and France (Echchabi and Echchabi, 2013). These studies have covered both Islamic banking in general, and also covered specific sub-sets of Islamic banking and finance, including Islamic insurance, Islamic retail products, and Islamic equity products.

It is noteworthy that the scope of these studies is relatively limited, which leaves the Islamic banking arena misty, especially in some MENA countries with majority Muslim population and a long and rich history of Islamic existence. Furthermore, most of these countries have either experienced Arab uprising or have been influenced by it by some way. This is particularly the case of Yemen which has passed through many months of uprisings resulting in a major change of political regime in 2011 accompanied with major social, economic and political reforms that were claimed by the Yemenis for many decades. The Yemeni context is currently still under-researched and under-scrutinised, though the country witnessed a considerable development of the Islamic banking and finance systems in the past few years.

Accordingly, it is also argued that the Yemeni people are religion and culture oriented; therefore, it is hypothesised that their adoption of any new product or service would usually depend on the Islamic aspect –its compliance with *shari'ah*. For instance, when a local insurance company called "United Insurance" introduced Islamic insurance services in 2008, around 80 percent of the existing customers shifted to these services (Saif, 2012).

Furthermore, Saif (2012) argued that this experience made the insurance sector in Yemen to realise the importance of Islamic finance services in attracting the Yemeni customers and investors, and therefore leading the Yemeni financial institutions to introduce Islamic finance services and to launch new institutions offering Islamic finance services.

Hence, the objective of this chapter is to examine the factors that influence the acceptance of Islamic banking services in Yemen in light of the changes that occurred in the

31

country after the Arab uprising. In this regard, the previous studies have identified that TPB has a higher explanatory power compared to the remaining models (Armitage and Conner, 2001). Hence, the study applies TPB to achieve the aforementioned objective.

The original idea behind TPB emanated from the early work by Fishbein and Ajzen (1975) which emphasised the internal and external attitudinal aspects of the human behaviour. This effort amounted to the establishment of TRA which suggest that the human behaviour is a result of a set of internal factors, namely the attitude toward behaviour, and a set of external factors, namely, subjective norms. Subsequently, Ajzen (1991) formally established TPB by including a third dimension, namely, the control over the behaviour i.e. perceived behavioural control.

Specifically, attitude refers to the individual's positive or negative feelings about performing a given behaviour. Attitude has two main dimensions, namely, the belief about a specific behaviour and the evaluation of the outcome from this behaviour.

Subjective norm (SN) is defined as the perception of the individual's main referent groups (people important to the individual) concerning the behaviour. SN has two interrelated dimensions i.e. the determination of the main referent groups to the individual, and their perception about the behaviour.

Finally, perceived behavioural control (PBC) is the extent to which the individual feels able to perform the behaviour. PBC has generally two aspects, firstly the ability to perform the behaviour and secondly the extent to which the individual feels confident to perform the behaviour.

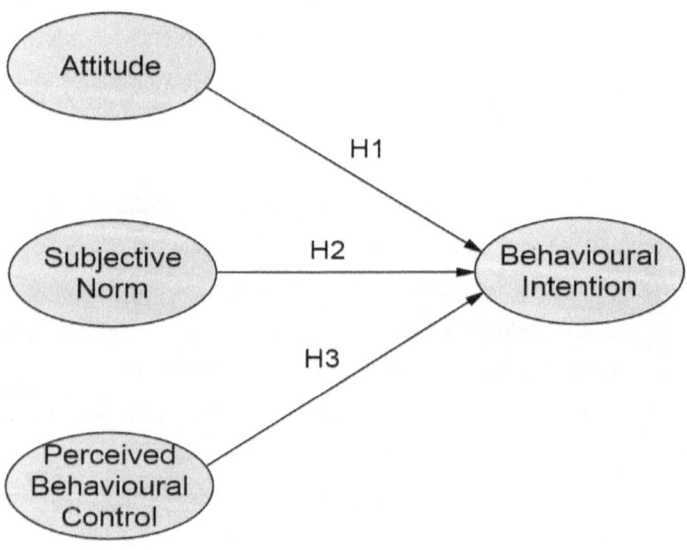

Figure 1: Theoretical model

Based on the model in Figure 1, attitude, subjective norm and perceived behavioural control have positive influence on the behavioural intention. Hence, the following hypotheses are posited and are tested in the following sections:

H1: Attitude has a positive influence on the usage of Islamic banking services in Yemen.

H2: Subjective norm has a positive influence on the usage of Islamic banking services in Yemen.

H3: Perceived behavioural control has a positive influence on the usage of Islamic banking services in Yemen.

In the Chapter

The chapter focuses on the Yemeni context. The target sample size was 300 respondents, out of the distributed questionnaires only 202 were properly and completely filled up and returned. Thus, a response rate of over 67 per cent was achieved, which is an acceptable rate (Dusuki and Abdullah, 2007).

The survey questionnaire was designed to collect information about the perception of the customers towards the attributes of the Islamic banking services as well as their intention to adopt and/or continue using it in their future transactions. For measuring this information, Likert type scaling was used (1 = Strongly Disagree and 7 = Strongly Agree). 20 items were listed in this section and most of them were derived from the previous studies conducted in other countries as highlighted above, as well as from current Islamic banking and finance literature with necessary adaptations made for the specific context of the study. The second section of the questionnaire explored information about respondents' profile, i.e. gender, age, marital status, employment status, etc. The questionnaire was made in English and was subsequently translated into Arabic and distributed as such.

The data were subsequently analysed using structural equation modelling, one sample *t*-test and descriptive statistics. The choice of this technique was inspired from Hair, Black, Babin and Anderson (2010) as well as from similar studies conducted in this area. It is worth mentioning that the analysis was done through AMOS 18 and SPSS 18.

The sample included customers using Islamic banking services, customers using conventional banking services, as well as non-banking customers. In this respect, 66.8 per cent are Islamic banking customers, 1 per cent are conventional banking customers, 9.4 per cent use both Islamic and conventional banking services, while 22.8 per cent are non-banking customers.

Furthermore, the respondents' profile indicates that 95 per cent of the respondents are male, while 5 per cent only are female respondents. This small portion of female respondents

33

might mainly due to the traditional and religious Yemeni culture, which is conservative by nature. Among these respondents, nearly 74 per cent are married, while 26 per cent are single.

Similarly, the table shows indicates that 63.4 per cent of the respondents are between 20 to 30 years old, 28.2 per cent are between 31 and 40 years old, 5 per cent are between 41 and 50 years old and 3.5 per cent are above 50 years old. On the other hand, nearly 60 per cent of the respondents hold a Bachelor's degree, 23.3 per cent are holding a Diploma, 8.9 per cent are holding professional certificates, and 5.9 per cent are holding Master's degree, while 2.5 per cent of the respondents are holding PhD degree. In addition, over 60 per cent of the respondents are working in the private sector, 25.3 per cent are holding positions with the public sector, 6.9 per cent are self-employed and the other 6.9 of the respondents are students.

Table 1: Respondents' Profile

Demographics	Categories	Percentage
Gender	Male	95
	Female	5
Age	20 to 30 years	63.4
	31 to 40 years	28.2
	41 to 50 years	5
	Above 50 years	3.5
Education Level	Diploma	23.3
	Professional Certificate	8.9
	Bachelor's Degree	59.4
	Master's Degree	5.9
	PhD Degree	2.5
Marital Status	Married	73.8
	Single	26.2
Occupation	Public Sector	25.3
	Private Sector	60.9
	Self-Employed	6.9
	Student	6.9
Usage of Banking Services	Islamic Banking	66.8
	Conventional Banking	1
	Both	9.4
	None	22.8

Results

Reliability and validity measures

The mean values in Table 2 show high values that are also significantly greater than the neutral value of four. These values indicate that the customers have a positive perception regarding the principles and operations of Islamic banking.

Furthermore, subjective norm is also marked by high mean values that are also significantly greater than the neutral value of four. These values indicate that the decision making by the Yemenis is generally collective, whereby due reference is usually made to the opinions of parents, siblings, peers and colleagues prior to decision making. This is compatible with the cultural and religious orientation of majority of the Yemeni population.

In addition, the mean values for perceived behavioural control are significantly greater than the neutral value of four. This indicates that the Yemenis have the necessary requisites to use Islamic banking services, including basic knowledge and awareness of Islamic banking principles and operations, the financial and logistic ability, and the environmental readiness to support Islamic banking services. This may justify by the lengthy period of existence of Islamic banking in Yemen since 1996.

Finally, the mean values for behavioural intention are significantly greater than the neutral value of four. This reveals the willingness of the Yemenis to opt for Islamic banking services and/or their satisfaction about their performance.

Table 2: Mean, Standard Deviations and *t* values

Items	Mean	Standard deviation	t
Attitude	5.8257	1.24578	20.829***
AT1	5.4059	1.36901	14.596***
AT2	5.9158	1.48888	18.288***
AT3	5.9455	1.39723	19.790***
AT4	5.8812	1.47811	18.088***
AT5	5.9802	1.43156	19.660***
Subjective Norm	5.0602	1.39876	10.772***
SN1	4.9257	1.65401	7.955***
SN2	4.8267	1.83245	0.412***
SN3	5.1400	1.69881	9.538***
SN4	5.3366	1.56311	12.153***
SN5	5.0429	1.61129	9.199***
SN6	5.0891	1.58726	9.752***

Items	Mean	Standard deviation	t
Attitude	5.8257	1.24578	20.829***
AT1	5.4059	1.36901	14.596***
AT2	5.9158	1.48888	18.288***
AT3	5.9455	1.39723	19.790***
AT4	5.8812	1.47811	18.088***
AT5	5.9802	1.43156	19.660***
Subjective Norm	5.0602	1.39876	10.772***
Perceived Behavioural Control	5.6254	1.32082	17.490***
PBC1	5.5545	1.53549	14.388***
PBC2	5.8168	1.34242	19.235***
PBC3	5.5050	1.41860	15.078***
Behavioural Intention	5.7409	1.20753	20.490***
INT1	5.7376	1.55671	15.864***
INT2	5.8663	1.24467	21.311***
INT3	5.5728	1.44328	15.488***
INT4	5.5842	1.39128	16.183***
INT5	5.6150	1.46494	15.668***
INT6	6.0693	1.17399	25.052***

Note: *** indicates significance at 1%

In order to address the reliability and validity of the estimations, two main measures are emphasised, namely, convergent and discriminant validity. The former refers to the requirement that a number of items measuring a given construct should share high proportion of common variance, while the latter refers to the basic requirement that each construct in the model is significantly distinct from the remaining constructs.

Convergent validity is usually assessed via three measures, namely the Cronbach reliability Alpha, the Average Variance Extracted (AVE) and the factor loadings. It is suggested that a Cronbach Alpha greater or equal to 0.6 is acceptable, similarly, an acceptable level of AVE and factor loadings should be 0.5 and above (Hair, Black, Babin and Anderson, 2010). The results in Table 3 indicate that the Cronbach Alpha and AVE values are greater than 0.5, thus these are acceptable reliability values. Similarly, all the factor loadings are found to be greater than 0.5. Hence, convergent validity is achieved in this model.

Table 3: Reliability Measures

	Cronbach Alpha	AVE
Perceived Behavioural Control	.910	.850
Attitude	.919	.764
Subjective Norm	.918	.714
Behavioural Intention	.937	.766

On the other hand, discriminant validity is assessed by fixing the correlation between the model constructs to 1 and the resulted fit indices are subsequently compared to those of the baseline model. In this respect, the model is suggested to achieve discriminant validity if the two models' fit indices are significantly different.

In this regard, Table 4 displays the Chi square and degree of freedom for the baseline and restricted models, as well as the difference between them. The Chi square value for the baseline model is 648.092 and 711.591 for the restricted model. Similarly, the baseline model has 157 degree of freedom and 163 for the restricted model. Hence, the change in Chi square is 63.499 and 6 for degree of freedom. By comparing the Chi square difference and the tabulated Chi square value corresponding to a degree of freedom of 6 and a confidence margin 0.05 i.e. 12.59, it can be seen that the Chi square difference is greater than the tabulated Chi square value (63.499>12.59). Hence, the fit indices for the baseline and restricted models are significantly different, which signifies that discriminant validity is achieved in this model.

Table 4: Discriminant Validity

Elements	Chi square	DF
Baseline model	648.092	157
Restricted model	711.591	163
Change	63.499	6

Finally, the results indicate that the model's Comparative Fit Index (CFI) is 0.888 and RMSEA value is 0.125, and a normed Chi square value of 4.128. These values are acceptable for the mentioned indicators (Broyles, Leingpibul, Ross and Foster, 2010; Singh, Sandhu, Metri and Kaur, 2013; Kim and Forsythe, 2010), hence, the overall model is validated.

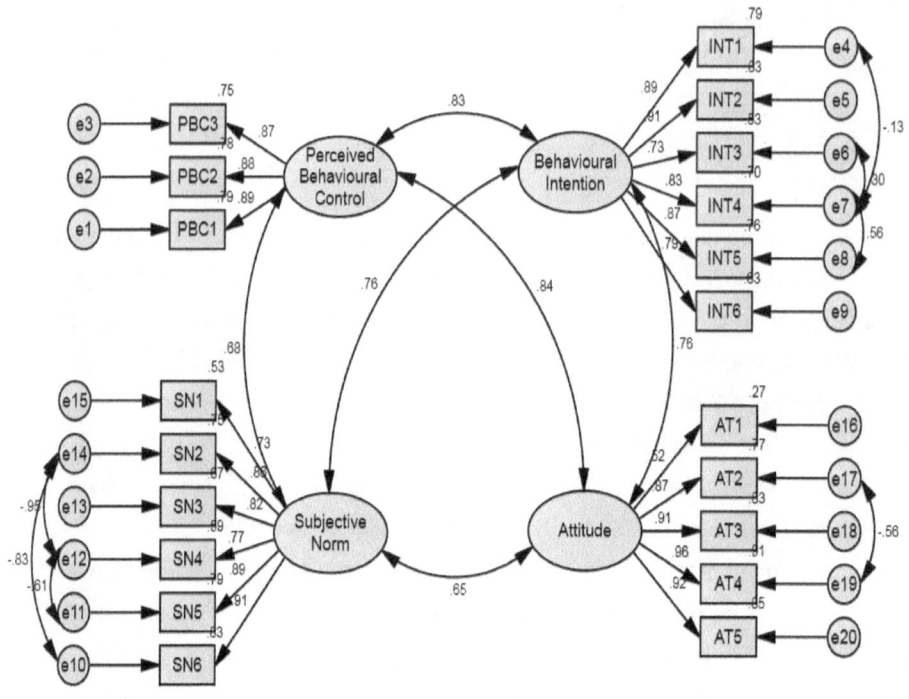

Figure 2: Measurement Model

Structural model

The results in Table 5 and Figure 3 indicate that attitude does not have a significant effect on the intention to use Islamic banking services in Yemen. Hence, hypothesis 1 is rejected. This contradicts TPB (Ajzen, 1991). This implies that the mere economic perceived superiority of Islamic banking services and their compliance with *Shari'ah* is not sufficient in attracting the Yemeni customers; rather, other dimensions seem to be more weighing. This includes the influence of the customers' main referent groups as well as their own ability to opt for Islamic banking services, especially in the current era which was highly marked by post-Arab uprising social and economic reforms.

On the other hand, subjective norm is found to have a significant positive effect on the intention to use Islamic banking services in Yemen. Hence, hypothesis 2 is supported. This is in line with TPB (Ajzen, 1991). This actually implies that the decision of the Yemeni customers to opt for Islamic banking services is highly dependent on referent groups' perceptions and opinions, including parents, siblings, and peers. Hence, the marketing strategies for Islamic banks in Yemen should be collective in nature and should target these groups of individuals.

Finally, perceived behavioural control has a significant positive impact on the intention to use Islamic banking services in Yemen. Hence, hypothesis 3 is supported. This is in line with TPB (Ajzen, 1991). This reveals that the Yemeni customers perceive they are able –in terms of decision control, in terms of means and also in terms of knowledge- to subscribe to Islamic banking services if they are willing. In this regard, it is worth noting that the overall social, political and economic arena in most of the Arab countries –especially those that experienced the Arab uprising- started improving in light of the Arab uprising, this includes various economic, social and political reforms that enhanced the overall wellbeing of the society. These reforms are believed to have contributed, and will continue contributing to the development of Islamic banking system in the region.

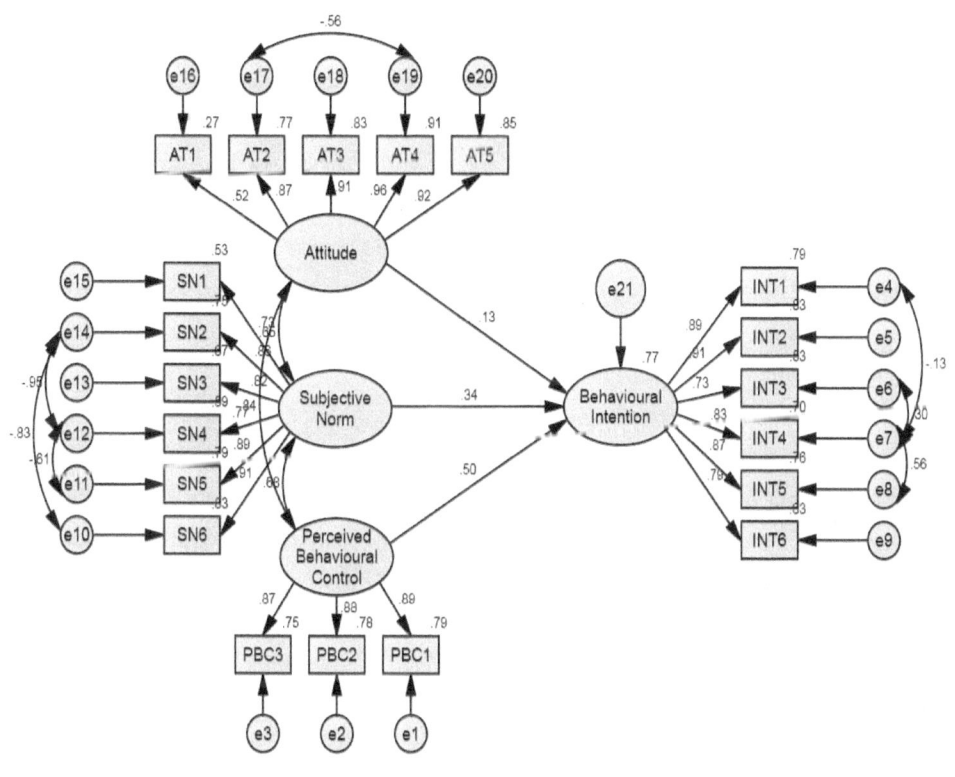

Figure 3: Structural Model

Table 5: Standardised Total Effects

	Attitude	Subjective Norm	Perceived behavioural control
Intention	.126	.343*	.496*

Thus, among the three explanatory variables initially included, two factors are found to be significantly influencing the intention of the Yemeni customers to opt for Islamic banking services instead of their conventional counterpart. Specifically, subjective norm and perceived behavioural control both explain 65 per cent of the variation in the behavioural intention.

Discussions and conclusions

The main purpose of the chapter was to examine the factors that influence the Yemeni customers to adopt Islamic banking services. The results indicate that generally the Yemeni customers are willing to adopt Islamic banking services. On the other hand, the findings indicate that the environmental influence and the extent of decision-making control are the main factors that influence the adoption of Islamic banking services in Yemen.

These findings have significant implications for the theory, for the policy makers and regulators as well as for the practitioners. Particularly, the study is an extension of the theory of planned behaviour to a different setting and to a different area that has been under-researched previously. Hence the study proves the applicability of this theory in this new context. Similarly, the current study provides insights to the practitioners and policymakers on the important dimensions to be emphasised to promote the Islamic banking industry in Yemen and similar countries. Particularly, much emphasis should be on the cultural and religious aspects that are important dimensions of the Yemeni identity.

The current chapter has a number of limitations that should be taken into account in the future studies in this area. Firstly, the sample size is relatively limited, though accurately calculated, hence the results cannot be generalised to the whole region. Thus, the future studies are recommended to select a larger and more representative sample size, in order to generalise the results to the whole country. The future studies are also recommended to extend these findings to other contexts and preferably using other models as well.

Reference

Abduh, M. and Omar, M. A. (2010), "Who patronizes Islamic banks in Indonesia?" *Australian Journal of Islamic Law, Management and Finance,* Vol. 1 No. 1, pp. 46-53.

Abdul-Razak, D. and Abduh, M. (2012), "Customers' attitude towards diminishing partnership home financing in Islamic banking", *American Journal of Applied Sciences,* Vol. 9 No. 4, pp. 593-599.

Ajzen, I. (1991), "The theory of planned behaviour", *Organisational Behaviour and Human Decision Process,* Vol. 50, pp. 179-211.

Alam, S. S., Janor, H., Zanariah, Che Wel, C. and Ahsan, N. (2012), "Is religiosity an important factor in influencing the intention to undertake Islamic home financing in Klang Valley?", *World Applied Sciences Journal,* Vol. 19 No. 7, pp. 1030-1041.

Amin, H. and Chong, R. (2011), "Is the theory of reasoned action valid for Ar-Rahnu? an empirical investigation", *Australian Journal of Basic and Applied Sciences,* Vol. 5 No. 10, pp. 716-726.

Amin, H., Abdul-Rahman, A.-R. and Abdul-Razak, D. (2013), "An integrative approach for understanding Islamic home financing adoption in Malaysia", *International Journal of Bank Marketing,* Vol. 31 No. 7, pp. 544-573.

Armitage, C. J. and Conner, M. (2001), "Efficacy of the Theory of Planned Behaviour: A meta-analytic review", *British Journal of Social Psychology,* Vol. 40, pp. 471-499.

ATKEARNEY (2012), *The future of Islamic banking,* ATKEARNEY, Seoul, South Korea.

Broyles, S. A., Leingpibul, T., Ross, R. H. and Foster, B. M. (2010), "Brand equity's antecedent/consequence relationships in cross-cultural settings", *Journal of Product & Brand Management,* Vol. 19 No. 3, pp. 159-169.

Central Bank of Yemen (2009). *Islamic Banking law,* Central Bank of Yemen, Hadramawt.

Dusuki, A. W. and Abdullah, N. I. (2007), "Why do Malaysian customers patronise Islamic banks?", *International Journal of Bank Marketing,* Vol. 25 No. 3, pp. 142-160.

Echchabi, A. and Aziz, H. A. (2012), "Empirical investigation of customers' perception and adoption towards Islamic banking services in Morocco", *Middle-East Journal of Scientific Research,* Vol. 12 No. 6, pp. 849-858.

Echchabi, A. and Echchabi, F. (2013), "Islamic insurance in the European countries: Insights from French Muslims' perspective", *WSEAS Transactions on Business and Economics,* Vol. 10 No. 3, pp. 125-132.

Echchabi, A. and Olaniyi, O. N. (2012), "Using theory of reasoned action to model the patronisation behaviour of Islamic banks' customers in Malaysia", *Research Journal of Business Management,* Vol. 6 No. 3, pp. 70-82.

Echchabi, A., Olorogun, L. A. and Azouzi, D. (2014), "Islamic insurance prospects in Tunisia in the wake of the Jasmine revolution: A survey from customers' perspective", *Journal of Islamic Accounting and Business Research,* Vol. 5 No. 1, pp. 15-28.

41

Fishbein, M. and Ajzen, I. (1975) *Belief, attitude, intention, and behaviour: An introduction to theory and research,* Addison-Wesley, Reading, MA.

Gumel, A. M. and Othman, M. A. (2013), "Reflecting customers' innovativeness and intention to adopt Islamic banking in Nigeria", *Business and Management Quarterly Review, Vol.* 4 No. 3/4, pp. 27-37.

Hair, J. F., Black, W. C., Babin, B. J. and Anderson, R. E. (2010), *Multivariate Data Analysis (7th Edition),* Prentice Hall, Upper Saddle River.

Khalek, A. A. (2014), "Young consumers' attitude towards halal food outlets and JAKIM's halal certification in Malaysia", *Procedia - Social and Behavioral Sciences,* Vol. 121, pp. 26-34.

Kim, J. and Forsythe, S. (2010), "Factors affecting adoption of product virtualization technology for online consumer electronics shopping", *International Journal of Retail & Distribution Management,* Vol. 38 No. 3, pp. 190-204.

Lada, S., Tanakinjal, G. H. and Amin, H. (2009), "Predicting intention to choose halal products using theory of reasoned action", *International Journal of Islamic and Middle Eastern Finance and Management,* Vol. 2 No. 1, pp. 66-76.

Said, P., Ahmad, I. and Javaid, F. (2009), *Handbook of Islamic banking products and services,* State Bank of Pakistan, Karachi, Pakistan.

Singh, R., Sandhu, H., Metri, B. and Kaur, R. (2013), "Modeling supply chain performance: A structural equation approach", *International Journal of Information Systems and Supply Chain Management,* Vol. 6 No. 4, pp. 18-41.

Chapter 4

Consumer Perceptions of *Takaful* Companies in Brunei Darussalam

Mohamed Sharif Bashir

Al-Imam Muhammad Ibn Saud Islamic University, Kingdom of Saudi Arabia

Nor Hafiizah Hj Mail

Ministry of Finance, Brunei Darussalam

Introduction

Customers are considered as a vital part of the stakeholders of any company. Their perceptions are very important for *takaful* (Islamic insurance) companies because they are the ones who purchase *takaful* products. Regarding Brunei's *takaful* industry, *takaful* operators, are concerned about and are considering offering an educational program to educate Bruneians about *takaful* policies. Bruneians should be educated on the value of insurance and develop the needs of saving culture. In the past, insurance was not seen as a priority for Bruneians. This was due to the extensive social welfare system provided by the Brunei Government to its local citizens. The gratis high-quality health service also practically eliminates the need for health insurance. However, in recent times, the government of Brunei has been considering the future of its social and welfare provision and the need to further develop the saving culture of its citizens. This is likely to benefit players in the life insurance segment [6], [15], [16].

Overview on Islamic Banking, Finance and *Takaful* in Brunei

Brunei Darussalam is a small and wealthy economy that is growing at a slow and steady rate. Brunei is the fourth largest oil producer in Southeast Asia and the ninth largest exporter of liquefied natural gas worldwide. It has remained stable with an average inflation rate of 1.5% over the past two decades. It is considered to have the second highest quality of life in the Association of Southeast Asian Nations (ASEAN) region, and Brunei has an estimated US$31,000 per capita income [7], [16].

Brunei's Islamic banking system is currently served primarily by two groups: The Bank Islam Brunei Darussalam (BIBD) and Tabung Amanah Islam Brunei (TIAB). Over the years, these two institutions have gone through a number of structural changes. The Tabung Amanah

Islam Brunei (TAIB) was the first Islamic financial institution to offer savings and financing launched in 1991, followed two years later by the Islamic Bank of Brunei. They were joined in 2000 by the Islamic Development Bank of Brunei. In line with its mission, the BIBD has two subsidiaries: Takaful BIBD Sdn. Bhd., which primarily provides insurance coverage, and BIBD At-Tamwil Bhd., a finance company that provides hire or purchase financing for vehicles and consumer products [9].

Over the past two decades, Islamic banking in Brunei Darussalam has grown rapidly. Although it makes up a small proportion of the country's financial market, consumer interest in this industry is shown by the fact that they hold 40% of whole banking sector's assets compared to conventional counterparts that account for 60%. Islamic bank deposits also constitute 36% of total bank deposits compared to conventional bank with 64%, while loans accounted for 48% from Islamic banks compared to 52% from conventional banks. The Brunei Government has thus issued over BN$7.23 billion worth of short-term *Sukuk Al-Ijarah* securities since the maiden offering on 6thApril 2006, and the total holdings of the Brunei Government *Sukuk* outstanding until 17thApril 2014 stood at BN$800 million.

The insurance industry was established in Brunei more than 30 years ago. However, the *takaful* business started just 18 years ago with the establishment of Insurance Islam TAIB on March 3, 1993. As an Islamic state, Negara Brunei Darussalam is keen to promote Islamic financial institutions, which include Islamic banks and *takaful* institutions, in its economy [7], [9]. It is interesting to conclude that Brunei Darussalam is among the Muslim countries that are very active in promoting Islamic Financial Institutions (IFIs) in its economy. *Takaful* companies are among the popular IFIs in Brunei. *Takaful* companies were established in Brunei 18 years ago. The first *takaful* company incorporated in Brunei Darussalam was Insurance Islam TAIB Sdn Bhd, which was inaugurated on March 3, 1993. Currently, there are two *takaful* companies in Brunei Darussalam, namely Insurance Islam TAIB Sdn Bhd and Syarikat Takaful Brunei Sdn Bhd. As official statistics show, the contribution of the insurance sector to Brunei's GDP is still below 2%, but in recent years it has been growing at a significant pace [15], [16], [22].

Table 1. Total Assets, Gross Premium, and Claims of *Takaful* and Conventional Insurance Companies in Brunei, 2008-2010 (%)

	Total Assets			Total Gross Premium			Total Claims		
	2008	2009	2010	2008	2009	2010	2008	2009	2010
Takaful Companies	18.6	19.9	20.0	31.1	39.0	41.9	15.1	19.4	26.3
Conventional Insurance Companies	81.4	80.1	80.0	68.9	61.0	58.1	84.9	80.6	73.7

Source:[7].

As shown in Table 1, conventional insurance companies' share in total gross premium decreased at 68.9%, 61.0%, and 58.1% in 2008, 2009, and 2010, respectively. While *takaful* companies' share in total gross premium increased at 31.1%, 39.0%, and 41.9% in 2008, 2009, and 2010, respectively. These increases were indicative of the public awareness and interests toward *takaful* products based on the profit-sharing approach that is not offered by conventional companies. Regarding gross claims, the total claims contribution by *takaful* companies increased at 15.1%, 19.4%, and 26.3% in 2008, 2009, and 2010, respectively. Conventional insurance companies' contribution in total claims declined from 84.9%, 80.6%, and 73.7% over those three years, respectively. As for *takaful* companies, their shares in total assets increased at 18.6%, 19.9%, and 20.0% in 2008, 2009, and 2010, respectively, while the shares of conventional companies declined from 81.4%, 80.1%, and 80.0% in 2008, 2009, and 2010, respectively [7].

The Islamic insurance industry is tightly regulated, with Takaful Order 2008 being the central document setting out the terms and conditions under which the industry operates. This order was issued in October 2008 and was enforced beginning from the following month. The order codified *takaful* operations, ensuring that the industry as a whole was based on a firm foundation and that its products offered and activities met the requirements of Islamic law [6], [7].

There are two types of insurance companies in Brunei Darussalam: conventional and *takaful*. Both types offer a wide range of non-life and life insurance products. Currently, there are two *takaful* operators in Brunei Darussalam: Insurance Islam TAIB Sdn Bhd and Takaful Brunei Darussalam Sdn Bhd (Takaful Am Sdn Bhd and Takaful Keluarga Sdn Bhd) [2], [9], [12]. Besides the *takaful* companies, there are also nine conventional insurance companies operating in Brunei Darussalam: American International Assurance Co. Ltd, Audley Insurance Co. Sdn Bhd, MBA Insurance Company Sdn Bhd, ETIQA Insurance Bhd, National Insurance

Company Bhd, Standard Insurance Sdn Bhd, TOKIO Marine Insurance Singapore Ltd, TM Asia Life Singapore Ltd, and Great Eastern Life Assurance Co. Ltd. Both *takaful* and conventional insurance companies are now under the supervision of the newly established Brunei Darussalam Monetary Authority (AMBD), pursuant to the *Autoriti* Monetary Brunei Darussalam Order of 2010, which took effect January 1, 2011. It was previously under the supervision of the Ministry of Finance's Insurance Section. However, both are governed by two different regulations. *Takaful* companies are regulated under Takaful Order 2008, and conventional insurance companies are governed by Insurance Order 2006 [6], [10], [21]. The *takaful* companies in Brunei started in the early 1990s and developed rapidly. They are successfully doing business on a competitive basis with conventional insurance companies in Brunei's insurance market [2], [9], [15].

Insurance Islam TAIB Sdn Bhd

Insurance Islam TAIB Sdn Bhd was the first *takaful* company established in Brunei Darussalam. It is a wholly owned subsidiary company of Perbadanan Tabung Amanah Islam Brunei (TAIB), a statutory company. The company was first incorporated on March 3, 1993, under the name Takaful TAIB Sdn Bhd. In July 1997, the company changed its corporate entity to Insurance Islam TAIB Sdn Bhd. The authorized capital of the company is BN$20 million and the paid-up capital is BN$10 million [2], [9]. The company's corporate mission is to provide competitive *takaful* products and services that comply with *Shariah* principles as well as to give sound and professional consultation services to customers through well-trained, highly courteous, and efficient personnel supported by the use of the latest advanced information technologies.

There are three types of *takaful* businesses offered by Insurance Islam TAIB Sdn Bhd: general *takaful*, family *takaful*, and special risk *takaful*. There are about 16 *takaful* schemes offered under the general *takaful* business, 10 *takaful* schemes in family *takaful* business, and eight *takaful* schemes under the special risk *takaful* business. All three *takaful* businesses use a *mudarabah* (profit-sharing) model as their *takaful* concept [9].

For the general *takaful* business, the contributions received will be divided into two parts: a *tabaru'* (gift) fund and an investment fund. The *tabaru'* fund will be utilised and deducted with the costs of managing the fund and other related expenses such as claims settlement and reserves, business acquisition costs, *re-takaful* costs, and other technical reserves that are required by statutory regulations or business practices [14], [18], [19]. The investment fund will be invested in *Shariah* compliant investment instruments. The surplus from the fund and the investment returns will make-up the profit for the fund. The profit produced will be shared between Insurance Islam TAIB (as the manager of the fund) and the participants at a ratio determined by Insurance Islam TAIB from time to time (known as *Al-Mudarabah*). Most of the *takaful* products offered by Insurance Islam TAIB are based on the *mudarabah* model, but they offer one *takaful* product based on the *al-wakalah* model, *takaful sinar*, which relates to protection of life and against critical illnesses [9].

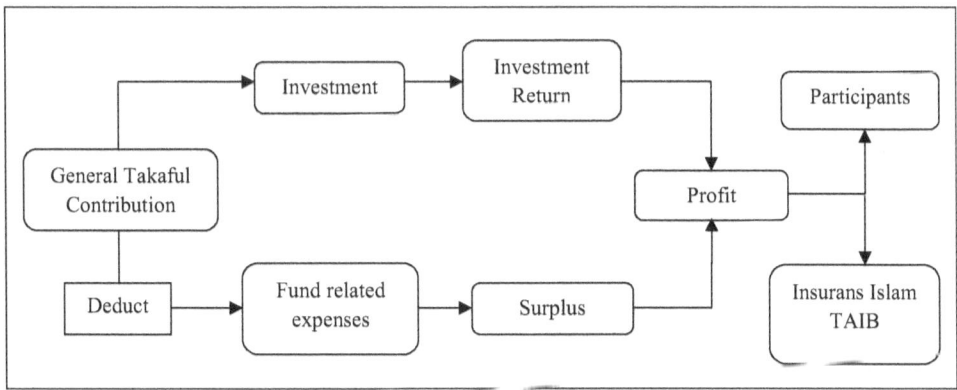

Figure 1. Flow Chart of General Takaful Business

For the family *takaful* business, the *takaful* contribution received from the participants (policy holders) will be allocated into two accounts, namely a participants account (PA) and a participant special account (PSA). The participants account is the saving element in the contribution, whereas the participants special account is the *tabaru'* element in the contribution. PA will be deducted with death, surrender, and partial withdrawal benefits, and PSA will be deducted with claims and *re-takaful* costs. Investment return from the PA and PSA will be distributed between Insurance Islam TAIB and policy holders according to the pre-agreed ratio. As of the date of this book, Insurance Islam TAIB is still operating a composite *takaful* business and has yet to segregate their family *takaful* from their general *takaful*, but it is noted that Insurance Islam TAIB does comply with the capitalisation requirements under Takaful Order 2008 by making provisions for minimum capitalisation of B$8 million for each of its *takaful* business classes [6], [9].

Syarikat Takaful Brunei Darussalam

Syarikat Takaful Brunei Darussalam Sdn Bhd is a holding company that consists of two *takaful* operators as its subsidiaries, Takaful Brunei Am Sdn Bhd (formorly known as Takaful IBB Berhad) and Takaful Brunei Keluarga Sdn Bhd (formerly known as Takaful BIBD Sdn Bhd), in order to comply with the Takaful Order of 2008. On November 13, 2010, Syarikat Takaful Brunei Darussalam held its official launching on the change of name and logos of its subsidiaries Takaful Brunei Am Sdn Bhd and Takaful Keluarga Sdn Bhd. The companies were renamed to reflect their future respective business functions in line with the requirements of the Takaful Order of 2008. Takaful Brunei Am Sdn Bhd, which was formerly known as Takaful IBB Berhad, now will be only focused on general *takaful* products [14], [16], [21], [22].

In contrast, Takaful Brunei Keluarga Sdn Bhd, which was formerly known as Takaful BIBD Sdn Bhd, will now focus only on family *takaful* products. The merging of the two *takaful* operators is seen as a positive development in the country's Islamic financial sector. Furthermore, it is hoped that the combination and synergy of both companies' expertise and experience can strengthen and further develop the *takaful* industry and provide a wider scope of services throughout the country. It is foreseen that this merger will provide awareness within Negara Brunei Darussalam as to the benefits and the advantages of prudent *takaful* practices as well as greatly contribute toward the country's Islamic finance with its vision for 2035. This is also in line with the mission and vision of developing and cultivating a savings culture in Brunei Darussalam through the use of *takaful*.

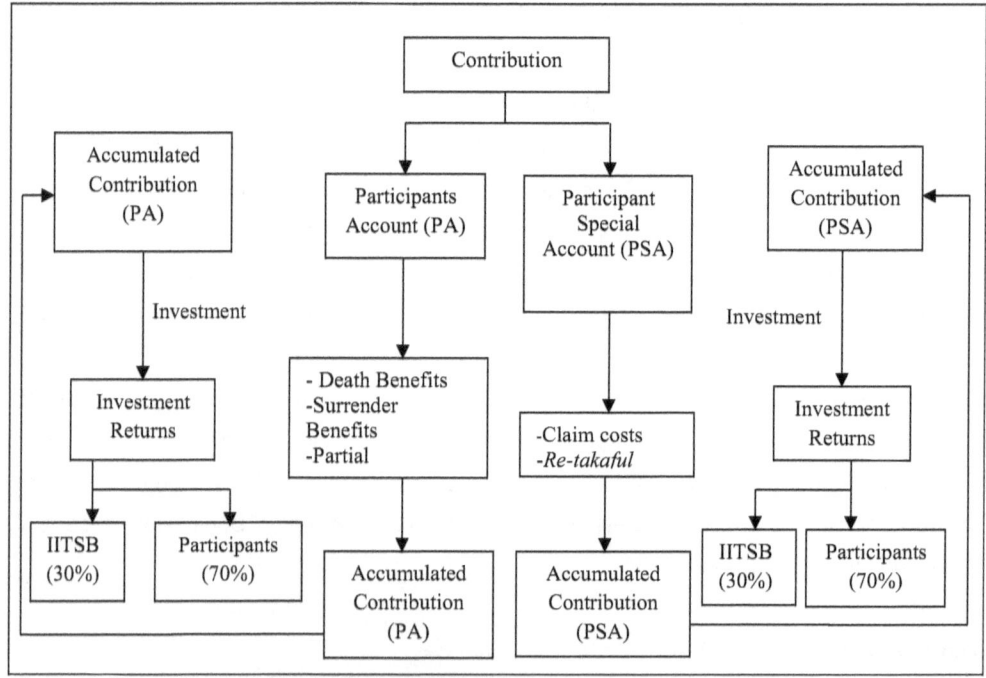

Figure 2. **Flow Chart of Family Takaful business**

Syarikat Takaful Brunei Darussalam Sdn Bhd, through its two subsidiaries, offers both family *takaful* (*takaful keluarga*) and general *takaful* (*takaful am*). The majority of the products offered by the operators are *wakalah* model-based. While the *wakalah* model is employed for short-term *takaful* products (*takaful am* products that are between 1 and 2 years long), the *mudharabah* model is employed for longer-term *takaful* products (investment-linked and life-savings insurance plans) [8], [14], [17], [20].

Notably, under the *wakalah* model, the operators (shareholders) are paid a fixed fee (upfront) as commission on participants' contributions and all expenses are paid for by the operators. Under this model, the operators do not have a share in any profits from investments or surpluses from the underwriting fund. Under the *mudarabah* model, the operators earn a percentage from the net profits, such as 30% for management of *takaful* operator and the remaining share ratio 70% for policyholders. According to *mudharabah* requirements, the operators are responsible for all operating expenses incurred (previously it was charged to participants) [3], [5], [9], [11]. A review of the types of models employed in Brunei reveals that there is a mixture of the two models, *wakalah* and *mudharabah*, both within a company and among companies with a preference for *mudharabah* in one and *wakalah* in the other [14], [16], [18], [21].

Types of *Takaful* Business

There are two types of *takaful* business that are mainly offered by *takaful* operators worldwide, namely general *takaful* business or *takaful am* (short-term maturity) and family *takaful* business or *takaful keluarga* (long-term maturity). *Takaful* operators have the flexibility to operate both *takaful* businesses with different models, but both classes of *takaful* business are required to be kept segregated. There are two types of models that are commonly used by *takaful* operators, namely the *Al-mudarabah* model (profit sharing) and *Al-wakalah* (agent) model [4], [5], [8].

Al-Mudarabah Model

A *takaful* operator that uses the *al-mudarabah* model in their business has a variation in terms of management fees, product design, and distribution channels. In the *al-mudarabah* contract, the *takaful* operator acts as the *mudharib* (manager) and participants act as the *rabbul mal* (capital provider) [1],[13]. The profit from this transaction will be shared according to the agreed ratio between the *takaful* operator and participants. However, losses will be borne by participants as the capital provider. Nevertheless, to protect the participant, the *takaful* operator needs to follow strict requirements and not to invest in risky investments [1], [3], [14]. This model is the preferred *takaful* model in Brunei presently, although there is a move to shift to the *al-wakalah* model [8], [13], [17].

Al-Wakalah Model

The *al-Wakalah* model is different from the *al-mudarabah* model because in the *wakalah* model, the relationship between the *takaful* operator and participant is basically as agent and capital provider. The *takaful* operator acts as the participant's agent and will be paid fees for the services provided. The fees are charged as a fixed amount or percentage, or based on the agreed ratio from the investment profits [11], [12], [13].

In the Chapter

Instruments

In an attempt to examine consumer perceptions of Islamic insurance companies in Brunei, a survey was conducted. The questionnaire consists of 4 sections. Each section is designed specifically to derive relevant information from the respondents. In section 1, the questionnaire asked about the respondent's demographic characteristics. For section 2, the questionnaire asked about the respondent's insurance policy. In section 3, the questionnaire asked about the respondent's understanding and knowledge about the performance of *takaful* companies in Brunei Darussalam. There are 20 statements given in this section asking them to score each of the 5 appropriate answers on a Likert-type scale of 1 to 5. Lastly, in section 4, the respondents are required to give their opinions and suggestion on the given questions.

Data Sources

All the data collected for this chapter were obtained from both primary and secondary sources. Primary source data were obtained from the survey that was conducted specifically for this chapter. Among the objectives of conducting the survey was to examine the customer's perceptions of *takaful* companies in Brunei Darussalam. For this survey, 100 questionnaires were distributed randomly to the public. The secondary data were generally obtained from the *takaful* companies, namely Syarikat Takaful Brunei Darussalam Sdn Bhd and Insurance Islam TAIB Sdn Bhd, and from government-published documents.

Results and Discussion

Respondents' Demographic Characteristics

Table 2 shows that 56% of the respondents are male and 44% are female. Most of them fall between ages 19-29 and 40-49 (29% each), followed by age group 30-39 (28%), with 14% of respondents who said they were more than 50 years of age. Of the respondents, 90% are Malays, followed by 8% Chinese, 1% Indian, and 1% other. It also shows that 92% of the respondents are Muslim, followed by 6% who are Buddhists, and 2% who are Christian. Of the respondents, 1% just graduated from primary school, 47% graduated from secondary school, 38% graduated from university, and 14% have other educational levels including national diploma and postgraduate degrees.

Table 2. **Respondents' Demographic Characteristics**

Characteristics	Frequency
Gender	
Male	56
Female	44
Age	
19-29	29
30-39	28
40-49	29
50 and above	14
Race	
Malays	90
Chinese	8
Indian	1
Others	1
Religion	
Islam	92
Buddh	6
Hindu	2
Other	0
Education Level	
Primary	1
Secondary	47
Graduate	38
Other	14

Table 3. **Respondents' Employment & Salary**

	Frequency
Employment	
Government	75
Private	15
Student	6
Unemployed	4
Salary Range	
Above 3000	23
3000-2001	24
2000-1000	40
Below 1000	13

Table 3 shows that 75% of the respondents work in the government sector, followed by 15% working in the private sector, 6% who are students, and 4% who are unemployed. In terms of monthly salary levels, around 40% of the respondents make BN$1000-BN$2000, followed by 24% who make BN$2001-BN$3000, 23% who make more than BN$3000, and 13% who make less than BN$1000.

4.2 Respondents' *Takaful*/Insurance Policy

Table 4. **Respondents' *Takaful*/Insurance policy**

Question	Frequency
Do you have insurance (conventional and *takaful*) policy?	
Yes	100
No	0
Where do you subscribe the insurance policy?	
Takaful Brunei Am	39
Takaful Brunei Keluarga	11
Insurance Islam TAIB	60
Conventional	3
Why do you choose the above company?	
Reputation	34
Price	28
Product	32
Other	11
Type of insurance policy you have	
Family:	
Health	4
Life	21
Other	4
General:	
Car	92
Fire / House	13
	2
Which part inside the policy you wish to understand more?	
The product	29
Claiming Process	36
Fees	20
Takaful terms	47
Other	2

Is there any policy (s) that you wish to purchase but not offer by *takaful* company in Brunei?	
Yes	6
No	94

Table 4 indicates that all of the 100 respondents have insurance/*takaful* policies. The survey is especially confined to those who have insurance/*takaful* policies. This is to meet the objective of the survey to examine the customer's perception of the *takaful* companies in Brunei. Almost 53.1% of the respondents bought their policy from Insurance Islam TAIB Sdn Bhd, followed by 34.5% respondents bought from Takaful Brunei Am Sdn Bhd, 9.7% respondents bought from Takaful Keluarga Sdn Bhd, and 2.7% of the respondents who said they have conventional insurance policies.

Also, in Table 4, about 32.4% of the respondents chose reputation as their reason for choosing the *takaful* company, while 30.5% respondents chose the products, 26.7% chose the price, and 11% have other reasons. The other reasons are such as through recommendations from family, friends, and insurance agents, because of personal reasons, and because *takaful* companies are *Shari'ah*-based institutions. The most common insurance policy held by the respondents is car insurance (67.7%). Second highest is life Insurance (15.4%). Third highest is fire insurance (9.6%). About 2.9% of respondents have other insurance policies (family *takaful*) beside the listed plan, such as travelling and domestic housemaid *takaful* plans. It also showed that 1.5% of the respondents have other insurance policies through general *takaful* products beside the listed products, such as student *takaful* plans. About 47% of the respondents want to know more on the *takaful* terms, 26.9% of the respondents want to know about the claiming process, 21.6% want to know about the product, and 1.5% want to know about topics other than those listed point in tho questionnaire such as tho investment projects for family *takaful* businesses.

Table 4 indicates that the most respondents (94%) do not have any *takaful* products that they wish to purchase. On the other hand, 6% of them wish purchase other *takaful* products beside those already on the market such as investment-linked insurance, insurance for laptops, insurance for personal valuable items such as gold, jewellery, and securities such as notes, bonds, etc.

Cross-Tabulation Analysis

A cross tabulation analysis has been chosen for showing how respondents answered on two demographic characteristics at the same time. It shows a distribution between responses made for two variables such as gender and age, gender and employment, and employment and age.

Table 5 shows that a plurality of male respondents is between 30-39 years old and a plurality of female respondents is between the ages 19-29. Moreover, the overall highest respondent's age is between the ages of 19-29 or 40-49.

Table 6 indicates that 75% of the respondents work in the government sector. This is followed by 15% of respondents who work in the private sector, 6% who are students, and 4% who are unemployed. From the age part, it shows that most of the respondents who work for the government are 40-49 years old. On the other hand, most of the respondents who work in the private sector are 19-29 and 30-39 years old. For respondents who are students, most are 19-29 years old, and most of the respondents who are unemployed are 19-29 years old or older than 50.

Table 5. **Gender and Age**

Gender	Age			
	19-29	30-39	40-49	above 50
Male	10	21	14	11
Female	19	7	15	3
Total	29	28	29	13

Table 6. **Employment and Age**

Employment	Age			
	19-29	30-39	40-49	above 50
Government	18	20	26	75
Private	6	6	3	15
Student	3	2	0	6
Unemployment	2	0	0	4

Table 7 shows that among the 56 of the male respondents, 75% of them work in the government sector, 14.3% work in the private sector, 3.6% are students, and 7.1% are unemployed. On the other hand, among the 44 female respondents, 75% work in the government sector, 16% work in the private sector, and 9% are students.

Table 7. **Employment and Gender**

Employment	Gender	
	Male	Female
Government	42	33
Private	8	7
Student	2	4
Unemploymen t	4	0

Table 8 indicates that most of the respondents (who work in the government sector) receive a monthly salary between BN$1000-BN$2000. It is similar with respondents who work in the private sector. The highest number of respondents (9) have monthly salaries between BN$1000-BN$2000. For the respondents who are students, most had incomes less than BN$1000 per month. On the other hand, the 2 unemployed respondents have incomes between BN$1000-BN$2000 per month. Thus, most of the respondents (40%) have salaries between BN$1000-BN$2000 per month.

Table 8. **Employment and Monthly Salary**

Employment	Monthly Salary (in BN$)			
	Above 3000	3000-2001	2000-1000	Below 1000
Government	20	20	28	7
Private	2	2	9	2
Student	1	1	1	3
Unemployment	0	1	2	1

Table 9. **Insurance Policy and Employment**

Insurance policy	Employment			
	Government	Private	Student	Unemployment
Health	3	1	0	0
Life	17	2	1	1
Car Insurance	70	14	5	3
Fire	12	1	0	0

Table 9 shows that the highest insurance policy that the respondents purchased is car insurance. The second highest is life insurance, followed by fire and health insurance. The table also shows that the highest *takaful* participants (78.5%) are respondents who work in the government sector. This is followed by the respondents who work in the private sector, students, and the unemployed.

Table 10. **Insurance Policy and *Takaful* Companies**

Insurance policy	Insurance Company		
	Takaful Am	Takaful Keluarga	Insurans TAIB
Health	1	1	2
Life	5	4	15
Car Insurance	37	10	53
Fire	8	2	8

Table 10 shows that about half of the respondents (53.4%) subscribe to their *takaful* policy through Insurance Islam TAIB Sdn Bhd. This is followed by Takaful Brunei AM Sdn Bhd (35%) and Takaful Brunei Keluarga Sdn Bhd (11.6%). The table also shows that the highest *takaful* policy being subscribed to at all *takaful* companies was for car insurance.

The Performance of *Takaful* Companies in Brunei

Table 11 showed that 50% of the respondents agree that a *takaful* company is better than a conventional insurance company, and 21% said that they strongly agreed. On the contrary, 4% of respondents disagreed and 2% of respondents strongly disagreed. From 100 respondents, 23% do not have any opinion about whether a *takaful* company is better than a conventional insurance company. Based on respondents' opinions on products, it showed that 58% of respondents agreed that *takaful* companies offer more beneficial products than other insurance operators, and 20% strongly agreed. This was followed by 18% who agreed and 4% who disagreed. Regarding *takaful* policy, 61% of respondents agreed that *takaful* policies are affordable, and 18% of the respondents strongly agreed and 13% did not have any opinion. However, 8% of the respondents disagreed on this. Based on the question about obtaining claims from *takaful* companies, the above result showed that 37% of the respondents agreed that obtaining claims from *takaful* companies is easier and faster than from other insurance operators. Out of 100 respondents, 14% strongly agreed about this. However, 31% did not have an opinion about this. On the other hand, 14% disagreed and 4% strongly disagreed.

As shown in Table 11, about 61% of the respondents agreed that *takaful* products are simpler and easier to understand. This was followed by 15% who strongly agreed. However, 11% of the respondents disagreed and they found *takaful* products complicated. From 100 respondents, 13% did not have an opinion about this. In regards to premiums required for *takaful* products; the above result showed that 39% of the respondents do not know if *takaful* products require higher premiums than those of other insurance operators. Around 29% of the respondents, agreed and 8% strongly agreed that higher premiums are required for *takaful* products. Conversely, 20% disagreed and 4% strongly disagreed.

In regards to employee attitudes and training skills, 60% of the respondents agreed that *takaful* employees are polite and respectful. On top of this, 30% strongly agreed; however, 8% of the respondents did not know and only 2% disagreed. Employees of *takaful* companies are well trained and can clearly explain the product. Table 9 shows that 58% of the respondents agreed that the *takaful* employees are well trained, 19% strongly agreed, 12% did not know, and 11% disagreed. It also indicates that 47% of respondents strongly agreed and 41% agreed that Bruneians should be better exposed to and educated more about *takaful* products and services. However, 3% of the respondents strongly disagreed and 1% disagreed. The other 8% did not know about this. It shows that 49% of the respondents strongly agreed and 43% agreed that *takaful* companies should offer more products. About 5% did not know and 3% disagreed about this matter.

Table 11 shows that 48% of the respondents strongly agreed and 40% agreed that the *takaful* company promotes Islamic ethics and teachings inside their products and services. Around 9% of respondents did not have any idea, 2% disagreed, and 1% strongly disagreed. About 37% of respondents agreed and 22% strongly agreed that Bruneians are not exposed to other insurance products beside car insurance. In contrast, 25% said they were not aware of this, while 12% disagreed, and 4% strongly disagreed about this statement. The above table showed that 49% of the respondents agreed and 45% strongly agreed that *takaful* companies need to advertise more of their products and services. Conversely, 5% of the respondents did not know, and 1% disagreed about this. The above result showed that 50% of the respondents strongly agreed and 44% agreed that *takaful* companies need to have an updated website that can be easily accessed by customers. Conversely, 5% did not know and 1% strongly disagreed on this matter.

Table 11 shows that 54% of the respondents strongly agreed and 40% agreed that *takaful* companies should give more rewards to their customers. About 4% had no comment on this matter and 1% strongly disagreed and 1% disagreed. The above table showed that 49% agreed and 46% strongly agreed that a regular survey should be done to improve the service quality of *takaful* companies. On the other hand, 3% did not have a comment and 1% each either strongly disagreed or disagreed on this matter. Almost 48% agreed and 45% strongly agreed that it is important to have insurance policies. On the other hand, 6% did not have an opinion and 1% disagreed about this. As shown in the above table, 50% of the respondents strongly agreed and 45% agreed that awareness should begin at an early age. In contrast, 5% did not have an opinion about this matter. Nearly 33% were unaware about this. Moreover, 22% disagreed and 12% strongly disagreed. However, 18% of the respondents agreed and 15% strongly agreed that Bruneians were not interested in purchasing insurance/*takaful* policies. Almost 44% strongly agreed and agreed that insurance/*takaful* is useful to protect life and property. Conversely, 8% did not have any opinion about this, 3% of the respondents strongly disagreed and 1% disagreed.

The mean response on table 11 shows that the consumer's response to the items listed were more on agreed and strongly agreed than disagreed and strongly disagreed. The mean values range from 3.23 to 4.30 which reveal that all twenty statements listed in the table could reflect consumer perceptions of *takaful* business and enhance better performance *takaful* companies in Brunei.

Table 11. **Consumers Response on** *Takaful* **Products and Services in Brunei Darussalam**

No.	Statements	Responses					Mean response
		SD	D	NT	S	SA	
1	*Takaful* company is better than conventional insurance company	2	4	21	23	50	4.15
2	*Takaful* company offers more beneficial products	0	4	20	18	58	4.30
3	*Takaful* policy is affordable to purchase	0	8	18	13	61	4.27
4	It is easier and faster to obtain claim from *takaful* company	4	14	14	31	37	3.83
5	*Takaful* products are simpler and easier to understand	0	11	15	13	61	4.24
6	Higher premium is required for *takaful* product	4	20	8	39	29	3.69
7	The employees are polite and respectful	0	2	30	8	60	4.26
8	Employees of *takaful* company are well trained and can clearly explain the product	0	11	19	12	58	4.17
9	Brunei should expose and educate more on *takaful* products and services	3	1	47	8	41	3.83
10	*Takaful* company should offer more products	0	3	49	5	43	3.88
11	*Takaful* company promotes Islamic ethics and teachings inside their products and services	1	2	40	9	48	4.01
12	Bruneian is not exposing to other insurance products beside car insurance	4	12	22	25	37	3.79
13	*Takaful* company need to advertise more of their products and services	1	0	45	5	49	4.01
14	*Takaful* company needs to have up-dated information website that can be easily access by the customers	1	0	50	5	44	3.91
15	Give more rewards to customers as a token of appreciation	1	1	54	4	40	3.81
16	Regular survey should be done to improve the service quality	1	1	46	3	49	3.98
17	It is important to have insurance policy	0	1	45	6	48	4.01

18	Awareness should be done at the early age example to pre university student	0	0	50	5	45	3.95
19	Bruneian is not interested to purchase insurance/*takaful* policy	12	22	15	33	18	3.23
20	Insurance/*takaful* is useful to protect life and property	3	1	44	8	44	3.89

Respondents' Opinions

The respondents were requested to give their opinions and suggestions on the booktopic. Based on their experiences dealing with *takaful* companies, some of the respondents have encountered the following problems and difficulties:

1. Long waiting time, especially during peak periods.
2. Very difficult to obtain claims. The processes are too bureaucratic and complicated.
3. The computer system sometimes does not work. Thus, everything needs to be done manually and this makes the processing time consuming.
4. One of the respondents found that the price of the insurance policy suddenly increased because of the merger of two *takaful* companies.
5. The renewal process is too tedious because too many procedures need to be done. For example, the car's blue card is sometimes at a different place. In that case, the customer needs to go to the bank (where the loans are taken) to take the blue card and pay a deposit of $50. After that, the customer has to go to the *takaful* company to renew the insurance. Then, the customer needs to return the blue card to the bank.

Some of the ideas and suggestions given by the respondents to improve the performance of *takaful* companies in Brunei are as follows:

1. The *takaful* companies need to improve their service delivery and need to conduct road shows to educate the public on the importance of *takaful*.
2. The *takaful* companies need to be more competitive with other insurance operators, especially in terms of price. The public needs to be exposed to insurance and its importance through more advertisements and promotions.
3. Open more counters and extend operation hours, especially during peak periods. This is to prevent the customer from waiting too long. Companies also should provide up-to-date information and promotions on company websites.
4. Provide clearer and simpler explanations on *takaful* products so that customers can understand and avoid misunderstanding. Conduct talks about the importance and

benefits of *takaful* at every school in Brunei Darussalam, especially at secondary schools, (including lower and upper levels), vocational schools and universities.

5. The *takaful* companies should have online facilities to enhance more of their services provided. In line with this, the company's IT system should be upgraded with more training for the *takaful* employees, especially regarding customer service and product explanation.

Descriptive Analysis

This analysis mainly focuses on section 3 of the questionnaire. Table 12 shows all preferred answers of the 20 statements given. Specifically, when asked which is better, the results show that the mean is 3.88 (Std. deviation = 0.88), which means on average the respondent strongly agreed that the *takaful* company is better than conventional insurance companies. When asked about beneficial products, the results show that the mean is 3.90 (Std. deviation = 0.73), which means on average the respondent strongly agreed that the *takaful* company offers more beneficial products than conventional insurance companies do. When asked which policy is affordable to purchase, the results show that the mean is 3.79 (Std. deviation = 0.77), which means on average the respondent strongly agreed that the *takaful* insurance policies are more affordable to purchase than those of conventional insurance companies. When asked which is faster for obtaining claims, the mean is 3.77 (Std. deviation = 1.02), which means on average the respondent strongly agreed that it is easier and faster to obtain claims from a *takaful* company. When asked about understanding of products, the results show that the mean is 3.76 (Std. deviation = 0.82), which means on average the respondent strongly agreed that the *takaful* products are simpler and easier to understand than those of conventional insurance companies. When asked which amount of premium paid is higher, the results show that the mean is 3.79 (Std. deviation = 1.27), which means on average the respondent strongly agreed that the higher premium is paid by *takaful* participants.

When asked about employee politeness, the results show that the mean is 3.74 (Std. deviation = 0.63), which means on average the respondent strongly agreed that the *takaful* company has polite and respectful employees. When asked about employees' skills, the results show that the mean is 3.71 (Std. deviation = 0.82), which means on average the respondent strongly agreed that *takaful* company employees are well trained and explain products clearly. When asked about promoting products and educating efforts, the results show that the mean is 3.50 (Std. deviation = 0.79), which means on average the respondent strongly agreed that Bruneians should be more exposed and educated about *takaful* products and services. When asked which company offers more products, the results show that the mean is 3.50 (Std. deviation = 0.64), which means on average the respondent strongly agreed

60

that *takaful* companies should offer more products. When asked about promotion of ethics and knowledge that appeared in products, the results show that the mean is 3.67 (Std. deviation = 0.72), which means on average the respondent strongly agreed that the *takaful* company promotes Islamic ethics and teachings on their products and services. When asked whether Bruneians are exposed to other insurance products besides car insurance, the results show that the mean is 3.67 (Std. deviation = 1.10), which means on average the respondent strongly agreed that Bruneians are not exposed to other *takaful* products besides car insurance.

When asked about advertisement efforts provided, the results show that the mean is 3.57 (Std. deviation = 0.64), which means on average the respondent strongly agreed that the *takaful* company needs to advertise more of their products and services. When asked about updating company website information, the results show that the mean is 3.52 (Std. deviation = 0.64), which means on average the respondent strongly agreed that the *takaful* company must have a website that can be easily accessed by customers and is updated with current information. When asked about rewards given to the customers, the results show that the mean, is 3.45 (Std. deviation = 0.64), which means on average the respondent strongly agreed that the *takaful* company should give more rewards to their customers as a token of appreciation. When asked about usefulness of conducting consumer surveys, the results show that the mean is 3.52 (Std. deviation = 0.62), which means on average the respondent strongly agreed that a regular survey should be conducted to improve *takaful* companies' service quality.

Table 12. **Descriptive Statistics**

No.	Category	Mean	Std. Deviation
1	Better than	3.88	0.879
2	Benefit	3.90	0.732
3	Affordable to purchase	3.79	0.769
4	Faster to obtain claim	3.77	1.153
5	Simple to understand	3.76	0.818
6	Higher premium	3.79	1.266
7	Polite employees	3.74	0.630
8	Well trained employees	3.71	0.820
9	Educate more on *takaful*	3.50	0.785
10	Offer more products	3.50	.644
11	Promote Islamic ethics	3.62	.722
12	Not exposing to other products	3.67	1.101
13	Advertisement	3.57	0.640
14	Website	3.52	0.643
15	Rewards	3.45	0.642
16	Survey	3.52	0.627
17	Importance	3.59	0.621
18	Awareness	3.55	0.592
19	Buying insurance or *takaful*	3.38	1.441
20	Usefulness	3.53	0.784

When asked about importance of having insurance or *takaful* policy, the results show that the mean is 3.59 (Std. deviation = 0.62), which means on average the respondent strongly agreed that it is important to have insurance or *takaful* policies. When asked about awareness, the results show that the mean is 3.55 (Std. deviation = 0.59), which means on average the respondent strongly agreed that awareness on the importance of having insurance should target a generation in its youth, for example pre-university students. When asked about buying insurance or *takaful* policy by Bruneian, the results show that the mean is 3.38 (Std. deviation = 1.44), which means on average the respondent strongly agreed that Bruneians are not interested in buying insurance or *takaful* policies. Finally, when asked about usefulness of insurance or *takaful*, the results show that the mean is 3.53 (Std. deviation= 0.78), which means on average the respondent strongly agreed that *takaful* or insurance is useful to protect life and property.

Conclusion and Policy Implications

The findings can be summarized as follows:

1. Regarding the availability of the educational programs conducted by the government as well as the *takaful* companies, there are only a few educational programs conducted. Bruneians still need to be better exposed and educated on the importance

of insurance, especially of *takaful* products. This statement is supported by 47% of the respondents who strongly agreed and 41% who agreed.

2. The majority of the respondents subscribed to their *takaful* policy at Insurance Islam TAIB followed by Takaful Brunei Am and Takaful Brunei Keluarga. Moreover, the majority of respondents who participated in a *takaful* policy chose it because of the *takaful* company's reputation, followed by product and price, respectively.

3. The majority of the respondents have car insurance. Only a few of them have other policies. This result proved that most Bruneians are not exposed to other insurance policies besides car insurance. Most of the survey respondents also agreed on this. The reason for this may be that car insurance is required by law for every car in Brunei.

4. The most common problem encountered by *takaful* policyholders regards the claim process. Most of the policyholders expressed unhappiness that it was difficult to obtain their claims. The processes are too bureaucratic and complicated. *Takaful* companies should find a better solution to this problem.

5. The majority of respondents suggested that *takaful* companies should better train their employees about their products and also on customer service. This is very important because when the employees have proper training on this matter, they can provide excellent service to customers and this can benefit the company and its reputations. Therefore, *takaful* companies should take this issue very seriously.

6. Another suggestion is on improving or upgrading *takaful* company computer systems. Their current computer systems do not meet good standards. Frequent breakdowns do not present a good image to the customer. *Takaful* companies should invest more in improving their computer system so that they can provide higher quality and more innovative services.

7. Besides the problem of the claim process, another common problem encountered by the policyholders was long waiting time. This problem is getting worse during peak periods. To solve the problem, *takaful* companies are suggested to have online registration so that the customers can register early and just come to pay for the insurance.

One of the current issues concerning the *takaful* industry relates to educating the public on the importance of *takaful*/insurance policies. As mentioned earlier, recently the Brunei Government began seriously considering its citizens' social and saving culture. This can benefit the life insurance business. The most common problems that the majority of customers encountered were long waiting periods, bureaucracy, and complicated claims processes. Less action has been done by *takaful* companies to address these problems. Most of the survey respondents who are also *takaful* customers expressed their unhappiness about these matters. Therefore, *takaful* companies in Brunei Darussalam should put more effort into solving these problems.

The findings suggest several policy implications as follows:

1. *Takaful* companies should take the opportunity to offer an innovative life insurance product that can benefit the public, especially Bruneians. Most of the Brunei population is Muslim, therefore *takaful* companies have a greater advantage in this regard.

2. *Takaful* companies should provide more training to their employees, especially on how to explain their products more effectively and understandably. Besides this, the employees should be given more training on customer relationship services. A properly trained employee can provide excellent service to customers and this can benefit the company and its reputation as a whole.

3. *Takaful* companies should improve their computer system to provide faster service. This will avoid customer frustration, which can give the companies a bad.

4. There is a need for frequently conducting surveys on customer perceptions about products and services. Companies can receive useful feedback from their customers, and this feedback can be used to improve their products and services.

References

AAOIFI (2004/2005), *Accounting, Auditing and Governance Standards for Islamic Financial Institutions, No 12*, AAOIFI, Bahrain.

Abdul R. and Abdul, K. (1998), *A Brief Description of Islamic Insurance (Takaful)*, The Islamic Bank of Brunei Bhd, Bandar Seri Begawan.

Abouzaid, A. (2007), *Takaful Market: The Challenges of the Fast Growing Industry*, Retrieved from:

http://www.takaful.coop/doc_store/takaful/Challenges%20of%20Takaful%20sector%20September%202007.pdf.

Ali, E. R. and Odierno, H. (2008), *Essential Guide to Takaful*, CERT Publications, Kuala Lumpur.

Ali, E. R. (2010), *Panduan Asas Takaful*, CERT Publications, Kuala Lumpur.

Government of Brunei Darussalam (2008), *Takaful Order 2008*, Government of Brunei Darussalam. Bandar Seri Begawan.

Government of Brunei Darussalam (2011), *Financial Institution Division*, Ministry of Finance, Bandar Seri Begawan.

Hashim, N. H. (2006), "Life Insurance Purchasing Decision: A Preliminary Study", *The Journal of Muamalat and Islamic Finance Research*, Vol. 3 No. 1, pp. 153-170.

Insurance Islam TAIB (2011), *Annual Report*, Insurance Islam TAIB, Bandar Seri Begawan. Retrieved from http://www.bruneidirecthys.net/about_brunei/insurance.html, February 18, 2011.

Matraji, S. (2006), "Journey from the Commercial Insurance Contract to Takaful", *First International Forum on Islamic Economics, Finance and Business for Young Scholars*, Universiti Teknologi MARA and Islamic Research & Training Institute, Islamic Development Bank, Sheraton Perdana Resort Langkawi, Malaysia, 18-20 April, pp. 211-241.

Metussin, B. (2004), *Ugama dan Insurance Islam Di Negara Brunei Darussalam*, Bandar Seri Begawan.

Mohd, M. B. (2007), *Applied Takaful and Modern Insurance*, Sweet & Maxwell Asia, Kuala Lumpur.

Mohd, M. B. (2002), "Legal Capacity to Contract of Takaful: An Islamic Jurisprudential Consideration", *International Journal of Islamic Financial Services*, Vol. 4 No. 1, pp. 20–32.

Oxford Business Group (2008), *Brunei Darussalam Report 2008*, Retrieved from www.oxfordbusinessgroup.com, May 25, 2011

Oxford Business Group (2009), *Brunei Darussalam Report 2009*, Retrieved from www.oxfordbusinessgroup.com, May 25, 2011

Pravaiz, S, (2011), *Takaful Concept*, Retrieved from: http://www.al-wasl.com/downloads/dhaka/Takaful_Concepts_Final.pdf, April 18, 2011.

Ramliy, J., Mansor, N. M. and Rahman, M. Z. (2007), *Asas Takaful Buku Panduan*, Islamic Banking and Finance Institute Malaysia (IBFIM), Kuala Lumpur.

Saiful, A. R. (2007), *Critical Issues on Islamic Banking and Financial Markets*, Dinamas Publishing, Kuala Lumpur.

Salahuddin, A. (2007), *Islamic Banking Finance and Insurance: A Global Overview*, A. S. Noordeen, Kuala Lumpur.

Shaffaii, S. (2008), *Brunei approves Islamic Banking Order 2008*, Brunei Times, Bandar Seri Begawan, November 25. Retrieved from: http://islamicfinanceupdates.wordpress.com/2008/11/28/brunei-approves-islamic-banking-order-2008/, May 25, 2011.

Siddiqui, S. A. and Athemy, A. A. (2008), "Resolving Controversial Issues and Setting Goals for Islamic Insurance: An Evaluation of Takaful Companies of Brunei", *Journal of Islamic Economics, Banking and Finance*, Vol. 3 No. 2, pp. 129-158.

Chapter 6

Islamic Finance: Growth and Prospects in Singapore

Habibullah Khan, PhD

GlobalNxt University
Omar K M R Bashar, PhD

Swinburne University of Technology

Introduction

Islamic finance, which dates back to 1975 with the establishment of Bank Faisal in Egypt, is developing at a remarkable pace. The growth of Islamic finance industry has been very strong over the past few years. Currently, there are over 300 Islamic financial institutions in more than 75 countries though they are mainly concentrated in the Middle East and Southeast Asia, but are also gaining popularity in Europe and the United States. It is estimated that the industry will grow at a rate of 15 to 20 percent annually, from current assets of US$300 billion (Al-Salem, 2008).

The importance and potential of Islamic banking prompted the International Monetary Fund (IMF) to facilitate the establishment of the Islamic Financial Services Board (IFSB) (the Islamic equivalent of IMF) in 2002, the idea being addressing the need for a suitable regulatory framework, new financial instruments and institutional arrangements for Islamic finance operations. Recently, the Singapore government has also recognized the need for establishing Islamic banking in order to be complete as an international financial centre.

Islamic Finance: Principles and Products
Principles of Islamic Finance and Advantages

Islamic finance operates under religious beliefs and cultural characteristics of Muslim societies. According to Shari'ah (Islamic law), the Islamic mode of finance should emphasize profit and loss sharing and prohibit fixed-returns. In other words, any predetermined payment over and above the actual amount of the principal (i.e. interest) is prohibited. The Shari'ah also prohibits activities related to uncertainty, risk and speculation. A modern interpretation is that interest may be paid only for taking investment risk but not for time value risk-free investment. As such, asset-based lending is allowed under Shari'ah while paper or financial-based lending is not. The law also prohibits investment in "un-Islamic" activities, such as lending for constructing a casino or trading of alcohol.

In sum, the guiding principles regarding Islamic finance include the following: First of all, any predetermined payment over and above the actual amount of principal is prohibited. Secondly, the lender must share in the profits or losses arising out of the enterprise for which money was lent. Thirdly, making money from money is not acceptable by Islamic law. Money is only a medium of exchange, and therefore should not be allowed to give rise to more money, via fixed interest payments, simply by being put in a bank or lent to someone else. Fourthly, *Gharar* (uncertainty, risk or speculation) is also prohibited. Finally, investments should only support practices or products that are not forbidden (or discouraged) by Islam.

There are several advantages of Islamic system which is based on the principle of profit-sharing. First of all, profit-sharing channels investible funds to the projects with the highest expected profitability as opposed to the interest-based system where funds go to the most creditworthy borrowers whose projects may not necessarily be the most profitable ones. In fact, the 'quest for profit' is the main driving force behind the development of modern businesses and it was clearly reflected in the powerful writings of Adam Smith in *The Wealth of Nations (1776)*. Adam Smith argued that even though self-interest is the prime mover of economic activity, the end result is the allocation of goods and services that serves society's collective interests in the best possible manner. If produces offer 'too much' of one product and 'too little' of another, profit opportunities immediately would alert entrepreneurs to the fact and provide incentives for them to change the line of production. In other words, the system based on profitability will ensure 'economic efficiency' leading to optimality in production, consumption, and exchange. Secondly, profit-sharing is more conducive to economic growth, as this would increase the supply of risk capital for investment and greater incentives for undertaking such risks due to expected profitability. Finally, the Islamic system promotes an 'integrated' economic development as it encourages the use of money for facilitating trade in goods and investment in productive capacity rather than creating money for the sake of money. Such a system is likely to be more stable and is less vulnerable to financial crisis that can be caused by speculative activities.

Islamic Financial Products

The following is a brief description of Islamic financial products:

i) **Profit sharing financial products**

These products include *Musharakah, Mudarabah, Qard Hasan, Wakalah,* and Hawalah. In case of *Musharakah,* all partners participate in terms of equity, investment, management, profit (based on pre-agreed ratio) and, loss (based on equity contributions). In *Mudarabah accounts,* one contributes capital, others provide entrepreneurship. Profit is shared on a pre-agreed ratio. Under *Qard Hasan,* charitable loans free of interest and profit-sharing margins are being provided and repayments are being made by instalments. Modest service charge is permissible. In case of *Wakalah*, a bank is authorized to conduct business on behalf of customers. *Hawalah* is an agreement by the bank to undertake some of the liabilities of the customer in return for a service fee. The customer pays back the bank when the liabilities mature.

ii)   ***Advance purchase financial products***

These financial products that are purchased in advance include the following: *Murabahah*- a contract between the bank and its client for the sale of goods at a price that includes a profit margin agreed by both parties. *Istithna'*- a contract for acquisition of goods by specification or order, where the price is paid progressively in accordance with the progress of job completion. *Mu'ajjal*- a sales contract that allows purchase with deferred delivery. *Ijarah*- a leasing contract under which a bank buys and leases out for a rental fee equipment required by its clients.

iii)   ***Deposit products***

The well-known deposit schemes include the following: *Wadi'ah*- deposits, including current accounts *(giro wadi'ah)*. *Mudarabah*- deposit products based on revenue-sharing between depositor and bank, including savings products that can be withdrawn any time and time deposit products. *Qard al-Hasanah*- unremunerated deposit products, usually for charitable purposes.

iv) *Insurance products*

Takaful is the most well-known Islamic insurance concept based on the principle of shared responsibility and cooperation as practised by Muslims under the Islamic law. For details on Takaful and all other financial products described above, please refer to Imady and Siebel (2006).

Islamic Finance in Singapore

Status of Islamic Finance in Singapore

Islamic finance received attention of the Singapore government in recent years. The following is a brief description of Singapore's recent development in Islamic finance:

Regulatory treatment

In June 2006, the Monetary Authority of Singapore (MAS) gave its approval to banks to engage in non-financial activities, such as commodity trading, to facilitate *Murabahah* transactions for clients' investments. Prior to this, banks had been forbidden to engage in non-financial activities such as trading, which is not normally associated with banking and finance. This move shows that MAS recognizes the fundamental characteristics of *Murabaha* - a key form of Islamic financing in the Middle East (Asmani, 2006).

Tax treatment

The Singapore government recognizes that given the nature and structure of Islamic financial products, they tend to attract more tax than their counterparts. The overall policy approach has been to align tax treatment of Islamic contracts with the treatment of conventional financing contracts they are economically equivalent to. In line with this policy, the Finance Ministry announced several changes in the 2005 and 2006 budgets.

In 2005, Singapore waived the imposition of double stamp duties in Islamic transactions involving real estate and accorded the same concessionary tax treatment on income from Islamic bonds that are applicable to conventional bonds.

In 2006, income tax and GST (goods and services tax) applications on some Islamic products were further clarified. The government identified three Shari'ah-compliant products and ensured that they do not suffer more taxes due to the nature of their structuring. In addition, to level the tax playing field for *Sukuk* (Islamic equivalent of a bond), remission will be granted on stamp duty on immovable property, incurred under a *Sukuk* structure, that is in excess of that chargeable in the case of an equivalent conventional bond issue.[4]

Growth and development of financial products

In July 2001, Maybank, Malaysia's largest bank started Islamic banking in Singapore with the introduction of Singapore Unit Trusts Ethical Growth Fund that complies with the principles of the Shari'ah.[5] In November 2005, the bank introduced Shari'ah-complaint online savings account and Shari'ah-compliant savings cum checking account (Siow, 2005).

In February 2006, the first Shari'ah-compliant term deposit in Singapore was launched by OCBC Bank. The bank targets wholesale to Muslim companies, financial institutions, mosques and non-profit organizations (Yee, 2006).

Islamic insurance or Takaful has also been successful in Singapore with over S\$500 million Takaful funds under management. For instance, HSBC (Singapore) launched Takaful Global Fund in September 1995 while Takaful Sinaran Fund was launched in May 2005. Returns from these funds are not subjected to income tax. There are about S\$2 billion Shariah compliant real estate funds managed out of Singapore.[6]

---

[4] Ng, Nam Sim, Executive Director, MAS, Opening Remarks at the IQPC Islamic Finance, Singapore 2006.
[5] Source: Singapore Unit Trusts website www.sut.com.sg/main/fund sutegf.asp (accessed on 28 May 2008).
[6] MAS, Annual Report 2005/2006.

Islamic equity index

In recognition of increasing interest of Middle East investors in diversifying and tapping the growth opportunities in Asia, the first Shari'ah-compliant pan-Asian equity index was launched in Singapore in February 2006. This index serves as a benchmark for Shari'ah-compliant funds investing in Asian equities, and paves the way for the growth of Shari'ah-compliant funds seeking Asian exposures.

IFSB membership

MAS is a member of IFSB. MAS joined the IFSB in December 2003 as an observer member and became a full member in April 2005. MAS currently participates in the Islamic Money Market Taskforce, the Supervisory Review Process Working Group and the Special Issues in Capital Adequacy Working Group.[7]

Education

Another significant move in the development of Islamic finance in Singapore has been the announcement by the Singapore Islamic Scholars and Religious Teachers Association (PERGAS) that some Islamic religious scholars would be trained in banking and finance to assist Singapore's aim of becoming a hub for Islamic finance. PERGAS also mentioned in September 2006 that in order to develop *Asatizah* (religious teachers), it would introduce a Shari'ah Advisers Training Programme organized jointly with the Kuala Lumpur-based International Institute of Islamic Finance (Venardos, 2006, pp 208-209).

Exchange traded fund

Singapore moved a step forward in the development of its Islamic finance industry with the first listing of a Shari'ah-compliant exchange traded fund (ETF) on 27 May 2008. Daiwa Asset Management Co. Ltd.'s first ETF offers an investment channel into Japanese companies that fully complies with Shari'ah investment principles.[8]

Prospects of Islamic Finance in Singapore

Singapore is a relatively new market player in Islamic finance. The domestic market is quite small and there is not sufficient public awareness about Islamic finance. Regionally, Malaysia is leading Islamic finance industry. Yet Singapore has good prospect for positioning itself in a niche market. For instance, as of 2006 there are nearly 227 million Muslims in Southeast Asia,

---

[7] MAS, Annual Report 2006/2007.
[8] "Singapore's de facto Central Bank sees 'promising growth' in Islamic Finance". Source: Forbes website www.forbes.com/afxnewslimited/feeds/afx/2008/05/27/afx5048208.html (accessed on 28 May 2008).

which is about 40 percent of total population in the region.[9] Being a regional financial hub, Singapore could target a big pie of this Muslim community since Islamic finance in Southeast Asia is not as far advanced as in the Middle East despite strong growth potential. For example, Islamic finance in Indonesia is not nearly as well developed as it is in Malaysia with Islamic banks holding only a 0.12 per cent share of the assets in the banking system. The lack of comprehensive and appropriate framework and instruments for regulation and supervision has impeded the development of Islamic finance to its full potential. Indonesia is the world's most populous Muslim nation and Singapore could eye on this potentially huge market.

The Middle East and South Asia could also offer a unique opportunity for Singapore's development in Islamic finance industry. Singapore could attract relatively wealthier Muslims from the Middle East, Pakistan, Bangladesh and India. Besides, non-Muslims could also be educated on Islamic finance products and targeted in the long-run. Singapore's reputation as a stable and open financial hub is expected to play an important role in luring investors in this industry.

In order to strengthen its presence in Islamic finance industry, Singapore has refined its regulatory framework and tax structures over the years. The initiatives include granting of a 5 percent concessionary tax rate for income derived from Shari'ah-compliant fund management, lending and insurance and re-insurance. The MAS will also be developing a facility for the issuance of Singapore dollar denominated sovereign-rated *Sukuks* in response to the needs of financial institutions conducting Shari'ah-compliant activities in Singapore.[10]

Conclusion

Islamic finance is a relatively new concept in Singapore. Small domestic market and lack of public awareness do not offer strong growth potential for Islamic finance industry within the Republic. Over the years, Singapore revised its regulatory framework and tax structure and introduced various Shari'ah-compliant financial products. The city-state Republic also faces strong competition from Malaysia in providing Islamic products regionally. However, the country can still find a niche market in Southeast Asia (particularly Indonesia), the Middle East and South Asia given the reputation of being regional financial hub and its overall attractiveness as a business location. Singapore's neutral stance to all religious beliefs and practices and its harmonious development of various race relations within the community at large has further added to its strength. Another important point is worth mentioning Singapore is pursuing a strategy of integrated development of financial and real sectors as it believes

---

[9] Source: **Muslim Population Worldwide website www.islamicpopulation.com (accessed on 31 May 2008).**
[10] **"Singapore's de facto Central Bank sees 'promising growth' in Islamic Finance". Source: Forbes website www.forbes.com/atxnewslimited/feeds/afx/2008/05/27/afx5048208.html (accessed on 28 May 2008).**

that the two can reinforce each other. Singapore has just completed a free trade agreement (FTA) negotiation with Gulf Cooperation Council (GCC) and this is likely to facilitate trade and investment between two sides. With deeper trade and investment links, there will be greater opportunity for financial integration that could open new promises for Islamic finance and the related products.

References

Al-Salem, F. (2008), "The Size and Scope of the Islamic Finance Industry: An Analysis", *International Journal of Management,* Vol. 25 No. 1, pp. xx-xx.

Asmani, A. (2006), *Banks Get Light to Offer Another Islamic Product*, The Straits Times, Singapore, 13 June.

Imady, O. and Seibel, H. D. (2006), *Principles and Products of Islamic Finance,* Working Paper No. 2006-1, Development Research Center, University of Cologne, Germany.

Monetary Authority of Singapore, *Annual Reports (various issues).*

Siow, L. S. (2005), Maybank Launches Islamic Banking, The Business Times, Singapore, 26 November.

Venardos, A. M. (2006), *Islamic Banking and Finance in South-east Asia: Its Developments and Future*, Asia-Pacific Business Series, Vol. 3, World Scientific Publishing Co., Singapore.

Yee, L. (2006). *OCBC Scores on 5-year Risk-adjusted Returns*, The Business Times, Singapore, 9 February.

Chapter 7

Quality Perception of the Customers towards Domestic Islamic Banks in Bangladesh

Assoc. Prof. Dr. Abu Umar Faruq Ahmad
International Shari`ah Research Academy for Islamic Finance (ISRA)

Mamunur Rashid,
Nottingham University Business School

Abul Kalam Muhammad Shahed, PhD
International Islamic University Chittagong, Bangladesh

Islamic Banking in Bangladesh: An Overview

The debiting and crediting of interest, which is one of the major features of the modern financial system and is central to financial operations all over the world, including the Muslim countries, is prohibited under the Islamic banking system for moral as well as economic reasons. In view of this unequivocal and categorical prohibition of *riba*, a society that is committed to establishing its socio-economic relations on Islamic values is bound to search for an alternative to the conventional banking system. The near-consensus amongst Islamic economists and jurists suggests that while Islam wants to discard all interest-bearing schemes in loan/investment operations, it aims at establishing an economy where equity participation becomes the primary mode of financial operations (Ahmad, 2006).

While comparing the two banking systems one will observe that the most important departure of Islamic banking system from conventional banking system is the prohibition of *riba*, and the concentration on *bai`* or selling and buying activities. Thus, if an Islamic bank were to be compared with an existing conventional bank, one may say that while the latter earns the major share of its profit from its revenues and expenses associated with interest, the former earns the same on the basis of profits arising from trade. Again, the former actually participate in production and commerce by taking an equity stake, whereas the latter's interest in commerce and production is limited to the interest it can receive in addition to recovering the principal. Furthermore, Islamic banking is a risky business, but it is this risk sharing that justifies profit sharing and hence the return on capital in an Islamic system (Ahmad, 2003).

The Shari`ah does not prevent Islamic banks from conducting transactions with conventional banks provided that the conventional banks follow the rules of Shari`ah, and structure their instruments or transactions accordingly. These conventional institutions should be encouraged and supported in such endeavours since they have the knowledge and experience to enrich the Islamic banking. They could introduce viable investment opportunities due to their large market and accumulated expertise. The entrance of such institutions increases competition provides broader diversification of markets and risks, and better liquidity arrangements. It also allows wider interaction between conventional and Islamic systems, which will facilitate better understanding for both and lead to the globalisation of financial markets (Hassan et al, 2001).

With the Islamic resurgence occurring all over the world, there have been attempts to set up an Islamic bank in this third largest Muslim country in the world. An Islamic bank thus appeared in Bangladesh in March 1983, for the first time in its history in the midst of conventional banks. The impact of this growth on the Muslims of the Peoples' Republic of Bangladesh has been tremendous (Ahmad, 2006). There are many factors that contribute to the successful growth of Islamic banking in Bangladesh, but its continued success will depend on its efficiency and profitability and its competitiveness with interest-bearing investments. The system must give proper consideration to the need to minimise the risk to customers and to the legitimacy of its operations from the Shari`ah point of view. The Bangladeshi experiment is fascinating and rich, illustrating the effectiveness of a pragmatic approach to solving the problems of Islamic banking.

We describe the banking system as well as the rules and regulations followed by the Islamic banks in Bangladesh in this chapter. Specifically, we suggest how Islamic banking can become a viable alternative banking system in Bangladesh. In this regard, we have utilised data collected from both primary and secondary sources to point out the operational differences of these two-banking system in Bangladesh. To this end, the study conducts an analysis of deposit and investment mechanisms of Islamic and conventional banking in Bangladesh. We conclude the chapter with specific policy recommendations.

Table 1: Banking sector performance in Bangladesh

	2010			2011		
Bank types	Branches	% of industry assets	% of industry deposits	Branches	% of industry assets	% of industry deposits
SCB	3404.00	28.50	28.10	3437.00	27.80	27.40
DFI	1382.00	6.10	4.90	1406.00	5.60	4.80
PCB	2810.00	58.80	60.90	3055.00	60.00	61.80
FCB	62.00	6.60	6.10	63.00	6.60	6.00

Source: Bangladesh Bank Annual Report (2012)

Genesis of Islamic Banking in Bangladesh

Banking System of Bangladesh: An Introduction

Information collected from Bangladesh Bank website on January 2014 shows that the banking system of Bangladesh consists of Bangladesh Bank (BB) as the central bank, 4 nationalised commercial banks (SCB), 4 government owned specialised banks (DFI), 28 private commercial banks (PCB) and 9 foreign commercial banks (FCB). There are 8 Islamic banks currently operating in Bangladesh. Table 1 illustrates briefly a performance comparison of various types of banks based on their ownership for the year 2010 and 2011. SCBs' are gradually losing their importance as the major percentage of industry assets and deposits have been shared by the private commercial banks. During 2010 and 2011, almost 60% of the industry deposits and assets were owned by the private commercial banks.

Figure 1: Islamic Banking in Bangladesh – thinking to experimentation

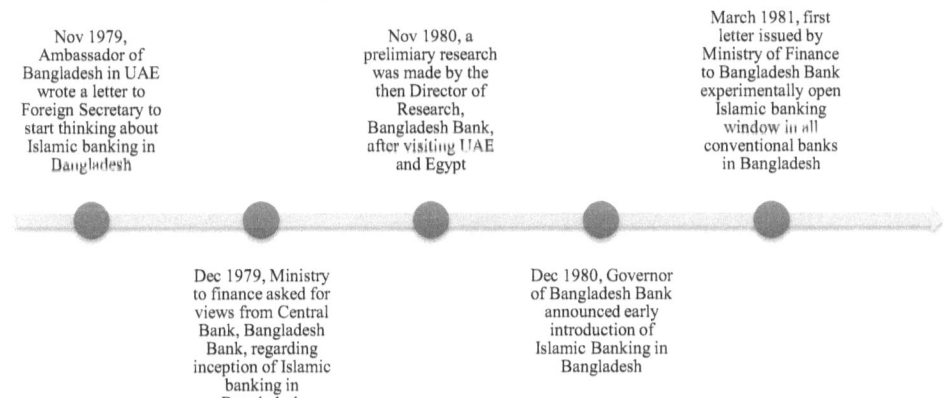

Islamic Banking in Bangladesh: History and Operation

In Bangladesh, Muslims wish to lead their lives as per instructions given in *Al-Qur`an* and the *Sunnah*. Bangladesh at its birth in March 1971, inherited an interest-based banking system that was introduced during the British (1757-1947) and Pakistani (1947-1971) rule. Since the conventional banking system is fully operated on *riba*-based transactions and which is absolutely prohibited in Islam, the people of Bangladesh have been looking forward to an alternative to interest-based banking in favour of their normal values and faith. This desire was specially revived when in the early 1970's there was a successful move to establish the Islamic Development Bank in Jeddah, and Dubai Islamic Bank being the first Islamic Commercial Bank to be followed by a number of other similar institutions in many other Islamic countries. As one of the twenty-six founder members, the Government of Bangladesh signed the Charter of the Islamic Development Bank (IDB) in the Finance Ministers' Conference held at Jeddah in August 1974, and committed itself to reorganise its economic and financial system according to Islamic norms and values. By adopting the above provisions of IDB charters, the subsequent governments also reiterated commitment of Bangladesh to bring its economic, financial and banking activities in line with the Shari`ah. The implicit undertaking was later explicitly stated in number of international conferences. In pursuant to the Government policy and commitment, figure 1 shows the timeline of official level actions that were taken the introduction of Islamic banking in the country (Huq, 1982).

These activities marked the introduction of the first Islamic bank of Bangladesh, Islami Bank Bangladesh Limited (IBBL), on 30 March 1983. Table 2 provides a sketch of Islamic banking performance in Bangladesh. Overall, there are 16 banks offering Islamic banking services, of which 8 are purely Islamic banks. Around half of the banking sector is influenced by Islamic activities. List of these 16 banks are given in Table 3. Table 2 shows that only around 20 percent of the deposits and investments are maintained with Islamic Shari`ah principle. This is crucial for a country like Bangladesh where 95 percent of the population is Muslim. In Table 2, dual banking is collection of banks those are purely Islamic and other conventional banks that are offering Islamic window services. '% of Islamic banking' is the percentage of banks, deposit and investments in purely Islamic and Islamic window banking with respect to total banking sector. Figures, except for percentage, are in Billion Taka, where one USD is equal to 82 Taka at the time of writing this report.

Table 2: Islamic banking in Bangladesh

	Islamic Banks		Dual Banking		% of Islamic to total banking sector	
Particulars	2010	2011	2010	2011	2010	2011
Islamic banks	7	7	16	16	49.00%	49.00%
Deposits	627.6	751.2	48	56.2	17.51%	18.26%
Investments	587.2	693	41.6	45.8	19.07%	20.28%

Source: Bangladesh Bank Annual Report (2012)

Table 3: List of banks offering Islamic banking in Bangladesh

No	Pure Islamic Banks	Islamic Window Banking
1	Islami Bank Bangladesh Limited	Prime Bank Limited
2	Al-Arafah Islami Bank Limited	Dhaka Bank Limited
3	Social Islami Bank Limited	Southeast Bank Limited
4	ICB Islamic Bank Limited	The Premier Bank Limited
5	Export Import Bank of Bangladesh Limited (EXIM)	Jamuna Bank Limited
6	First Security Islami Bank Limited.	HSBC Amanah

7	Shahjalal Islami Bank Limited	Standard Chartered Bank
8	Union Bank Limited	The City Bank Limited
		Arab Bangladesh Bank Limited

Source: Bangladesh Bank Annual Report (2013)

Figure 2: Performance of Islamic banks in Bangladesh

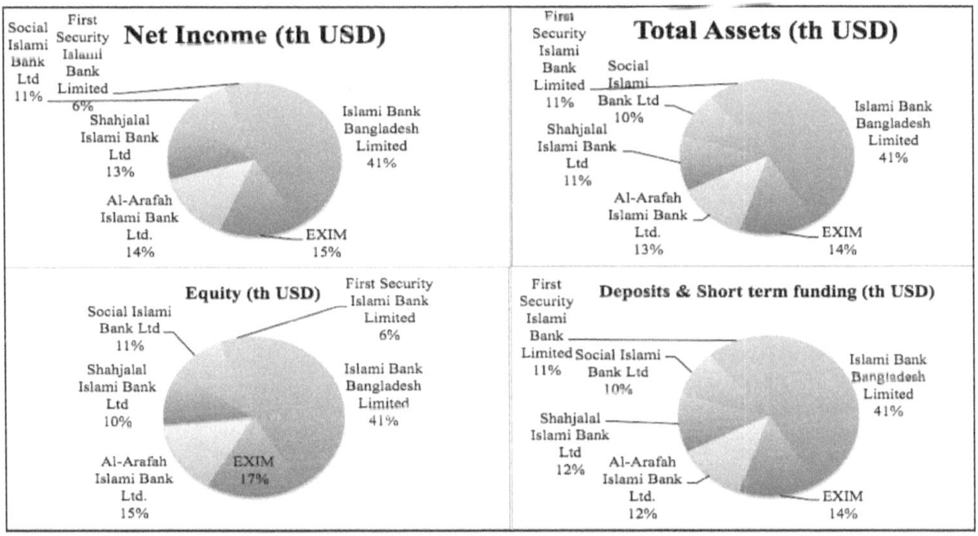

Source: Bankscope (retrieved in January 2014)
Note: Six of seven banks are shown. One Islami bank reported negative figures and was discarded to bring a balance to the comparison

Figure 2 shows recent performance of Islamic banks in Bangladesh. Around 40 percent of the net income earned in the industry is credited to Islami Bank Bangladesh Limited (IBBL) followed by the second highest 15 percent that belongs to EXIM Bank, a converted Islamic bank in operation from the year 2003. Interestingly, around 41 percent of the total assets, equity, and deposits and short-term funding belong to IBBL. EXIM Bank stays in the second position in total assets, equity and deposits with 14, 17 and 14 percent of the Islamic industry respectively. Al-Arafa Islami Bank Limited can be ranked as third largest bank that captured around 12 percent of net income, total assets, equity and deposit of the industry. The most recent addition to the list of Islamic banks, First Security Islami Bank Limited, is the lowest performer in all the four criteria. The generation effect is not entirely visible as the new comers are more efficient than old. However, experience of IBBL is a serious reckon as the bank dictates over almost half of the market. There is always the other side of the story. As the market is growing in population and new entrants in the list of Islamic banks, there is no doubt that efficiency will be the sole determinant of success in near future.

Islamic Banking in Bangladesh: The Regulatory Framework

Regulations in any country are authoritative and binding legal instruments. The prime objectives of regulating the banks are to reduce risk of collapse and to achieve certain desired social objects. Banking regulations are usually set to provide working framework for banking companies, which accept deposits from public for lending or investment. They are also designed to prevent commercial banks from becoming too risky and thus uphold public confidence in the country's financial system. Like conventional banks, Islamic banks need to be supported by a strong regulatory and supervisory framework in order to ensure their sustainable growth and stable development.

To offer banking services all Islamic Banks in Bangladesh like their conventional counterparts and non-bank financial institutions have to obtain licenses from the Bangladesh Bank under the Bank Companies Act 1991. In order to be eligible for getting a license, all intending banks have to be registered with the Registrar of Joint Stock Companies under the Companies Act 1994, and collect Certificate of Incorporation. Moreover, to collect capital through public offerings of shares, intending banks have to obtain permission from the country's Securities and Exchange Commission which is established to regulate institutions engaged in capital market activities (Securities and Exchange Commission, n.d.).

The Bangladesh Bank is empowered to regulate and supervise the country's financial system. Bangladesh Bank's basic authority comes from various laws and acts including the Banker's Books Evidence Act 1891, Insolvency Act 1920, Banking Companies Ordinance 1962, Bangladesh Bank Order 1972, Foreign Exchange (Regulation) Act 1986, Money Loan Court Act 1990, Banking Companies Act 1991, Financial Institutions Act 1993 and Rules 1994, Companies Act 1994 and Bankruptcy Act 1997 (Bangladesh Bank, n.d.).

Laws that directly regulate the banking system of Bangladesh are: the Bangladesh Bank Order 1972; Bank Company Act 1991; Companies Act 1913 and 1994; the Securities and Exchange Commission Act 1993, Deposit Insurance Order 1984; Bankruptcy Act 1997; Insolvency Act 1920; Financial Court Act 1990; Foreign Exchange (Regulation) Act 1986; Financial Institutions Act 1993; Financial Institutions Rules 1994; and Co-operative Societies Ordinance 1984 (Bangladesh Bank, n.d.). Laws that indirectly influence the banking system and for which references are made in the Banking Company Act 1991 are: Code of Civil Procedure 1898; Code of Criminal Procedure 1898; Evidence Act 1872; General Clauses Act 1897; Limitations Act 1908; Negotiable Instruments Act 1881; Penal Code 1860; Trust Act 1882; Transfer of Property Act and Bangladesh Chartered Accountant Order 1973 (Bangladesh Bank, n.d.).

As regards the supervision and inspection of the banks, an equal treatment is being followed for all conventional and Islamic banks by the Bangladesh Bank. However, considering the lack of Islamic financial markets and instruments of products in the country, the Bangladesh Bank had granted some preferential provisions for smooth development of Islamic banking in the country. Among these provisions, the following are of great importance.

1. Since there are no Profit and Loss bearing securities in Bangladesh, Islamic banks have been allowed to maintain their Statutory Liquidity Requirement (SLR) with the Bangladesh Bank at the rate of 10% of their total deposit liabilities, while it is 20% for the conventional banks (Bangladesh Bank, n.d.). This discriminating provision had facilitated Islamic banks to hold more liquid funds for more investment thereby generate more profit.

2. Under the indirect monetary policy regime, Islamic banks were allowed to fix their Profit and Loss Sharing (PLS) ratios and mark-ups independently commensurate with their own policy and banking environment. This freedom in fixing PLS ratios and mark-up rates provided scope for Islamic banks to follow the Shari`ah principles independently for realising their aims and objectives in accordance with the Islamic Shari`ah.

3. Islamic banks could reimburse 10% of their proportionate administrative cost on a part of their balances held with the Bangladesh Bank. This facility has given some scope for enhancement of their profit base.

Islamic banking that has developed in Bangladesh over the last two decades has evolved as an integral part of Islamic financial system that operates in parallel with, and is able to compete with conventional banking system. An effective legal and regulatory framework within which banks and non-banking financial institutions function is just as necessary and desirable in Islamic banking as it is in conventional banking to reduce risks to the soundness of the banking system and enhance banks' role as active players in the development of the economy. To help this goal, a number of standards and best practices established by the Bank for International Systems' (BIS) Basel Committee on Banking Supervision (BCBS) are useful and provide a valuable reference. These internationally recognised standards have not yet emerged in Islamic banking. However, aiming at bringing the infrastructure of Islamic banking and finance industry the establishment of a number of institutions with the key role played by the Islamic Development Bank is indeed, a major development in this regard (Ahmad, 2010)

In Bangladesh, there is no complete Islamic banking act or any specific laws or independent regulations that control, guide and supervise the functions of Islamic Banks. The Bangladesh Bank exercises authority over Islamic Banks under laws and regulations engineered to control and supervise conventional banks whose goals and functions are different from Islamic Banks. Moreover, the Bangladesh Bank does not have separate department to control and supervise the operation of Islamic banks. Inspection and supervision of Islamic banks' operation are being scrutinised by the Bangladesh bank as per general rules and guidelines set for conventional banks. However, as stated earlier that all existing Islamic Banks of the country are incorporated as companies limited by shares, thus they are subjected to the Companies Law of the country. They are incorporated as interest-free Shari`ah based commercial banks and Public Limited Companies with limited liabilities as well, under the Companies Act, 1994 (Act No. 18 of 1994, section 2) [The Companies Act (Bangladesh), 1994]. Besides, all kinds of commercial banking services of Islamic Banks in Bangladesh are provided by them with their branches to their customers following the provisions of the Bank Companies Act 1991 (Act No. 14 of 1991), Bangladesh Bank's directives and the principles of Islamic Shari`ah. Among the provisions in these Company Laws, are the effects of incorporation, matters related to finance, management and control of the company, and its liquidation.

There are also various requirements to be adhered to by Islamic banks like other companies in Bangladesh. One of the most important requirements in this regard is that Islamic banks have to have their own constitutions called Memorandums and Articles of Association where they have to include in addition to some common provisions following two more clauses or articles in their Articles of Association: firstly, a clause that prescribes that their operations are free from any element of interest, and secondly, a clause pertaining to the appointment of a Shari`ah Council/Board.

Perception of the Stakeholders
Perception of the bankers and customers towards the deposit and investment mechanisms of Islamic banking versus conventional banking in Bangladesh

Performance evaluation is an important pre-requisite for the sustained growth and development of any institution including the banking sector. Furthermore, the performance evaluation of government business enterprises had become a high priority in the climate of microeconomic reform in the recent past. It is customary for commercial banks to evaluate its goals and objectives because in financial markets, bank performance provides a signal to depositors and investors as to whether they will deposit/invest or withdraw their funds from the bank. Likewise, it gives feedback to bank managers/financiers as to whether to improve their services aiming at running the business successfully. With the changes in their goals and objectives, the criteria for evaluation of an Islamic bank as shifted overtime. To this end, this study examined deposit and investment mechanisms of Islamic and conventional banking in Bangladesh.

Purposive random sampling was used to collect data on a series of questions regarding Islamic banking practices. Data for the study was collected from both primary and secondary sources. Through interviews, two sets of a pre-approved questionnaire were administered, among customers and bankers of selected Islamic and conventional banks in Dhaka City (Hassan & Ahmed, 2001). The study included four Islamic and four conventional private banks. The four Islamic banks were: Islami Bank Bangladesh Ltd., Al-Arafah Islami Bank Ltd., Social Investment Bank Ltd. and Al-Baraka Bank Bangladesh Ltd. The four conventional banks were National Bank Limited (NBL), International Finance and Investment Corporation (IFIC) Limited, Arab Bangladesh Bank Limited (ABBL) and City Bank Limited (CBL). Since all these banks were established in the same year, i.e., in 1983, we assumed that the officers of the selected banks and their customers have a common exposure to the banking practices of Islamic and conventional banks. Ten questionnaires were pretested among five bank officers and five customers. The final sample consists of twenty-five bank officers and customers of each bank. Overall, 200 bankers and 200 customers were interviewed to gather their opinions about possible similarities between Islamic and conventional banks. Findings of the study were verified with the aid of the available literature and executives of the banks to confirm their reliability and acceptability.

Analysis of Deposit Mechanism of Islamic and Conventional Banking

Although the various types deposit services provided by Islamic banks look similar to those of conventional banks, a deeper scrutiny will show that they are indeed different. Payment of profit on deposits by Islamic banks is not equivalent to payment of fixed interest on deposit by conventional banks.

The conventional bank accepts deposits to supply money to the income generating activities of entrepreneurs. The major source of funds for conventional banks is customer deposit, on which the bank pays a fixed interest rate. This deposit is a form of debt given to the bank by a bank customer. The bank has to pay to the depositor the principal as well as interest, regardless whether the bank makes a profit from the money or not. In case of a bad loan, the bank has to pay the depositor from its own resources. The depositor has not shared any risk with the bank, but is getting paid for his deposit with the bank. Islam views such transaction as unjust because it allows for the unequal treatment of creditors (depositors) compared to the debtors (the bank).

On the other hand, Islamic banks accept deposits with the condition that the money will be put to work through the skills and management expertise of the banks. The depositor gets back his principal together with a share of profit after the expiry of the contract. In fact, the depositor agrees to put his money in the bank's investment account and to share profits with the bank. In this case, the depositor is the supplier of capital and the bank is the manager of capital. The depositor does not earn interest at a fixed rate in Islamic banking system, but accepts some of the business risks and earns a share of the profit. The depositor is not guaranteed any pre-determined return on the nominal value of his deposit like interest-bearing banks, but is treated as a shareholder of the bank and as such, is entitled to a share of the profits made by the bank.

Similarly, if the bank incurs losses, the depositor share in these losses and the value of his/her deposit is reduced. Therefore, any shift to the asset positions of Islamic banks is instantaneously reflected by changes in the value of shares (deposits) held by the public in the bank, and therefore, the real value of assets and liabilities of an Islamic bank would be equilibrated at all times. However, in the conventional banking system, because the nominal value of deposits is fixed, a similar shift could cause a divergence between real assets and real liabilities. Since the Islamic bank engages in a two-way contract with depositors and borrowers, the bank does not trade money for money, which is forbidden in Islam. Rather, the bank lends money, which is put to work by the borrower, and shares profit/loss of the invested capital. The Islamic equity system has proven to be a mechanism of efficiency, justice, welfare and fair growth (Akkas, 1966). Therefore, we conclude that although monetary benefits are paid to depositors in both Islamic and Conventional banks, they are not the same. Payment to depositors by Islamic banks may vary while payment to depositors by conventional banks is fixed.

Analysis of Investment Mechanism of Islamic and Conventional Banking

The Short-term trade financing techniques (*bai`-murabahah, bai`-mu'ajjal, bai` al-salam, and 'ijarah*) used by Islamic banks are alleged to be similar to interest-bearing short-term lending by conventional banks because of the following reasons:

a.   Fixed charges as a percentage increase with time in the form of compensation for violation of the agreement for repayment schedule of investment obtained by the entrepreneur from the bank;

b.   Dated payment obligations may not synchronise with a firm's cash flow;

c.   The borrower has to make payments whether or not he is succeeding in his/her business;

d.   Security/collateral (by way of a pledge) is essential for investment;

e.   Returns are practically calculated on the benchmark of an interest-based bank.

Islamic banks earn profit either from investment in trading (*bai`*) and leasing (*`ijarah*) or in production/manufacturing. When Islamic banks become directly involved in trade and industry, Islamic banks perform functions of both an intermediary and of a manager. Lack of expertise in appraising and monitoring different types of industries and long drawn court procedures for the recovery of bad loans in case of default by borrowers have made Islamic banks hesitant to engage in long-term *mudarabah* or *musahrakah* modes of lending (investment). Consequently, '*bai*' and '*ijarah*' modes of investment have become dominant forms of financing by Islamic banks (Hassan & Ahmed, 20001).

It is argued by some Muslim scholars that a fixed price in a deferred sale does not mean a fixed return on capital because of the uncertainty and risk incorporated in such transactions (Ahmad, 2006). Other scholars, however, reject this proposition and suggest that the time value of money can only be determined ex-post (Khan, 1987). Finally, some Shari`ah scholars recognise the value of time but only in relation to real transactions (Saadallah, 1992). Therefore, the value of time is related to an actual transaction and its outcome. The postponement of liability justifies a greater return to capital under a *riba*-based system. However, in actual transactions, the return to capital is linked to ownership of real goods, which carries an element of risk with it.

Given the above, the profit of Islamic banking consists of several factors including the time required to complete the actual transactions. *Riba* does not consider risk sharing, whereas profit loss takes into account risk-sharing. As a result, the capital involved in trade may grow or decline over time, while in *riba*-based transactions, capital automatically increases over time.

Islamic banking is involved indirectly with commodity trading, as a manager of funds based on the request of the client. The business relationship between the bank and client considers every aspect of assurance of profitability, such as credit risk, liquidity risk, maturity risk and inflation risk. A prudent lending decision on behalf of the bank makes the probability of risk negligible. In case of genuine default, the Islamic bank recovers only the principal without any compensation for bearing risk. In case of wilful default, there is no alternative to the Islamic bank except demanding compensation for bearing risk. However, Islamic banks do not count this compensation as part of its income; rather they distribute these monies to the poor.

The instruments of *bai`* *murabahah* and *ijarah* are devoid of interest. Although these two instruments are criticised as being very similar to those of interest-based banking and as not having brought much real change to the banking system, their use does carry an element of risk for the Islamic banks which makes them acceptable to the Shari`ah. The Qur'an clearly states that "*Allah has permitted trade and forbidden interest/usury*" (2: 275), and both cost-plus sales and leasing are forms of trade. For example, in the case of sale with cost-plus transactions, there must be a definite period during which the financier actually owns the commodity in question. This does not mean that he takes the physical possession of the commodity. He must be the legal owner for this period, bearing all risks, liabilities and benefits of this possession. He is, therefore, the genuine seller of the commodity and is entitled thereby to make a profit on the sale. It is the risk in trading which makes it an acceptable way of making profit. Fixed interest, on the contrary, carries no such risk and is, therefore, against Islamic principles as a way of making money (IIBI, n.d. p. 3). Although in face value, a number of Islamic financing modes look similar to those of interest-based banking, it is found that these are very different from each other in terms of justice, efficiency, stability and economic growth.

Questionnaire Survey Analysis of Banker-Customer Perception of Islamic and Conventional Banks

Results from the survey undertaken for this study indicate that an overwhelming group of the customers are businessmen. They total 57% of the sample. The remaining groups are: self-employed (13%), service holders (10%), housewives (7%) and others (3%) The whole sample consists of customers in the–age group 35-60 years, and 89% of them are male. Most respondents had a graduate degree (68%) but 17% had a postgraduate degree (17%) while only 15% had an undergraduate's degree. It seems that the attributes of the respondent customers are unique within the context of the conventional social fabric of Dhaka city.

However, the majority of bankers are officers (72%). Only 5% of the samples are senior executives. It is observed that the age, sex and education levels of the bankers are close to that of the customers under study.

Regarding a general understanding of the core of the profit and loss sharing system of Islamic banking and finance, results indicate that the bankers are more aware than the customers. Fifty-five percent of bankers believe that Islamic finance aims at both profit and losses. However, only 32 percent of the customers agree with bankers although most customers (62 percent) believe that Islam permits profit and forbids *riba*. The opinions vary due to the fact that the Islamic bankers get formal training on Islamic economics and banking and the conventional bankers are aware due to their professional consciousness.

However, both the bankers and customers know of the relation of profit, in lieu of interest, to Islamic finance. This awareness is the outcome of launching Islamic banking in the country in 1983. The basis of such observation is that 11% of the bankers and customers believe that Islamic finance always means investment in real assets, while 9% of them have mentioned that Islamic finance cannot earn *riba* in anyway.

A majority (69%) of the bankers and customers perceived that *zakah* has been mobilised through Islamic banking system. 12% of the respondents thought that welfare activities are organised through the Islamic banking system, while 10% believed that Islamic banking system has introduced new products. Again, 7% of respondents agree the concept of *halal* and *haram* is to be relevant in the case of investment, buying and selling, while few of them (2%) mention that mobilisation of financial resources to the real sector of the economy is well introduced. This indicates that Bangladesh has benefited from Islamic banking.

In response to the question, what is the basis of the development of Islamic banking system in Bangladesh, 55% of bankers and 69% of customers think that this is due to 'mere faith in Islam' of the Muslims in the country (they represent a total of 88% of its population). In contrast, 23% of them believe that the 'intention to earn profit' is the basis of development of Islamic banking system. However, 18% of the bankers hold the opinion that the 'tendency to avoid interest' is the basis for this banking system, while only 2% of the customers discount its relevance as a basis. Such discrepancy is again observed when 9% of the bankers said that 'to do welfare of the economy' is the basis; it is supported by only 3% of the customers. 3% of both bankers and customers agree that the basis is 'to ensure justice in the financial transactions.

It follows that the item 'to avoid interest' as a basis of development of Islamic banking system has not captured the attention of the majority of the respondents. Why is this? Do they believe that Islamic banks have opened the back door for continuation of transactions like interest-based banks?

Our survey results indicate that, in fact, all respondents believe in the existence of such a back door. 73% of the customers and 60% of the bankers believe that the trading and the rental modes of investments of Islamic banks do not differ much from the transactions of interest-based banks. The agreement of payment by instalment in due time and the extra payment for excess time of repayment of an investment under the trading and rental mode create the same financial burden on an investor customer. Additional arrangements (mortgage, security, registration etc.) for getting an investment loan from Islamic banks are the same as those of conventional banks.

On the other hand, 14% of the respondents believe that the degree of risk that the present system of Islamic banking shares is not enough to give good reason for claiming itself as PLS of banking. It is followed by 11% of the respondents, who views that Islamic banks are working along the lines of the interest-based banks. Finally, 8% believes that the products of current Islamic banks serve the purpose of interest-based banks.

In response to the question: what are the causes of the lagging interest in the Islamic banking system, 45% of respondents replied that exploitation is going on through Islamic banking. Alternatively, 19% mentioned two other causes: (i) the products of Islamic banks have failed to remove the curse of interest-based banking; and (ii) the bankers lead the Islamic-banking system to the garb of interest. 16% believe the cause to be the fact that Islamic banking has been introduced in a society, which is not founded on Islamic principles. It seems that the bankers and customers are concerned about the interest factor, and this tends to make both Islamic and conventional banks similar.

The next question is what are the reasons that these Islamic banks do not act strictly in accordance with the Shari`ah principles (do not comply fully with the Shari`ah) in their operation? In response, the majority (35%) of the respondents have mentioned that the level of profit earning cannot be the sole criterion of success for an Islamic bank. 32% think that the status of the Shari`ah Council is advisory in nature, not supervisory in the system of Islamic banking. 20% believe that Islamic banks do not ensure justice and welfare in financial transactions. A minority of respondents (12%) believe that exploitation still remains in the Islamic banking system. As a result, many Muslim businessmen and industrialists do not really patronise the Islamic banks. About 73% believe that potential patrons do not find any business difference between Islamic and conventional banks. 20%attribute the lack of customers to confusion about Islamic banking while few respondents (8%) believe that people are not properly motivated to participate in Islamic banking.

When asked to consider the risk dimension of Islamic banking respondents stated that most of the Islamic modes of investment practiced by Islamic banks do not really share risk for a number of reasons. While a majority of them (66%) believe that the risks are covered by the insurance companies rather than shared by the bank, 21% said that Islamic banks do not do practice buying and reselling the objects physically. 10% observe that buying and selling arrangements of Islamic banks are almost risk-free. Only 3% of the respondents believe that Islamic banks do business with depositors' money. Therefore, if any risk is there, it is borne by the depositors.

Most importantly, the respondents indicated that many customers are not interested in dealing with Islamic banks because they feel that only the name of the banks has been changed but that interest in a real sense has not been eliminated. The survey uncovers some causes underlying these perceptions. For example, many respondents (73%) feel that mark-up profit has created a financial burden similar to the interest burden of conventional banks. Other reasons that were mentioned are: (i) repayment of the amount financed by the bank in instalments (10%), and (ii) the failure of payment of instalments that creates additional liability (7%). A few of them (6%) stated that Islamic banks, in most of the cases, do not consider themselves to be incurring business losses.

In the Islamic banking system, the possibility of deposit loss is an essential principle, but it may be harmful for deposit mobilisation. With this view in mind, our survey sought to find out whether the condition of deposit loss is or is not harmful for deposit mobilisation in Bangladesh? 43% of respondents believe that the profit and loss sharing system of banking cannot ultimately lead to a loss of deposit. While 23% are expresses their opinion that the condition of deposit loss does not mean total loss of deposit. However, 20% of respondents believe that the possibility of deposit loss is an actual element of investment, and it is what makes the profit on the Islamic bank's deposit *halal* (legitimate). 14% of respondents think that the condition of a deposit loss is insignificant to a true Muslim, who prefers an eternal life in the Hereafter. Overall, respondents expressed strong feelings in favour of Islamic banking.

Regarding the present modes of investment practiced by Islamic banks, both bankers and customers believe that it is tantamount to the interest factor of conventional banks. For example, according to the respondents, *bai` murabahah* and *bai` mu'ajjal* modes of investment are analogous to the Pledge and Hypothecation techniques of interest–bearing banking. 67% of the respondents believe that the finance process under both systems of banking have the same effect on business results. The remaining 33% view that both banks' motive is to ensure (i) justice *('adl)* and welfare *(`ihsan)* (ii) working side by side, and (iii) working in the same value loaded society.

Finally, a last question was asked about how to resolve that situation. They advocate for governmental reformation measures focusing on moral building and the eradication of false values of life, which would pave the way for Islamic banking. They also mentioned several causes to support their opinions. A majority of them (59%) feel that Islamic banks cannot work well in a dishonest society. While 17% have mentioned that governmental power can change social values, 13% believe that governmental reformation measures are a powerful instrument in the building of a moral society. About 10% of them have expressed that false values of life give a detrimental environment to Islamic banking. This indicates that the bankers and customers hold a very strong opinion in favor of governmental measures for reformation.

The above analysis of the misleading similarities between Islamic and Conventional banks, along with the understandings, values and attitudes of the bankers and customers about the Islamic banking system, indicates the degree of commitments to Islamic banks in Bangladesh.

Summary of Empirical Results

The prohibition of *riba* makes Islamic banking different from conventional banking. Of course, the investments of an Islamic bank must be channelled to Shari`ah approved sectors. The phenomenal growth of Islamic banks in Bangladesh has attracted the attention of bankers, business community and bank customers. It is also contended that Islamic banks are not very different from conventional banks. This debate raises a natural question: if Islamic banks are no different from conventional banks, why they are growing so fast? A survey analysis of the deposit and investment mechanisms and the opinions of the bankers and the customers of both Islamic and conventional banks helps our understanding and identification of this debate. The theoretical analysis undertaken for this study shows that Islamic bank practices are indeed different from those of conventional banks.

Islamic banking maintains *Al-Wadi`ah* Current, *Mudarabah* Savings and Term Deposit accounts, and conventional banks maintain Current Deposit, Savings Deposit, and Term Deposit accounts. An analysis of these deposit mechanisms shows parallel processes. both Islamic and conventional banks pay money for the deposits of the customers, which is termed as profit in Islamic banking or interest in conventional banking respectively. While payment of return on deposit in Islamic banking contains element of risk, payment of interest in conventional banking does not contain the element of risk. Only payment on deposit apparently generates misunderstanding in the minds of bank customers whether Islamic banking is indeed different from conventional banks.

In terms of financing techniques, the prevalence of short-term financing in Islamic banks raises the efficiency, equity and justice of Islamic banks. In addition, this also brings up questions such as whether or not Islamic banks pay profit or interest in the name of profit. It is found that, although apparently similar, the Islamic banking financing mechanism is different from those of conventional banks. The misleading similarities between Islamic and conventional banking products are the result of the following observations (1) fixed charges in percentage, which increases with time as compensation for violation of an agreement for repayment schedule of investment taken by the entrepreneur from the bank, (2) dated payment obligations that may not synchronise with the firm's cash flow, (3) payment obligations that are mandatory whether or not the business is making a profit, (4) a security or mortgage being required for investment, and (5) returns that are practically based on the benchmark of an interest-based bank.

The survey analysis shows that both the bankers and bank customers have confusing notions about Islamic banking practices. There are valid reasons to argue that this misconception is partly due to the incomplete knowledge in the fundamentals of Islamic finance and due to the over-reliance on short-term trade financing. The investment portfolio of Islamic banks has generally favoured trade-related over production-related activities, short-term profitability over long-term profitability, and private profitability over social profitability. Almost 80 to 90 percent of investment has been made in short-term trade-related activities. Heavy reliance on a short-term asset portfolio makes Islamic banks vulnerable, increases its overall risk and threatens its stability. On the other hand, the borrowers prefer short-term trade loans to profit-loss sharing instruments, and this has weakened the bank's portfolio. The real rates of return of the Islamic bank's asset portfolio are lower than those of conventional banks.

Islamic banks have become, to an extent, successful in the field of deposit mobilisation, but socially beneficial and development-oriented utilisation of these deposits is yet to happen. Employment generation and a flow of resources towards the lower and middle classes, particularly in the rural areas, have not taken place so far (Ahmad, 2001). Still, Islamic banks are involved in the heroic role of eliminating *riba* from financial dealings in Muslim countries against a backdrop of regulation in the area of taxation, legal framework, and weak moral fabrics of society. In order to remove misconception from the minds of bankers and customers, there is no alternative to publicity, research and training of Islamic banking practices. Research should focus on the development of financial products that conform to Islamic Shari`ah, and training should be given to bankers, potential investors as well as bank customers.

Conclusions and Recommendations

Islamic banking is no longer an uncertain experience, but is now a reality in Bangladesh and is likely to keep growing rapidly. Although Islamic banks in Bangladesh are different from conventional banks in terms of mission, objectives and its practice, they are still subject to basically the same laws and regulations as their conventional counterparts and apply the same interest-based framework for regulatory and supervisory activities. The absence of such a supportive framework obstructs Islamic banking in its effective and smooth functioning in line with the principles of Shari`ah. It is true that a few regulations have been developed and foundations for regulatory instruments have been laid by the Bangladesh Bank in this regard, but it did not make any substantial steps towards developing effective services and operation of Islamic banks in line with the tenets of Shari`ah. Therefore, a well-defined regulatory and supervisory framework for Islamic banks in Bangladesh is needed. The key objectives of this framework would be the systematic stability, an adequate level of compliance to the Shari`ah principles and the international acceptance to Islamic banking operations. Islamic banks in the country have seemingly arranged themselves with the analogous application of conventional regulations. Although, to some extent, this does not seem to have been a serious threat of the future growth of Islamic banks in terms of their assets and numbers, regulatory authorities of Bangladesh should come forward and establish a well-defined and explicit legal and regulatory framework that, while consistent with Islamic Shari`ah, would at the same time, be realistic and flexible enough to meet internationally recognised prudential and supervisory requirements.

References

Ahmad, A.U.F. (2010), *Developments in Islamic banking practice: the evidence from Bangladesh*, Universal Publishers, Florida.

Ahmad, A.U.F. and Hassan, M.K. (2007), "Regulation and Performance of Islamic banking in Bangladesh", *Thunderbird International Business Review,* Vol. 49 No. 2, pp.251-277.

Ahmad, A.U.F. (2004), "Islamic banking in Bangladesh: Legal and Regulatory Issues", *Sixth Harvard University Forum on Islamic Finance,* Cambridge, MA.

Ahmad, A.U.F. (2000), "Legislations and Issues on Islamic banking in Bangladesh", *First International Forum on Islamic Economics, Finance and Business for Young Scholars,* Langkawi.

Ahmad, A.U.F. (2001), "Problems of Islamic banking in Bangladesh", *Islamic Economics Research Bureau Seminar,* Dhaka.

Ahmad, A.U.F. (2003), *Islamic banking in Bangladesh,* Unpublished Master's Thesis, University of Western Sydney.

Ahmad, A.U.F. and Hassan, M.K. (2006), "The Time Value of Money Concept in Islamic Finance," *American Journal of Islamic Social Sciences,* Vol. 23 No. 1, pp. 66-89.

Akkas, A.S.M. (1996), *Relative Efficiency of Conventional and* Islamic banking *System in Financing Investment,* Unpublished Doctoral Dissertation, Dhaka University.

Al-Arafah Islami Bank Limited, retrieved on: http://www.al-arafah.com.

Al-Azami, M.M. (2003), *The History of the Qur'anic Text from Revelation to Compilation: A Comparative Study with the Old and New Testament,* UK Islamic Academy, Leicester.

Al-Suyuti, J.A.D. (1987), *Al- 'Itqan fi `Ulum al-Qur'an,* Dar al-Kutub al-`Ilmiyyah, Beirut.

Bangladesh Bank, Dhaka, retrieved on: http://www.bangladeshbank-bank.org.

Doi, A.R.I. (1996), *Shari`ah: The Islamic Law,* A.S. Noordeen, Kuala Lumpur:

Exim Bank of Bangladesh Limited, "Management," Retrieve from: http://www.eximbd.com/management.html

Faruqi, R. (2003), "Islamic Finance - An Alternative Financial System: Global Opportunities and Challenges," *inaugural address given at the conference of London-based Institute of Islamic banking and Insurance on Islamic banking and Finance,* Abuja, Nigeria, 27-28 January.

Haron, S. (1997), *Islamic banking: Rules and Regulations,* Pelanduk Publications, Kuala Lumpur.

Hassan, M.K. and Ahmed, M. (2001), *Islamic Versus Conventional Banking: A Survey of Their Apparent Similarities and Differences,* Dhaka. Unpublished paper.

Huq, M.A. (1987), "Prohibition of Interest and Some Common Misgivings", In Ataul Hoque (ed.), *Readings in* Islamic banking, Islamic Foundation Bangladesh, Dhaka.

Huq, M.A. (1982), "Bangladesh Marches towards Islamic banking: Thoughts on Economics*", Journal of Islamic Economics Research Bureau,* Vol.3 No.5, pp. xx-xx

Huq, M.A. (1996), "Islamic banking in Bangladesh with a Brief Overview of Operational Problem", *Seminar of BIBM,* Dhaka, June.

Institute of Islamic banking and Insurance (N.D), *Islamic banking Diploma Module-1, Lesson 3.* Institute of Islamic banking and Insurance, London.

Iqbal, M. (1988), *Distributive Justice and Need Fulfillment in an Islamic Economy,* The Islamic Foundation, Leicester.

Iqbal, M. and David, T.L. (2002), *In Islamic banking and Finance: New Perspectives on Profit Sharing and Risk,* Edward Elgar Publishing Ltd., London.

Iqbal, Z. and Mirakhor, A. (1987), *Islamic banking*, International Monetary Fund, Washington DC.

Islami Bank Bangladesh Limited (IBBL), retrieved on: http://www.islamibankbd.com.

Kamali, M.H. (2000), *Law and Society: The Interplay of Revelation and Reason in the Shariah*, Oxford University Press.

Kamali, M.H. (2000), *Law and Society: The Interplay of Revelation and Reason in the Shari`ah, Oxford History of Islam*, Oxford University Press.

Khan, M.F. (1987), *Value of Time in Islamic Perspective*, IIIE, Islamabad.

Al-Omar, F. and Abdel-Haq, M. (1996), *Islamic banking: Theory, Practice and Challenges*, Zed Books Ltd., London.

Saadallah, R. (1992), *Concept of Time in Islamic Economics*, Islamic Development Bank, Jeddah.

Sarker, A.A. (1998), *Islamic banking in Bangladesh: Growth, Structure and Performance*, Unpublished Master's Thesis, Loughborough University, UK.

Shahjalal Islami Bank Limited, retrieved online on: http://www.shahjalalbank.com.bd.

Social Investment Bank Limited (SIBL), Annual Report 2000.

Social Investment Bank Limited (SIBL), "Balance Sheet as at December 31, 2013," retrieved October 30, 2004 from: http://www.siblbd.com/home.html

Southeast Bank Limited, "Branch Information", retrieved September 7, 2014 from: http://www.southeastbank-bangladesh.com/branch.htm

Tantawi, M.S. (1997), *Mu'amalat al-Bunuk Wa Ahkamuha al-Shar'iyyah*, Dar Nahdah Misr Li al-Tiba'ah Wa al-Nashr Wa al-Tawzi`, Cairo.

The Companies Act (Bangladesh) (1994), retrieved October 30, 2014 from: http://www.vakilno1.com/saarclaw/bangladesh/part2.htm

The Daly Star, Vol.5 No. 344, December 18, 2013, retrieved September 7, 2013 from: http://www.thedailystar.net/2005/05/17/d50517050551.htm

The Financial Express, May 24, 2014, retrieved September 4, 2013 from: http://www.thefinancialexpressbd.info/search_index.php?page=detail_news&news_id=34525

The Independent (Internet Edition), May 17, 2014, retrieved September 7, 2013.

The New Nation, August 16, 2008, retrieved September 4, 2013 from: http://nation.ittefaq.com/issues/2008/08/16/now30996.htm

The Premier Bank Ltd., retrieved September 7, 2013 from: http://www.premierbankltd.com/html/branches.php

Wehr, H. (1976), *A Dictionary of Modern Written Arabic*, Spoken Languages Services, New York.

Chapter 8

Islamic Banking in India: What More Needed?

Dr Fayaz Ahmad Lone,
Salman Bin Abdulaziz University, Al Kharj Saudi Arabia

Prof. Imamul Haque
Aligarh Muslim University, Aligarh India

Introduction

Although Islamic banking is for all irrespective of religion, but particularly for Muslims interest is forbidden and that is why Islam has its own economic system which is based on social justice. But as far as Muslim population is concerned, then Islam is the world's second largest religion after Christianity with over 1.0-1.8 billion adherents, comprising 20-25% of the world population while most estimates figures that there are 1.5 billion Muslims worldwide [11]. India is the second largest country in the world as far as population is concerned. It has been estimated that in July 2009, India has 1.17 billion populations. In India, Muslim population has been estimated to be 13.4 percent [12]. Banking in India is totally base on interest and in this country 88 scheduled commercial banks (SCBs) - 27 public sector banks (that is with the Government of India holding a stake), 31 private banks (these do not have government stake; they may be publicly listed and traded on stock exchanges) and 38 foreign banks. They have a combined network of over 53,000 branches and 17,000 ATMs. According to a report by ICRA Limited, a rating agency, the public sector banks hold over 75 percent of total assets of the banking industry, with the private and foreign banks holding 18.2% and 6.5% respectively. But unfortunately, there is not a single Islamic bank presently working in this country. Although some banks/institutions are working on the Islamic banking principles, but they are treated as Non-Banking Financial Companies (NBFCs). NBFCs are doing functions akin to that of banks, however there are a few differences:

- (i) A NBFC cannot accept demand deposits (demand deposits are funds deposited at a depository institution that are payable on demand -- immediately or within a very short period -- like your current or savings accounts.)

---

[11] http://www.adherents.com/Religions_By_Adherents.html

[12] http://www.state.gov/r/pa/ei/bgn/3454.htm

- (ii) it is not a part of the payment and settlement system and as such cannot issue cheques to its customers; and
- (iii) Deposit insurance facility of DICGC is not available for NBFC depositors unlike in case of banks.

Taking the above differences into consideration, Islamic banks/institutions are not becoming popular in India and that is why maximum population is unaware about the working of Islamic banks. Also, these institutions/banks have not showed good performance compared to conventional banks may be due to Government and public support.

Indian Banking Scenario

Banks in India can be categorized into non-scheduled banks and scheduled banks. Scheduled banks constitute of commercial banks and co-operative banks. There are about 67,000 branches of Scheduled Banks spread across India. During the first phase of financial reforms, there was a nationalization of 14 major banks in 1969. This crucial step led to a shift from Class banking to Mass banking. Since then the growth of the banking industry in India has been a continuous process. As far as the present scenario is concerned the banking industry is in a transition phase. The Public Sector Banks (PSBs), which are the foundation of the Indian Banking system account for more than 78 per cent of total banking industry assets. Unfortunately, they are burdened with excessive Non-Performing assets (NPAs), massive manpower and lack of modern technology.

On the other hand, the Private Sector Banks in India are witnessing immense progress. They are leaders in Internet banking, mobile banking, phone banking, ATMs. On the other hand, the Public Sector Banks are still facing the problem of unhappy employees. There has been a decrease of 20 percent in the employee strength of the private sector in the wake of the Voluntary Retirement Schemes (VRS). As far as foreign banks are concerned, they are likely to succeed in India. Indusland Bank was the first private bank to be set up in India. IDBI, ING Vyasa Bank, SBI Commercial and International Bank Ltd, Dhanalakshmi Bank Ltd, Karur Vysya Bank Ltd, Bank of Rajasthan Ltd etc are some Private Sector Banks. Banks from the Public Sector include Punjab National bank, Vijaya Bank, UCO Bank, Oriental Bank, Allahabad Bank, Andhra Bank etc. ANZ Grindlays Bank, ABN-AMRO Bank, American Express Bank Ltd, Citibank etc. are some foreign banks operating in India.

Islamic banks in India

The last decade has seen many positive developments in the Indian banking sector which is totally based on interest-based banking. The policy makers, which comprise the Reserve Bank of India (RBI), Ministry of Finance and related government and financial sector regulatory entities, have made several notable efforts to improve regulation in the sector. The sector now compares favorably with banking sectors in the region on metrics like growth, profitability and non-performing assets (NPAs). A few banks have established an outstanding track record of innovation, growth and value creation. This is reflected in their market valuation. However, improved regulations, innovation, growth and value creation in the sector remain limited to a small part of it. The cost of banking intermediation in India is higher and bank penetration is far lower than in other markets. India's banking industry must strengthen itself significantly if it has to support the modern and vibrant economy which India aspires to be. While the onus for this change lies mainly with bank managements, an enabling policy and regulatory framework will also be critical to their success.

- The failure to respond to changing market realities has stunted the development of the financial sector in many developing countries. A weak banking structure has been unable to fuel continued growth, which has harmed the long-term health of their economies.
- Indian banks which are based on conventional pattern have compared favorably on growth, asset quality and profitability with other regional banks over the last few years.

The banking index has grown at a compounded annual rate of over 51 per cent since April 2001 as compared to a 27 per cent growth in the market index for the same period. Policy makers have made some notable changes in policy and regulation to help strengthen the sector. These changes include strengthening prudential norms, enhancing the payments system and integrating regulations between commercial and co-operative banks. However, the cost of intermediation remains high and bank penetration is limited to only a few customer segments and geographies. While bank lending has been a significant driver of GDP growth and employment, periodic instances of the "failure" of some weak banks have often threatened the stability of the system. Structural weaknesses such as a fragmented industry structure, restrictions on capital availability and deployment, lack of institutional support infrastructure, restrictive labour laws, weak corporate governance and ineffective regulations beyond Scheduled Commercial Banks (SCBs).

Entry of New Banks in the private Sector:
As per the guidelines of licensing on new banks in the private sector issued in January 1993, based on review of experience gained on the functioning of new private sector banks, revised guidelines were issued in January 2001. The main provisions/requirements are listed below:
- Initial minimum paid-up capital shall be Rs.200 crore; this will be raised to Rs. 300 crore within three years of commencement of business.
- Promoters' contribution shall be minimum of 40 percent of the paid-up capital of the bank at any point of time; their contribution of 40 percent shall be locked in for 5 years

from the date of licensing of the bank and excess stake above 40 percent shall be diluted after one year of bank's operations.

- Initial capital other than promoters' contribution could be raised through public issue or private placement.
- While augmenting capital to Rs. 300 crore within three years, promoters need to bring in at least 40 percent of the fresh capital, which will also be locked in for 5 years. The remaining portion of fresh capital could be raised through public issue or private placement.
- NRI participation in the primary capital of a new bank shall be to the maximum extent of 40 percent. In case of foreign banking company or finance company (including multilateral institutions) as a technical collaboration or a co-promoter, equity participation shall be limited to 20 percent within the 40 percent ceiling. Shortfall in NRI contribution to foreign equity can be met through contribution by designed multilateral institutions.
- No large industrial house can promote a new bank. Individual companies connected with large industrial houses can, however, contribute up to 10 percent of the equity of a new bank, which will maintain an arm's length relationship with companies in the promoter group and the individual company/ies investing in equity. No credit facilities shall be extended to them.
- NBFCs (under which Islamic banks are covered in India) with good record can become banks.
- A minimum capital adequacy ratio of 10 percent shall be maintained on a continuous basis from commencement of operations.
- Priority sector lending target is 40 percent of the net bank credit, as in the case of other domestic banks; it is also necessary to open 25 percent of the branches in rural/semi-urban areas.

SWOT Analysis of Islamic Banking in India

When SWOT analysis of Islamic banking is done as far as India is concerned, it shows a good that Islamic banking has high Strengths India compared to Weaknesses. The following is briefly a summary of the same.

RBI and Islamic Banking

In the straitjacket world of Indian banking, something as fascinating as Islamic banking is a distant dream. Nonetheless, countless advocates of Islamic banking have been trying their best over the years to propagate the concept. In furtherance of this propagation the Reserve

---

Strengths

- population of Muslims in India is more than Muslim population in Bangladesh, turkey, Egypt, Iran, Nigeria, Afghanistan, Sudan, Iraq, Saudi Arabia
- Bridges the rising income disparity in India
- Demand for nitch products is increasing in India

Weaknesses

- Unawareness about the Islamic banking
- Lack of experts
- Modification in banking act regulation needed.

Opportunities

- Indian economy would benefit from inflow of funds from GCC countries
- Would add real estate boom
- Address the issue of financial inclusion
- A large number of Muslims that are considered unworthily of credit by commercial banks or who avoid banks due to sharia law would welcome this.

Threats

- Expected to become a political weapon
- Goes against secular fabric of nation
- May bridges financial segregation, so regulatory authority may oppose
- Microfinance is a good competitor

Bank of India (RBI) constituted a committee in 2007 [13] to examine the issue but viewed that Islamic banking cannot be offered by banks in India as well as the overseas branches of local banks under the present legal framework. Except a basic offering like current account, almost no other banking product in India can be modified to meet the conditions of Islamic banking. As a genre of financial services, Islamic banking shuns the very idea of interest rates, and

---

[13] **Reserve Bank of India to set up a committee headed by Mr Anand Sinha, chief general Manager in-charge, department of banking operations & development to look into the matter and the committee submitted the report.**

rests on profit-sharing principles. Based on the Shari'ah law, it abhors the business of making money out of money, upholding the belief that wealth is generated through actual trade and investment [14] The RBI has not put the report in the public domain[15].

While the final form of the report is not known, from the newspaper reports it can be collected that the members had pointed out how Indian banking laws come in the way of various Islamic banking principles. These are as follows:

Indian banking laws do not explicitly prohibit Islamic banking but there are provisions that make Islamic banking almost an unviable option. The financial institutions in India comprises of Banks and Non-Banking Financial Institutions. Banks in India are governed through Banking Regulation Act 1949, Reserve Bank of India Act 1934, Negotiable Instruments Act 1881, and Co-operative Societies Act 1961.

Certain provisions regarding this are mentioned below

* Section 5 (b) and 5 (c) of the Banking Regulation Act, 1949 prohibit the banks to invest on Profit Loss Sharing basis -the very basis of Islamic banking.

* Section 8 of the Banking Regulations Act (BR Act, 1949) reads, "No banking company shall directly or indirectly deal in buying or selling or bartering of goods…"

* Section 9 of the Banking Regulations Act prohibits bank to use any sort of immovable property apart from private use –this is against Ijarah for home finance

* Section 21 of the Banking Regulations Act requires payment of Interest which is against Sharia

As regards to partnership by Islamic banks in a firm, the bank has to make sure that the manager does not avoid his responsibilities or obtain other non-pecuniary benefits at the expense of non-participating partners and ensure the veracity of the profit statements. Monitoring of data about firms in which Islamic bank invests would involve exorbitant cost. However, Islamic banks need to set up monitoring cell to keep them informed of the internal function of their joint venture. The implication is that banks and entrepreneur have to function very closely.

Islamic banking needs to introduce corporate governance with transparent accounting standards. It needs to perform detailed evaluation before embarking Profit Loss Sharing Scheme, which demand a pool of highly trained professionals. The imparting of professional training is costly. Detailed principles are still to be laid down and techniques and procedures evolved to carry them out. It Is only after the satisfactory achievement of these that proper training can begin.

---

[14] www.economictimes.indiatimes.com/articleshow/2172818.cms
[15] The newspapers state that it might be because of the sensitive issues it was dealing

It is observed that inability to evaluate a projects' profitability has tended to act against investment financing. Some borrowers frustrate the banks appraisal efforts as they are reluctant to provide full disclosures of their business. These exercises are not limited to relatively few large loans but need to be carried out on nearly all the advances made by the bank. Yet, widely acceptable and reliable techniques are yet to be devised. Moreover, the borrowers do not observe business ethics which make it difficult to establish close bank-clientele relationship - a condition for successful Islamic banking. Adverse selection has been one of the major impediments in the world of Islamic banking.

Among the other disincentives from the borrower's point of view is the need to disclose his accounts to the bank if he were to borrow on the Profit Loss Sharing basis. However, many small-time businessmen do not keep any accounts, leave alone proper accounts. And large conglomerates do not like to disclose their real accounts to anybody. The widespread lack of business ethics among certain business community will be another major hurdle in the path of Islamic banking in India.

The practices in use by the Islamic banks have evoked questions of morality. Some critics view Sukuk (Islamic Bond) as unIslamic in nature. Others criticize that financing through the purchase of client's property with a buy-back agreement and sale of goods to clients on a mark-up, involved the least risk and are closest to the old interest-based operations. Bai' mu'ajjal (sale with deferred payment) and Murabaha (cost-plus financing) are permitted in the Sharia under certain conditions. What is being done in many countries are fictitious deals which ensure a predetermined profit to the bank without actually dealing in goods or sharing any real risk. This is against the letter and spirit of Sharia.

The BR Act even disallows an Indian bank from floating a subsidary abroad to launch such products, or offering these through a special window. Thus, the upshot of the findings is that such banking experiment is impossible without a new law or multiple amendments to the BR Act.

Another important consideration is the tax procedures. While interest is a passive income, profit is defiantly an earned income which is treated differently. If principles of Islamic banking are incorporated then how does it comply with the tax procedure is the moot question. Further RBI cannot act as the lender to such banks because such accommodation by the monetary authority is also interest based. Islamic banks cannot interact with conventional banks based on principles of interest.

Michael Porter Five Forces Analysis:

The five forces model of Porter is an outside-in business unit strategy tool that is used to make an analysis of the attractiveness (value) of an industry structure. The competitive forces analysis is made by the identification of 5 fundamental forces:

1. **Bargaining power of customers**. How easy or difficult is it for new entrants to start competing, which barriers do exist.
2. **Bargaining power of suppliers**. How strong is the position of sellers? Do many potential suppliers exist or only few potential suppliers, monopoly?
3. **Competitive rivalry among the existing players**. Does a strong competition between the existing players exist? Is one player vary dominant or are all equal in strength and size.
4. **Threat of substitute products**. How easy can a product or service be substituted, especially made cheaper.
5. **Threat of new entrants.** How easy or difficult it is for new entrants to start competing, which barriers do exist.

When applying Michal porter's five forces model to Islamic banking, it shows the results like this.

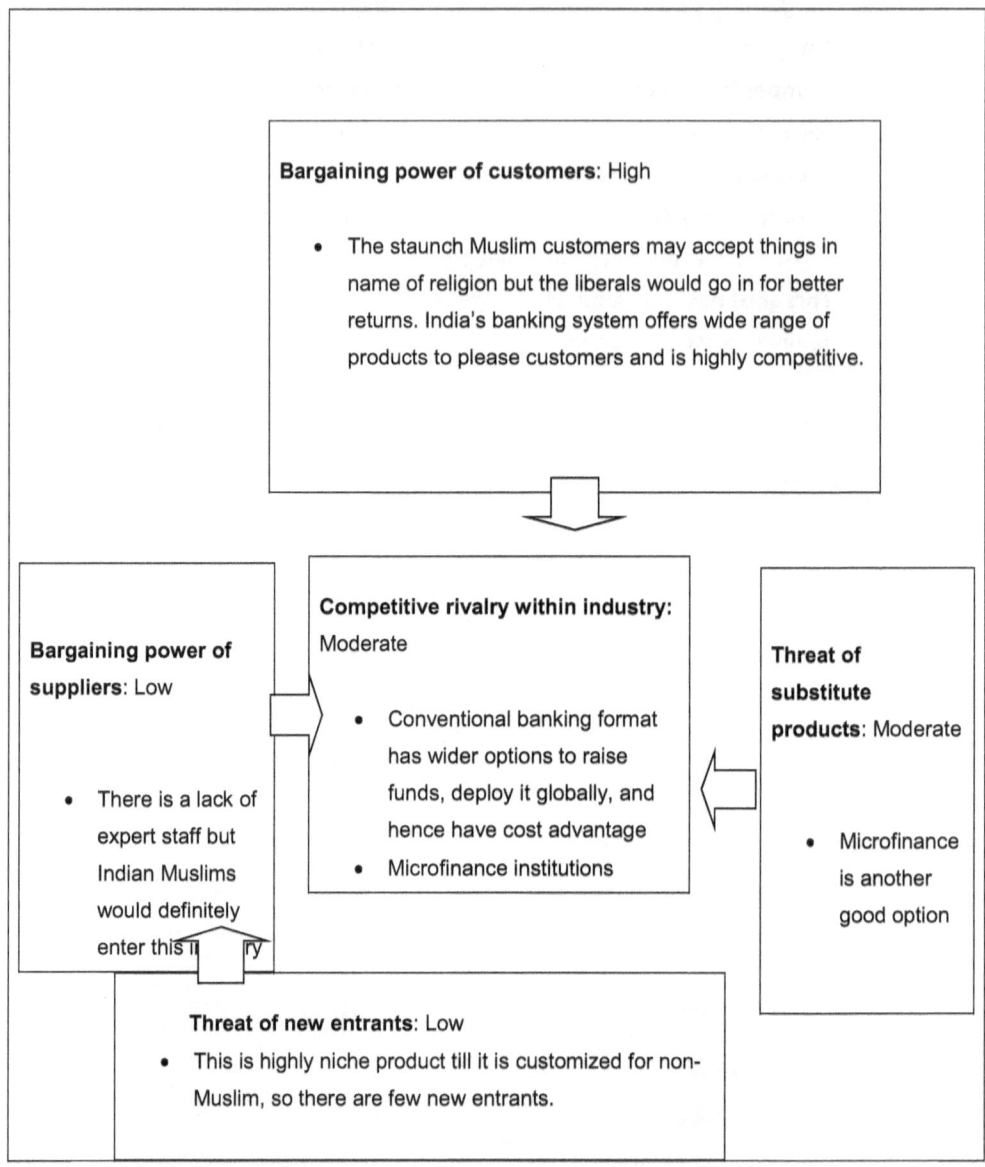

Bargaining power of customers: High

- The staunch Muslim customers may accept things in name of religion but the liberals would go in for better returns. India's banking system offers wide range of products to please customers and is highly competitive.

Bargaining power of suppliers: Low

- There is a lack of expert staff but Indian Muslims would definitely enter this industry

Competitive rivalry within industry: Moderate

- Conventional banking format has wider options to raise funds, deploy it globally, and hence have cost advantage
- Microfinance institutions

Threat of substitute products: Moderate

- Microfinance is another good option

Threat of new entrants: Low
- This is highly niche product till it is customized for non-Muslim, so there are few new entrants.

Present Status

There are several Baitul Mals working in cities as well as in villages. Only 10 to 15 Islamic banks with deposits of about Rs 75 crore are operating all over the country in various states. They are actually non-banking finance companies (NBFCs) which work on profits/loss basis.

Islamic banks by and large cater to the needs of local area except a few of them operating across districts or states. Their sources of funds are limited and as a result these banks have to operate on small scale missing the economies of scale. Islamic banks in India provide housing loan, on the basis of co-ownership, venture finance on mudarabah basis as well as on musharaka basis and consumers loans. Some banks finance transports also on the mark up basis via hire purchase. Education finance and skill development finance is also provided by them. Investments are made in government securities, small savings schemes or units of mutual funds. Investment in shares of companies is also made by some Islamic banks. Hire purchase and lease finance are other source of investments

Islamic banks in India do not function under banking regulations. They are licensed under Non-Banking Finance Companies Reserve Bank Directives 1997 RBI (Amendment) Act 1997, and operate on profit and loss based on Islamic principles. RBI has introduced compulsory registration system. In the Monetary and Credit Policy for the year 1999-2000, it was proposed that in respect of new NBFCs, which seek registration with the RBI and commence the business on or after April 21, 1999, the requirement of minimum level of net owned funds (NOF) will be Rs 2 crore.

Conclusion

Islamic banking is at an incipient stage. The existing legal framework does not permit Islamic Banking. Only selective activities like equity investment is possible, while trade finance aspects like taking title to goods is not possible. A lot of amendments need to be carried out in the prevalent legal set up. Appropriate models need to be selected and implemented to suit society's diverse financial needs. Islamic Bank of Britain, Islamic banks of Thailand, Singapore and USA may be glaring models for Indian bankers. The reputed domestic and international banks along with the collaboration of RBI should be involved in the process of determining and implementing Islamic Banking products.

The importance and relevance of Islamic banking in India in the context of "Financial Tsunami" that has taken place in recent times further enhances the need of Shari'ah banking. Also, the political parties need economic rationality to convince majority of voters that Islamic banking is not being introduced to please Muslim voters but to genuinely boost faster and inclusive growth for the Indian economy. Obnoxious politics in the name of religion must be avoided. we personally believe to refer 'Islamic Banking' as 'Interest Free Banking' so that it could be looked through the broad economic kaleidoscope and not a narrow religious prism.

Islamic banking could be a huge political issue. Certain parties might abhor the use of the word "Islamic" and could term it as anti-Indian. They might argue that the very concept of Shari'ah banking would go against the secular fabric of our country. We are already facing problems pertaining to Muslim Personnel Law and trying to implement Uniform Civil Code.

Therefore, at this juncture, if we introduce Islamic banking in India, it will create more problems than solving the issue. Moreover, it may bring financial segregation in the economy. The compartmentalization of Shari'ah compliant and Non-Sharia Compliant banking might be used by certain vested interest to communalize the finance sector in India. Such questionably sane but unquestionably dangerous trend must be prevented with full might

With only minor changes in their practices, Islamic banks can get rid of all their cumbersome and sometimes doubtful forms of financing and offer a clean and efficient interest-free banking. Participatory financing is a unique feature of Islamic banking, and can offer responsible financing to socially and economically relevant development projects. This is an additional service that Islamic banks offer over and above the traditional services provided by conventional commercial banks. Such a system will offer an effective banking system where Muslims in India.

Suggestions

India is eyeing a stake in the booming Islamic banking industry with its proposed implementation being assessed with great interest by the Indian policymakers. But they have to substantially modify the legal framework which governs the Indian banking system prior to offering Islamic banking financial services in the country.

- Under the current Indian banking laws, it is almost impossible for Islamic banking to be carried out in India due to the mandatory requirement for interest payments on deposits. The concept of profit-loss sharing or partnership is alien to the conventional banking framework of India and thus not allowed under the law. The tax treatment of Islamic finance products, unless reviewed, would be the biggest hindrance to the implementation of Islamic banking in India.

- India is ready to make waves in Islamic banking but not without their Government's permission to the conduct of Islamic banking in the country.

- With 150 million Muslim populations, India stood to gain advantage to pool around one trillion dollars Islamic investment funds from Gulf countries compared with its other non-Muslim counterparts. This will help the national current account and fiscal deficit in check.

- Regulators are still in doubts about the scope of Islamic banking, having understood that from a mere religious perspective. A committee to analyse the impact of Islamic banking to the Indian communities not withstanding their religious faith was never established. Thus, the potentials of Islamic banking to resolve India's real economic problems were not realized.

- The prejudices about Islamic banking still remained as there was not yet report on economic viability of Islamic banking and its impact on inclusive growth.
- There was also a fear that Muslims may dominate the Islamic banking industry in India. Islamic banking requires a professional expertise beyond one's religious belief because it deals with commercial projects than mere monetary credit and debit transactions. While Indian Muslims may have an edge in terms of Islamic ethics required for Islamic banking but they lack professional exposures to manage modern commercial banking on Islamic ethics.
- There would be viable opportunities to energise the Indian economy with the participation of Muslims in Shari'ah compliant banking who were previously excluded and the availability of funds for developments in India. It would help the poor and vulnerable as it allows the manufacturing and retail enterprise of unorganized sector and agriculture to obtain equity finance.
- The equity financing would also help India to fund irrigation, dams, roads, electricity, and communication projects along with other public infrastructure. These are areas where public finance is insufficient and debt finance may be a cause of deficit to the government.
- Islamic banking has one of the objectives as 'equal distribution of income', which in other words mean complete eradication of poverty. But it can be achieved only if Islamic banking is fully implemented in India.

References:

Bagsiraj M.I. (2000), "Islamic Financial Institutions of India, Their Nature, Problems and Prospects; A Critical Evaluation of selected representative units", *4th International conference*, Loughborough University, UK.

Bagsiraj M.I. (2001) "Islamic Financial Societies of India, Nature Problems and Prospects", *UGC National Seminar*, Islamiah College, Vaniyambadi.

Bahauddin, K. (1982), *Arab-wa-Dayare Hind (Urdu)*, Naqshe Nawayath, Bhatkal.

Baig, T. (2001), *"PLS Banking; Past, Present, and Future with special reference to India"*, Unpublished Paper.

Francis, J. and Clark, E. (1980), *Readings in Investments,* McGraw Hill Inc., New York.

Gulaid, M.A. (1995), *Financing Agriculture through Islamic modes and Instruments; practical scenarios and Applicability,* Research Paper No.34, IRTI, Jeddah.

Hassan, K.M. (2000), "Micro-Financial Services and poverty alleviation in Bangladesh; A Comparative analysis of secular and Islamic NGOs", *4th International Conference*, Loughborough University, UK.

Iqbal, M. (2000), *"Islamic and Conventional Banking in the 90s; A comparative study",* 4th *International Conference,* Loughborough University, UK.

Ahsanul, H. (2009), *"Islamic finance in India",* retrieved from: http://www.iosworld.org/islamic_finance_in_india.htm, May 14.

Iqbal, M., Ausaf, A. and Tariqullah, K. (1998), *Challenges Facing, Islamic Banking,* Occasional Paper No. 1, IRTI, IDB, Jeddah.

Khatkhate, M.H. (1997), "Islamic Investment Activities in India", *Second Conference on Islamic Banking and Finance,* Toronto, Canada, June.

Mahmud, A. (1995), "Islamic Banking Modes for House Building Finance", Seminar Proceeding Series No. 28, IRTI, Jeddah.

Mannan, M.A. (1993), *Understanding Islamic Finance; A Study of the Securities Market in an Islamic Framework,* IRTI, Jeddah.

Siddiqi, M.N. (1983), *Issues in Islamic Banking,* The Islamic Foundation, Leicester, UK.

Siddiqi, M.N. (1991), *Thirty Years of Muslim Fund (Urdu),* Muslim Fund Trust, Deoband.

Sumik, M. (2008), *Islamic banking in India-what is the future potential?* Management Development Institute Gurgaon, retrieved from http://www.crisil.com/crisil-young-thought-leader- 2008/dissertations, on April.

Sirageldin, I. (2000), "Elimination of poverty; challenges and Islamic Strategies", *International Conference,* Loughborough University, UK.

Wilson, R. (2000), "The Interface between Islamic and Conventional Banking", *4th International Conference,* Loughborough University, UK.

Khan, M.Y. (2001), "Banking Regulations and Islamic Banks in India: status and issues", *International Journal of Islamic Financial Services,* Vol. 2 No.4, pp. 1-7.

Sampath, G. (2009), "why not Islamic banking for India too", retrieved from http://www.dnaindia.com/report.asp?newsid=1204695, 22 May.

Chapter 9

Islamic Banking and Finance in Post-Soviet Central Asia with Special Reference to Kazakhstan

G.N. Khaki

Bilal Ahmad Malik

Kashmir University, Srinagar, India

Introduction

Islamic banking and finance industry, creeping out of its niche, has now become an integral part of the global finance industry. It has not only taken its roots in almost all of the Muslim countries but has also been under discussion and penetration in Western and Far Eastern jurisdictions. Presently the industry's working outlets are found in 75 countries of the world (Martin, Heiko, 2008). In today's depressed financial scenario; investors, retail banking customers and corporations are embracing Islamic banking and financing as a viable alternative in investments, lending and corporate financing (Zetti Aziz 2008). Although Islamic financial institutions have existed since the 1960s but the investment in Central Asia was on halt till the end of the communist regime. After independence in 1991, the Muslim republics of Central Asia and the southern Caucasus witnessed the arrival of Islamic banking and finance to the region (Geoffrey 2007).

In the mid-1990s, most Central Asian states joined the Organization of the Islamic Conference (OIC), allowing them to tap into the resources of the OIC's Islamic Development Bank (IDB) and get linked to Shari'ah based financial instruments. Moreover, triggered not least by the recent global financial crisis, political decision makers and financial entrepreneurs in the region were eager to develop new sources of capital. The Middle East and the Arab states, less touched by the meltdown of Western banks, were welcoming partners for fresh capital investment in the region. The need for new and fresh cash-flows, the search for an alternative form of banking and the rising discourse about interest free banking has opened a new chapter for Islamic and finance industry in the region (Mahmud 2012). Along with many other factors; the growth in the range of financial products and services, the increasing significance of the international dimension of Islamic finance, the growing economic and political relations between Central Asian countries and other money rich Arab countries are some of the essential factors which are believed to push-up the industry to become a dynamic and competitive form of financial intermediation in the region.

The purpose of this chapter is to take a general account of the emergence of Islamic banking and finance industry in Post-Soviet Central Asia and also to examine the actual demand for services and products offered by the industry to the majority Muslim populace of the whole region in general and Kazakhstan in particular. The emphasis shall be given to discuss the theoretical and empirical aspects regarding, feasibility of the industry and the kind of structure it employs in building alliance and linkage with important Kazakh stakeholders. The chapter will also investigate the role of Kazakh government in providing legal provision to the industry.

Reality of Islamic banking and finance

Years ago, Islamic finance was considered merely a wishful thinking. However, serious research efforts and development of Islamic products have shown that the Islamic finance is not only feasible but also an efficient and productive way of financial intermediation (Mohammad, Nadiyah, Khalid, Hajar, and Rohaya 2011). Islamic banking and finance are a generally used term to indicate all banking, financial and commercial transactions that are in compliance with Shari'ah (Islamic law). Since its relatively recent appearance, nearly forty years ago, Islamic banking and finance industry has increasingly become a mainstream banking activity with its major financial centers in Bahrain, Dubai, and Kuala Lumpur. While still considered to be in its infancy as compared to the conventional global financial industry, Islamic finance accounts for assets conservatively valued at over US$750 billion across 450 financial institutions based in 75 countries, all operating according to Islamic principles (Ernst & Young 2011). Most of the customers come to know about the industry only after recent global financial crisis. It was not less than a wonder to economists and financial experts that during global financial crisis 2007-2009 no Islamic bank failed or required government recapitalization in contrast to centuries old conventional banking giants. The industry has established its own regulatory authorities and standard-setting bodies. Being based on Shari'ah rulings, Islamic banking has moral principles ingrained in its core and its high-level goals aim for social justice and distributional equity. The characteristic features of Islamic banking and finance industry which differentiate it from its conventional counterpart are as:

• Risk and profit are shared between the two parties of a financial transaction.
• Speculation and uncertainty (*gharar*) in transactions is strictly prohibited.
• *Riba*, making money from money (i.e. interest) isn't justifiable at any cost.
• Certain activities like gambling (*maisir*) and game of chance (*qimar*), not beneficial to society, are banned.
• Transactions must be asset-based or asset-backed.
• Prohibition of investment in illegal and void (*haram*) businesses.

Emergence of Islamic banking and finance in the Post-Soviet Central Asia

In the late 1980s most, Central Asians were still deeply secular in outlook, a legacy of 70 years of communist rule. Yet from the bottom up, as well as from the top down, there was an impetus for enhancing the role of Islam in society. The collapse of Soviet Union marked end of the 'Iron-curtain, a period that ascertain limited access to the outer world and beginning of the 'Velvet-curtain' era, letting the regional people to peep in and out. The process of reformation and revival moved on very quickly as Islam always had deep roots in the region. Moreover, the newly freed region started to become a hub of dawah activism as many missionaries and funding agencies started to arrive from the outer mainstream Muslim centers to help the indigenous Muslims in rebuilding the mosques and other religious institutions. Increasingly, as the Central Asian states became integrated into the international community, so their responses to Islam began to resemble those that are found in other parts of the world, particularly in the Middle East.

Since the breakup of the Soviet Union, each of the Central Asian Republics has joined the largest Islamic banking institute Islamic Development Bank (IDB): Azerbaijan (1992); Kyrgyzstan (1993); Turkmenistan (1994); Kazakhstan (1995); Tajikistan (1996); and Uzbekistan (2003). By 1997, the IDB established a regional office in Almaty, Kazakhstan, to foster the Bank's efforts enhance the socio-economic development of the Muslim republics of Central Asia. The regional office in Almaty (ROA) has effectively become the hub for IDB group operations in the area. The regional decision makers and private bankers are gradually opening up to Islamic financial products. Responding positively to the growing customer demand, local governments like Kazakhstan, Kyrgyzstan and Azerbaijan have made some significant amendments in their respective state constitutions. Such amendments were also meant to provide some legal space for the industry where it could facilitate its Shari'ah based financial instruments and could generate a healthy market share. A healthy group of economic experts and financial analysts are of the opinion that the continuity of financial crisis, firstly hitting U.S and now rocking the Euro-Zone has encouraged the demand for some robust and risk-mitigated alternative in the Central Asian republics and there is better option than Islamic banking and finance industry. For example, in spite of the crisis, the Islamic financial market in Kazakhstan grew by 15% last year and in the last two years Kazakhstan's trade turnover with the Arab world reached 500 million dollars per year - more than any other Central Asian state (Oxford Analytica, 2009).

A brief overview of banking in Kazakhstan

Since its independence in 1991 Kazakhstan, a transitional economy has been carrying out a lot of reforms and innovatory fiscal trends towards a market-oriented economy and macroeconomic stabilization. The FDI inflow into oil and gas industry was enhanced, public sector was restructured, financial sector was liberalized, Soviet era Kazakhstan Republic's *Gosbank* was transformed to the National Bank of the Republic of Kazakhstan in 1993 and Russian ruble was replaced by Kazakh *Tenge* (KZT), the national currency (OECD report). The two-tier banking system was introduced with the National Bank as its first tier and all other commercial banks as the second one. The National Bank was empowered to fulfill traditional central bank's functions including money issue, currency control, monetary policy and banking regulation and supervision. Among all Central Asian countries, the banking system of Kazakhstan continues to be one of the strongest and comparatively stable since independence. The total banking assets cover around 10% of total GDP, and the National Bank of Kazakhstan commands sufficient resources to support the country's commercial banks. Consolidation in the banking sector continues, with liquidation of insolvent banks, privatization and mergers of others. Currently, NBK oversees 38 commercial banks, including one Islamic bank opened in 2010. NBK facilitated growth by strategies aimed towards international banking and finance standards in terms of accounting and reporting, information technologies and risk management, infrastructure and regulation.

Over the past decade, Kazakhstan's banking industry has experienced a pronounced boom and bust cycle. After several years of rapid expansion in mid-2000s, the banking industry collapsed in 2008, since then the role of the banking sector in the economy decreased significantly. The total Assets-to-GDP ratio fell down as much as twice to 47% at the end of 2011. Overall, despite economic recovery of the country and structural changes in the banks' balance sheet during last few years, the banking sector is still fragile. Already high NPL (non-paying loans) ratio may be even higher than official number, as indicated by 2012 IMF Kazakhstan banking sector report. At the same time the decreased Assets-to-GDP ratio designates a low penetration of the banking sector, promising a high potential for growth. It also reflects the possibility of new banking approach in contemporary Kazakh economy (Mahdi 2012).

Kazakhstan: A growing market for interest-free banking and finance industry
Kazakhstan holds a unique position among the countries that gained sovereignty after the collapse of the USSR. Kazakhstan, the ninth largest state in the world in terms of area, occupies more than 2.7 million square kilometers (over one million square miles). More than 70 percent of the residents of Kazakhstan are Muslims. For centuries, Islam has been the main religion for the whole region. However, during the period of Soviet regime, Kazakhstan faced a vehement wave of modernization and secularization. The country where thousands of

Islamic state figures and scientists lived and worked was subjected to violent elimination of religious values and potential abolishment of religious institution and as a result Islam was saved for domestic aspects of life only. Once Kazakhstan has gained sovereignty in the early 1990s after the demise of the Soviet Union, the process of the revival of Islamic values started with a vengeance (Kuralay 2008). Although, Kazakhstan does not have Islam as the state religion and according to Article 1 of the 1995 constitution Kazakhstan is a secular state but still one can witness the rapid increase of religious feelings among the people. The increase in number of Mosques (2.5 thousand compared to 63 during Soviet era), Madrasas, Islamic institutions of higher education, and Islamic publication of Islamic literature come as evidence of reactivation and revitalization of religious life in Kazakhstan (Saniya Edelbay 2012). The demand for Halal food and Islamically valid dressing was another sign of growing interest in religious activities. Meeting the public demand, in 2001, the Halal standard was introduced in Kazakhstan, resulting in a growing number of cafes and restaurants offering Halal food, and stores selling clothes that meet Shari'ah requirements (Saniya Edelbay 2012).

The most fascinating thing to see was the emergence of Shari'ah compliant banking and financial transactions. Kazakhstan, in this regard took some initials soon after independence. Though not to a large extant but Kazakhstan got practically involved with Islamic banking and finance after joining IDB in 2005.The statistical observations reflect that PLS (profit and loss share) industry in Kazakhstan is continuously spreading out to produce a better alternative in terms of policies and services in the near future. Kazakhstan's effort to develop Islamic finance has a short history and is closely intertwined with the effects of the global financial crisis starting in 2007. First initiatives for Islamic banking, however, were undertaken as early as 1990 in the republic. Still part of the Soviet Union, the Council of Ministers of the Kazakh SSR passed a resolution to found the "Al'baraka Kazakhstan Bank" as an international project in cooperation with Saudi-Arabian partners. Al'baraka Kazakhstan Bank opened on January 1, 1991 and survived the difficult years of the dismantling of the Soviet economy only to be renamed "Kaspi Bank" and re-structured into a conventional commercial finance institute in 1997. A similar fate was suffered by an initiative from "La riba", a riba-free operating US-based Bank that tried to enter the Kazakhstan market in the 1990s (Wolters 2013).

Kazakhstan was the first country in Central Asia to experience PLS system of banking and finance when in 1996 IDB opened its representative office in Almaty, then capital of the Russia, which is now covering the whole Central Asia, Azerbaijan and Albania. Since operations began, the IDB has spent almost 700 Mill.US-Dollar in Kazakhstan, which puts the republic ahead of its Central Asian neighbors in terms of received funding. As a player in the development aid market in Central Asia, the IDB follows the standards of operation provided for in this particular game. For its investments in Kazakhstan such standards demand a close cooperation with the state structures as the point of entrance to the market and it results in a predominance of funding and loans to state organized infrastructural projects. The money used for such activities stems from contributions generated in the member states of the IDB group. It is important to mention that for most of its engagement the bank employs conventional instruments, even if Shari'ah conformity is being observed on a case-by-case basis. As an important engine for the further development of Islamic finance in Kazakhstan the IDB has emerged, nonetheless, during the unfolding of the global financial crisis when it supported first attempts to launch reforms (Wolters 2013). Taking a move forward, Kazakhstan became the only IDB member country in the Central Asia Region which joined the Islamic Corporation for the Insurance of Investment and Export Credit (ICIEC) in 2002. During the Member Country Partnership Strategy (MCPS) Technical Mission, potential opportunities in the provision of Shari'ah-compliant export credit and investment insurance in Kazakhstan were identified. In order to enhance Islamic banking finance in the country the MCPS Work Program proposed the following programs and capacity development activities:

a. Technical Assistance to develop the Enabling Environment (regulatory and supervisory frameworks) for Islamic finance;
b. Technical Assistance for developing the Takaful sector;
c. Equity investment in an Islamic bank to expand the sector, as well as joint initiatives and programs with key institutions, including the Development Bank of Kazakhstan; and
d. Assistance to build capacity of the Zakat Fund (IBD Group 2012).

Kazakhstan banks demonstrated a strong interest in Islamic financial services since early 2000's. In 2003, Kazakhstan's largest bank, BTA, became the first Central Asian financial institution to draw on an Islamic-backed line of credit when it borrowed 250 million dollars from Arab, UK and Malaysian Islamic lenders. Since 2006, other Kazakh banks such as Centre Credit and Alliance have started using Islamic financial practices (Oxford Analytica 2009). The current instability in the international financial markets (e.g. the recent subprime mortgage crisis in the US) has had an impact on the local economy, and Kazakhstan's banks and regulatory authorities are increasingly turning their attention toward Shari'ah approved PLS transactions. With respect to the present domestic business environment and local clients' capabilities, *Murabaha,* which is the simplest type of Islamic financing, is also being practiced in Kazakhstan today. Other forms, specifically *Musharakah* (joint venture), *Ijarah* (leasing) *Sukuk* (Islamic bonds) and *Mudarabah* (profit/loss sharing) are currently under examination, and their introduction is being planned (Kuralay 2008). Islamic banking guidelines were first approved in 2003 by one of the major banks in Kazakhstan, Bank Turan Alem JSC (BTA Bank). From 2006, these were acceded to other leading domestic banks, Center Credit Bank,

Alliance Bank and Kazcommertzbank. In the spring of 2007, BTA Bank signed a memorandum of understanding with Dubai-based Emirates Islamic Bank to promote Shari'ah-compliant banking in Kazakhstan and other CIS states, where BTA has a number of subsidiaries (New Horizon 2007). Initiatives for the development of Islamic finance in Kazakhstan in 2007 did not only result in new legislation, but also led to new corporations and agencies being formed and established. First to appear was "Fattah Finance", a consultancy and financial broker for Islamic investment and securities. Fattah Finance and its staff were behind the establishment of the "Association for the Development of Islamic Finances" in 2009.

A clear lobby group, ADIF tries to develop contacts with state institutions in Kazakhstan to ease the reform of legislation and work on behalf of its members' interests. In 2012 seven members join ARIF, among them the only Islamic bank operating in the republic to this day, the Islamic Bank Al- Hilal. The bank was founded in 2009 based on an agreement between the governments of the Republic of Kazakhstan and the United Arab Emirates. In line with this agreement, Al-Hilal bank from Abu Dhabi owns 100% of the JSC Islamic Bank Al Hilal which has its headquarters in Almaty, with branches in Astana and Shymkent and each branch is targeting to offer a wide range of products for both retail and corporate customers. Al Hilal bank in Abu Dhabi in turn is 100% owned by the UAE government. The young bank, founded in 2008, has become a major player on the UAE financial market, with 97% of its activities in retail and only 3% in corporate financing. Quite to the contrary, Islamic Bank Al Hilal in Kazakhstan operates solely in corporate financing, with state holdings being the main recipient of investment and service, and big infrastructure projects as the target market segment for loans. Furthermore, having considered the need of an independent Shari'ah Panel as specified in the Al Hilal Islamic Bank's JSC charter and the Banking Law of RK (Article No. 52-2), the Bank's Shareholder has appointed the Islamic Finance Principles Board of scholarly qualified individuals to issue opinions (Fatwa) according to Shari'ah Principles with specialized and comprehensive knowledge in Islamic Jurisprudence, Finance, Banking and Laws. It has been put at the helm of the bank to ensure all the activities are carried out in strict compliance with Shari'ah rules and principles (Al-Hilal Audit Report 2012).

source: Al-Hilal Bank

The Bank's mission is to raise the profile of Islamic banking in the CIS countries whilst contributing to Kazakhstan's national growth and prosperity and also strives to understand its customers' needs and provide the right Islamic finance solutions to meet these needs. The bank plays an insignificant role in the financial market in the republic ranked 33 out of 39 Kazakh banks in 2011. According to the bank's annual report (Al Hilal bank, 2012) the main products offered to the corporate clients are commodity *Murabaha (58%)* and *Ijarah (42%)*. The retail banking presents a current account based on *Qard-Hassan* and a deposit based on *Mudarabah* contracts. It is supervised in its activities by the Islamic Finance Principles Board which consists of three members that are specialists in Shari'ah law and that yearly issue a fatwa on the bank's performances (Wolters 2013). The Government also plans to develop and promote Almaty as a Central Asia regional financial center, and mandated the Regional Financial Center Almaty, or RFCA, for achieving this goal. More recently, in November 2011, the National Bank of Kazakhstan was admitted as an Associate Member of the Islamic Financial Services Board, based in Kuala Lumpur, Malaysia. Furthermore, in July 2011, the President signed into law the amendment "On alteration and addition to some legislative acts of the Republic of Kazakhstan on the organization of Islamic finance", paving the way for issuance of *Sukuk* (IDB Group 2012). In July 2012 the Development Bank of Kazakhstan became the first in the region to issue *Sukuk*. In May 2013, the ICD announced its initiative to convert Zaman Bank into Islamic bank with an investment of up to 35% of capital. The local bank will be the second Islamic bank in the country. The ICD along with Zaman Group and other investors established the first *Ijarah* Company in the Republic with an authorized capital of US$36 million. A US$ 76 million debut *Murabahah* program carrying a 5.5% yield will mature in August 2017. Since independence, the government of Kazakhstan has been paying special attention towards the development of Islamic financial services sector but from the past few years, there has been a kind of drift in its policy. The industry is being supported through;

(a) Promulgation of specific legislation,

112

(b) Development of ambitious strategies,

(c) Setting up of special purpose departments,

(d) Hosting of events to deliberate on core issues in a transparent environment, and

(e) Reaching out to IDB and other institutions and experts for assistance.

Law of Kazakhstan and Government Road Map: New avenues and prospects

The economic researches convey that the market of Islamic banking and finance industry is growing 15-20% annually which reflects prospects of the industry in the coming years. Kazakhstan has joined the list of countries that have altered their legislation in order to facilitate Islamic banking and finance. Modern Islamic banking and finance legislation has originated not bottom up from the Islamic faithful, but top down from multinational businesses seeking a profitable market position (Maggs 2011) The Republic of Kazakhstan became the first country in the Commonwealth of Independent States (CIS) to introduce fundamental legislative amendments after indentifying the volume and future prospectus of Islamic finance in the country.

In 2009, after President Nursultan Nazarbayev ordered a bill on Islamic financing, the government revised existing laws on banks and the securities market and several other laws pertinent to Islamic financing. The country's powerful president has issued an edict calling for use of Islamic finance as a measure "for attracting resources for further development" (Maggs 2011). Such amendments were made to a number of Kazakhstan's legislative acts (the Civil Code, the Tax Code, the Law on Banks and Banking Activities, the Law on Financial Markets and others). An amendment to the Kazakhstan Banking Law in 2009 allowed Islamic banking activities, established a separate license for Islamic banks and stipulated the Islamic financing products. However, the law does not recognize Islamic 'window' operations. The main differentiating factor between conventional and Islamic banks is the accounting procedures for Islamic banks (IDB Group 2012). To develop these amendments, a group of specialists was formed that actively cooperated and continues to cooperate with government bodies on issues related to the development of Islamic finance in Kazakhstan. The main principles used in developing the amendments to Kazakhstan's legislation were the following:

•Equalization of the taxation of Islamic financial products with the taxation of conventional financial products
• Expansion of existing concepts to include specific definitions of Islamic financial instruments
• Extension of tax benefits applied to traditional financial products to Islamic financial products
• For tax purposes, Islamic financial products are classified as such only for the purposes of transactions carried out by Islamic banks.
The following main amendments to the Tax Code were also introduced:

• The list of types of income received by residents and non-residents was expanded to include income received from an investment deposit placed in an Islamic bank. Such an amendment allows the taxation of such income to be defined and makes the tax consequences of investing in Kazakhstan, including foreign investments, more transparent.

• The provision of Islamic financial products was generally exempted from value added tax, which is a significant achievement in equalizing the taxation of Islamic and traditional financial products.

The implementation of Islamic finance at the legislative level in Kazakhstan is expected to play an important role in the development of the country's economy and infrastructure. In particular, it extends the range of financial services, which makes Kazakhstan's financial market more competitive, and is a means of attracting investment capital and major players from the worldwide Islamic financial industry to Kazakhstan (Ernst &Young 2011). The Government and NBK continue to demonstrate a political will to support the new industry. The 41-point government road map "Road Map for Development of Islamic Finance by 2020", released on March 2012 (extending up to the year 2020), speaks about the concern of Kazakh government towards expansion of Islamic banking finance industry in the country. The Road-map includes main actions to be taken, responsible parties and time-frame for the following directions (Mahdi 2012):

1. Legislation Improvement;
2. Educating Market;
3. Islamic Finance Infrastructure Development.
4. Public Sector Development.
5. Islamic Financial Services Development;
6. Science and Education;
8. Investors Relations.

Growth of Sukuk and Takaful market and some other activities

In the medium term and in the context of favorable market conditions, the Government of Kazakhstan is considering the issuance of Sovereign *Sukuk* to finance fiscal deficit of the country and set the benchmark for local issuers. According to the estimates, the coupon rate of the *Sukuk* will be formed taking into account some risk premium. Overall, expected markup will be comparable to ones with traditional sovereign securities, as one of the key factors of price formation is the credit risk of the issuer. Issuance of *Sukuk* is being promoted by the Government, however, for this to materialize the pricing of the *Sukuk* will need to be competitive with the conventional bonds (Ernst & young 2011). On 3 August 2012 the Development Bank of Kazakhstan, a government owned financial investment institute with assets worth more than 6 Bill. US$, issued a *Sukuk*, an Islamic bond in the size of 75 Mill US$.

This was the first time an Islamic bond was issued in the former Soviet Union. For a market new to Islamic finance, the issuance by the Development Bank is believed to provide a good starting point for opening the market for other *Sukuk* issuers because of the bank's ties with the government of Kazakhstan. To begin with, the issuer, the Development Bank of Kazakhstan (DBK), was operating under uncertain legal conditions. The *Sukuk* was issued as a commodity *murabahah*, yet laws in Kazakhstan specified only *Sukuk* of the *Ijarah* and *Musharakah* type. In addition, according to representatives from the DBK, neither issuance procedures for Islamic bonds nor their listing procedures were clearly regulated. The launching of this bond was a test for all parties involved to examine the reaction of the market. To smooth the process, the *sukuk* was issued in Malaysian ringgit, using the Malaysian law and corresponding supervisory capacities in the Kingdom, namely approval from the Malaysian Central Bank and the Shari'ah Advisory Council of the Securities Commission of Malaysia for Shari'ah conformity. Listed at the Kazakh stock exchange and with a profit rate of 5,5% p.a. the *Sukuk* was aimed at investors from Malaysia to whom 62% of the bond were allocated, the remaining 38 to investors in Kazakhstan (Wolters 2013). Thanks to the state support and adoption of the new law on Islamic Finance in Kazakhstan, some Islamic financial institutions have been established and are successfully operating in the local markets. A number of legal entities have been registered in order to provide consultancy services on Islamic finance.

In order to coordinate activities of public entities involved in development of Islamic finance, the Government of Kazakhstan approved Road Map for Development of Islamic Finance in Kazakhstan by 2020, and its implementation will contribute to the creation of stable environment for development of Islamic financial industry, attracting the investors and market players. Definitely, to ensure efficient implementation of the Islamic finance in Kazakhstan further amendments and changes will be required to adapt the current legislation to the needs of this sector. Currently National Bank of Kazakhstan prepare a draft law "On the introduction of changes and amendments into the legal acts of the Republic of Kazakhstan related to insurance and Islamic finance", to further develop the Islamic finance in Kazakhstan through introducing principles of Islamic insurance, improving environment for Islamic banks, and developing infrastructure of the Islamic finance. The *Takaful* sector shows potential in Kazakhstan. The *Takaful* Association is busy in promoting the sector. Currently, it only offers health and accident coverage for *Hajj* and *Ummrah* travelers. The Financial Services Industry (FSA) has adopted a document which entails acceptance of necessary legislation of *Takaful* by 2012. The Hajj Fund (a 50:50 joint venture of Fattah Finance and Amana Raya) was launched at the WIEF in June 2011. The Ministry of Finance is keen to develop the Islamic microfinance sector, and has allocated funds for developing the microfinance in the country. It is proposing changes to national legislation for microfinance with a focus on rural areas. Kazakhstan's priorities are to strengthen the existing 800-1,000 microfinance institutions.

Applying Islamic financing instruments in Agri sector is a new market exposure for the Islamic finance industry in Kazakhstan. The country is among the world's top 10 exporters of wheat which is by far the country's most important agricultural commodity, well- known for its modernization of harvesting techniques. The International Islamic trade Finance Corporation (ITCF), a member of the Islamic development Group, put together an Islamic structured deal of US$40 million for financing exports of wheat in a Shari'ah-compliant manner. The deal in the form of a *Murabaha*-based financing structure serves as a model for future agricultural and supply chain transactions with a substantial reduction of the total pricing charged to the beneficiary and thereby rendering the financing structure more competitive (IRTI 2012).

Conclusion

Islamic banking and finance are emerging as a viable financial intermediation in the republics of Central Asia. The banking and financial pundits are of the opinion that the chances for Islamic banking are higher in Kazakhstan because of declining customer trust in years old conventional banking industry due to the impact of global financial and debt crisis on the local Kazakh banks. While the majority of Kazakhstan's citizens are Muslim, the country is largely secular, and Nazarbayev's policy has been to build good relations with all religions. However, he has been very much the driving force behind efforts to establish Islamic finance in Kazakhstan. The country of Kazakhstan has a lot to offer for Islamic banking and finance. The banking and business sector of country shows a promising potential for the industry. Taken alone by the numbers of international conferences and forums dedicated to Islamic finance and business, Kazakhstan has indisputably become the regional leader in promoting Islamic ideas of banking and doing business in the region. The "Seventh World Islamic Economic Forum" was held in June 2011, the "Second Islamic Finance Forum" took place in September 2011, the "Kazakhstan International Halal Expo '2012" and the "Third Kazakhstan Islamic Finance Conference" were both organized in October 2012. These events underline Kazakhstan's declared goal to develop the country into the regional center for Islamic finance in the former Soviet Union. The government is currently implementing a program of industrial and innovative development and to give this framework a practical shape, it needs foreign investment. The Muslim world, including Malaysia and the countries of the Middle East, has a huge amount of capital ready to flow into Kazakhstan once the right conditions are in place, and that is what the roadmap is for. The roadmap, primarily set out to provide all possibilities of regulating the Islamic banking and finance activities until 2020, is expected to enhance the market share of Islamic banking and finance industry in the coming years. From the industry side, the industry has to keep the local market requirements into consideration while developing new policies and only those Shari'ah complaint financial instruments which are equally effective in market penetration and customer satisfaction are to be promoted.

References

Ahrens, J. and Hoen, H.W. (2012), *Institutional Reform in Central Asia, Politico- Economic Challenges*, Routledge, London.

Awan, A.G. (2009), "Comparison of Islamic and Conventional banking in Pakistan", *Proceedings 2nd CBRC*, Lahore, Pakistan.

Akmambet, M. (2012), *How Attractive is Setting up an Islamic Bank in Kazakhstan?* Cass Business School, City University London.

Clare, N. (2011), *Support from the top for Islamic Finance Market in Investing in Kazakhstan*, New Desk Media, Washington, DC.

Frederick, V.P. and Scheherazade, S.R. (2011), "Globalization of Islamic Finance: Myth or Reality?", *International Journal of Humanities and Social Science*, Vol. 1 No. 19, pp. xx-xx.

Fuad, A. (2008), *Guerilla Islamic Finance: The Azerbaijani Way*, Azerbaijan in the world 1, no. 13, August 1.

Fuad, A. (2012), *The Politics of Islamic Finance in Central Asia and South Caucasus, Voices from Central Asia*, The Elliot School of International Affairs, Washington university.

Geoffrey, F.G. (2007) "The Rise of Islamic Banking and Finance in Central Asia", *The Fletcher School Online Journal for issues related to Southwest Asia and Islamic Civilization*, Vol. 2007, pp. 13-24.

Askari, H., Iqbal, Z., Krichene, N. and Mirkhor, A. (2007), *The Stability of Islamic Finance: Creating a Resilient Financial Environment for a Secure Future*, John Wiley & Sons (Asia) Pte. Ltd., Singapore.

Islamic Development Bank Group (2004), *Member Country Partnership Strategy for the Republic of Kazakhstan (2012-2014) Strengthening Competitiveness for Growth & Diversifications*, Islamic Development Bank, Jeddah.

Islamic Research and Training Institute (2012), *Islamic Finance in Practice Financing Agri-Business*, IRTI, Jeddah.

Istisnaa Corporation (2013), "Kazakhstan: The Golden Ticket to Islamic Finance in Central Asia", Online Islamic Finance News, retrieved on: http://www.istisna.kz/eng/?p=3003 20.10.2013.

Cihak, H. Hessel, H. (2008), *Islamic Banks and Financial Stability: An Empirical Analysis*, IMF Working Paper, WP/08/16.

Mohieldin, M. (2012), *Realizing the Potential of Islamic Finance*, The World Bank Economic Premise, No. 77.

Hanief, M. (2011), "Differences and Similarities in Islamic and Conventional Banking", *International Journal of Business and Social Science*, Vol. 2 No. 2, pp. 166-175.

Uthmani, M.M.T. (2010), *An Introduction to Islamic Finance*, Adam Publishers & Distributors, India.

Chapra, M.U. (2009), *The Global Financial Crisis: Can Islamic Finance Help Minimize the Severity and Frequency of Such A Crisis in The Future?* Center for Islamic Area Studies at Kyoto University (KIAS), Japan.

Oxford Analytica Ltd. (2009), *Central Asia: Islamic Finance Shows Promise*, Oxford Analytica Ltd., UK.

Maggs, P.B. (2001), *Islamic Banking in Kazakhstan Law*, Martinus Nijhoff Publishers, Leiden.

Bekkin, R. (2009), *Islamic Finance in the Former Soviet Union*, Moscow State Institute of International Relations, Moscow.

Sapir, J. (2008), "From financial crisis to turning point", Real world Economics Review, Vol. 46, pp. xx-xx.

Ilias, S. (2010), *Islamic Finance: Overview and Policy Concerns*, Congressional Research Service, USA.

Chapter 10

The Challenges of Conventional Banking Practice and Prospects of Introducing an Islamic Bank to Tajikistan

Ashurov Sharofiddin
Insaniah University

Introduction

Indeed, financial system is one of the most important designs of modern society. Its main duty is to transfer funds from saving sectors to investment sectors, to spend on the production of goods and services, investment in new equipment. It is generally recognized that the financial system plays a crucial role in the process of economic development and growth. As the economy grows, the financial system becomes increasingly more compound and its structure more sophisticated that is according to Davis (1989),

Furthermore, as mentioned by Oke (1989), the financial system of any country represents a function of the size of its economy. A developing economy places more responsibility on the financial sector in order to activate the needed capital in society to facilitate production, and generate employment and income. An economy that does not accelerate continuous growth is likely to have a very inactive financial sector as there is no incentive for investment. Through the process of growth, the financial system offers a wide range of collection options for savers and issuable instruments for investors; a function often referred to as financial intermediation.

In the other hand according to Makhmedov et al. (2012), all countries in Central Asia are to some degree affected by a financial crisis, but the two poorest countries, Kyrgyzstan and Tajikistan, are in awful conditions. Their own specialists foresee that in the next few years there will be "no teachers for their children and no doctors to heal them". In Tajikistan, power cuts in winter can last longer than twelve hours a day in the countryside. This is so common that it has become a tradition. Experts from Kyrgyzstan and Tajikistan are worried by the increasingly likely prospect of catastrophic systemic collapse, especially in the energy sector.

Besides, as it mentioned by Curtis (1996), Tajikistan has two main dimensions, first was the civil war soon after the collapse of the communist regime and the second has been the underdeveloped financial system. Although the country is moving toward a market economy, sixty-eight per cent (68%) of the population continue to live below the poverty line. Poverty in

Tajikistan differs from other countries by the speed for which it sets in and its magnitude. Poverty in Tajikistan emerged instantly in the 1990s due to the civil war which saw much of the population become poor and created an enormous class of new poor. Moreover, Tajikistan capital markets are non-existent and banks often prefer to lend to larger, well-established businesses that have a profitable track record and can offer stronger security (p.7).

According to Akramov (2012), low income countries such as Tajikistan have been open to global financial and economic crises. Tajikistan is a poor country that is highly dependent on food imports, and is feeling increasingly at risk due to the international financial crisis. More than half of the population continues to live below the absolute poverty line.

Akramov further highlighted that due to the financial and food crises, the country's terms of trade have considerably worsened in recent years while relative prices of its major imports of fuel and foods with respect to its main exports, aluminium and cotton, have significantly increased. Second, rising global food and fuel prices led to significant inflationary pressure in Tajikistan, and double-digit inflation was observed in the second half of 2007 and throughout 2008 and early 2009. Rising inflation became evident again in 2011; the annualized inflation rate rose from approximately 5 percent in mid-2010 to nearly 15 per cent in mid-2011.

As mentioned by Honohan et al (1996), many countries have experienced costly banking crises. The importance of the banking system in the development of the economy cannot be underestimated based on the significant role banks play in the mobilization and allocation of resources for productive economic activities. The collapse of the banking system can result in liquidity problems that make it difficult for the industry and business to access loans. As a result, the economy can be paralyzed. The recent financial crisis in mid-2007 that crippled the global economy started as a result of the collapse of banks in most developed and developing countries. The occurrence of failures in the banking system is as great in developing countries as in the industrial world.

According to Nichol (2014), the interest based financial system had become the dominant system during the colonial period and continued to be so in many Muslim countries even after their independence. Tajikistan experienced two types of economic and financial systems, namely the socialist and capitalist. The socialist system was adopted when Tajikistan was under the Soviet Union, whereas the capitalist system was introduced after independence until now. However, due to the collapse of leading Wall Street institutions and the bankruptcy of many banks specifically Lehman Brothers, the following global financial crisis and economic downturn caused professionals and economists all around the world to think of alternative financial solutions. One such alternative was Islamic Banking and Finance (Wilson, 2010). Hence, this chapter examines the challenges of current financial practices in Tajikistan to ascertain how it can accelerate the business cycle in Tajikistan. Of particular interest is the issue of the general lack of trust between banks and customers.

Of all solutions attempted for resolving the financial crisis, no solutions from the Islamic perspective have been sufficiently explored for the context of Tajikistan. Based on the continuous instability of banks that have defied all possible solutions, this chapter attempts to examine the challenges facing current financial practices in Tajikistan and the possibility of the adoption and public perception and awareness of Islamic banking and finance as an alternative to conventional finance in Tajikistan.

According to Meera (2008), Islamic finance is asset based rather than debt based and it is the lack of debt and the direct link to real assets that provide it with stability. The relationship between Islamic banks and the real economy has good potential to foster a stable financial sector that will play a positive role to reduce the unemployment rate and improve economic growth. In light of the relatively scarce literature on Islamic banking and finance in the context of Tajikistan, this chapter attempts to begin addressing this lacuna.

Accordingly, the main objective of this chapter is to investigate the challenges of conventional banking practices in Tajikistan and to analyse prospects, and public perception and awareness towards the introduction, adoption and acceptability of Islamic Banking as a part of solution to the challenges of the conventional banking system in Tajikistan.

Review of Tajikistan's Economy

Tajikistan is a small landlocked country located in the heart of Central Asia, and bordered by Afghanistan, China, the Kyrgyz Republic, and Uzbekistan. Roughly one-tenth of its 8 million total population lives in Dushanbe, the capital city. The country is blessed with abundant water resources, contributing to its specialization in cotton production. Tajikistan also has huge hydropower generation potential, abundant and inexpensive electricity has led to its other main specialization, aluminium production, contributing approximately one-half of exports. However, unlike other richer Central Asian countries e.g. Kazakhstan and Turkmenistan, Tajikistan has little to no oil, gas, and other such natural resources. Only 7 percent of its total land area of 143,000 square kilometres is liveable. High mountain ranges across its territory make communication between different parts of the country difficult, especially in winter. Up to 40 percent of the country's national workforce is employed abroad, mostly in Russia, and sends home remittances equal to more than one-third of its gross domestic product. The above factors have caused Tajikistan to become one of the poorest countries in Central Asia. Furthermore, Tajikistan's economic and financial situation remains fragile due to uneven implementation of structural reforms, corruption, weak governance, seasonal power shortages, and the external debt burden according to (Brbone, et al 2010),

In this regard, according to Mackie Falkowski, (2009), Tajikistan is the poorest country of the former Soviet Union. Tajikistan's GDP in 2007 was US$3.2 billion and it's per capital GDP was only US$578, its inflation rate stood at 19.8%, and the balance of trade turnover was negative at US$1.1 billion. The average salary in 2008 amounted to around US$68.

Besides, Tajikistan's economic development has been delayed by geographic and historical factors such as its bordering location, a recovering economy, its poorly developed industry and agriculture, an obsolete infrastructure, communication problems, and the absence of foreign investments and political difficulties after the break-up of the USSR, and the ruinous effects of the 1992-1997 civil war.

In addition, according to the "Asia-Plus" public newspaper (Ergashieva, 2010), Tajikistan's banking system does not satisfy the needs of the country's economy. The volume of loans is very low according to finance experts from the Association of Banks of Tajikistan (ABT). According to the results of a survey conducted in 2009, specific weight of credit portfolio of Tajik banks against GDP is only 26.4%. It was further stated that despite those measures that are being undertaken to reduce the refinancing rate, actual interest rates remain very high. This is mainly associated with the fact that the bank deposits of ordinary persons and legal entities that are deposited with high interest rates are being used as resources for these loans. To gain the confidence of the depositors and make deposits more attractive, banks tend to offer high interest rates.

However, according to ABT, in the first quarter of 2010 the average interest rate on fixed period deposits increased up to 19.21% from 16.92% in 2009. The increase was mainly connected with the global financial crisis and those measures banks have undertaken to prevent the outflow of deposits. Based on the fact that banks pay high rates on deposits, it is expected that interest rates on loans should also be high. Thus, in the first quarter of 2010, the average interest rate increased up to 22.72% compared to 22.63% in 2009.

According to Rashidov (2012)[16], in Tajikistan there is a general lack of public trust in the banking system as many Tajiks lost millions of Rubles (Russian currency) following the collapse of the social system. Although there has been slight improvement in regards to regaining trust in the banking system, suspicion remains deeply engrained in the Tajik public psyche. Another reason identified by Rashidov is the long process of documentation required in the banking sector

---

[16] www.ozodagon.tj retrieved on 4/05/2013

has turned many Tajiks off the banking system in Tajikistan. Exorbitant interest rate between 20 to 30 percent however is the main cause for customer displeasure. According to Tajik economists, the interest-based banking system could be another reason for the majority Muslim population to reject the banking system as the interest based conventional banking system is prohibited in Islam. Moreover, according to Salimpur[17] (2012) who quoted from World Bank statistics, only 14% of the population deals with banks in Tajikistan, while the majority prefers to keep their money in their house rather than deposit it in banks.

In this regard according to Niyozov (2011), the financial crisis is no strange occurrence in Tajikistan. The first major financial crisis in Tajikistan occurred after the collapse of the former Soviet Union. The collapse in the financial institution sparked high interest rates and the rate of inflation reached the highest level annually, which resulted in exorbitant prices of commodities. Moreover, the gravity and consequences of that crisis weighed heavily on the country's economy to the extent that it warranted a change of the national currency twice. Tajikistan was the last country among former Soviet Union countries to change its currency, and other member countries were using their old Russian currency (Rubles) to buy commodities from Tajikistan. This caused the price of commodities to rocket upwards due to the high demand of commodities and excess currency (Ruble) in Tajikistan, which resulted in a shrinking economy.

To date, many solutions have been developed and applied to mitigate the effects of economic turmoil but without success. As a result, Tajikistan continues to face many economic problems. In 2011, the International Monetary Fund (IMF) asserted that Tajikistan is one of the poorest countries in Central Asia, with the lowest per Capital Gross Domestic Product (GDP) among the 15 former Soviet Republics. This is due to the lack of employment opportunities in Tajikistan and that nearly half of the workforce works overseas.

The Adoption of Islamic banking in Muslim and non-Muslim Countries

An Islamic Banking, which is religiously based, is a financial institution that operates with the objective to implement and materialize the economic and financial principles of Islam in the banking arena. If we look for definition of Islamic bank is an entity as owned by its shareholders, established to conduct banking and investment activities in accordance with Shari'ah law (Kalaithasan & Mohamed, 2007).

Islamic banking area has been studied mostly by Muslim scholars and to some extant among non-Muslim as well. According to Erol and El-Bdour (1989), Kaynak and El-bdour (1990)

---

[17] www.ozodi.org retrieved on 6/7/2013

are among the earliest known researchers who identified three important keys selection criteria for Islamic banks: fast and efficient services, reputation and confidentiality, but religious motivation was not among primary criterion (Zarehan et al 2012).

Nevertheless, Metawa andAlmossawi (1998), Naser, Jamal and Alkhatib (1999) found obedience to Islamic tenets the primary criterion for selecting Islamic banks in Bahrain and Jordan. Likewise, Kader (1995), Othman and Owen (2002) and Wakhid and Efrita (2007) share the same findings in their studies in Malaysia, Kuwait and Indonesia respectively. Furthermore, Dusuki (2007) explained that Islamic bankers cannot longer depend on promoting the Islamic factor, but also service quality as well. The important factors which they found from the analysing 750 respondents are friendliness and customer services quality. Similarly, the study has been done by Muslim and Zaidi (2008), the Malaysian Muslims' awareness of Islamic banking products and services was high compared to non-Muslim customers. The relationship between service quality and customer satisfaction was significant. However, the authors have not addressed the possibility for the Islamic Banking system to be an alternative banking system in Malaysia. But there is no any study has been done before to study an awareness and adoption of an Islamic bank in Tajikistan.

Another study conducted by Zairani, Rohaya and Hafizi (2008), in Malaysia, measured the perceptions of employees in both Islamic and conventional banks about Islamic products and services, the training and experience gained in Islamic banking and the potential of Islamic banking in Malaysia. The study focused on the Northern part of Malaysia wherein questionnaires on Islamic banking were distributed to bankers. The results revealed that bankers in Islamic banks had positive perceptions of Islamic banking. Interestingly, few bankers possessed a relevant academic background or relevant experience in Islamic banking before entering this field. One of the issues identified by this study is that the bankers claimed that they had very limited knowledge in IB prior to working with the banks.

Therefore, the regulatory bodies of the banking and financial industry should provide skilled employee training and provide greater opportunities for those with knowledge of Shari'ah and conventional banking. Greater public adoption of Islamic banking can be facilitated through the inclusion of factors such as greater religiosity, improved product quality, and quality management among others.

Much studies have been conducted on the adoption of Islamic banking and finance in various countries. Such studies are instructive as they often offer rich field data concerning how Islamic banking has successfully been adopted by the public and obstacles they have had and continue to face. One example is the research by Thambiah, Eze, Tan, Nathan and Kim (2010),

212

who established a comprehensive conceptual framework for the adoption of Islamic retail banking services in Malaysia. In this study, the Roger's innovation diffusion model was used. Therefore, this chapter offers a theoretical discussion on the historical growth of Islamic banking through its literature review of conventional and Islamic banking in Tajikistan, together with its application of the TID Model.

The Role of Islamic Banking in Economic Development

According to Ahmad (2004), Islamic banking is globally recognized as an emerging alternative to conventional banking and has grown rapidly over the last decade not only in Muslim countries, but in non-Muslim countries as well. Islamic banks have achieved high growth rates in both size and number and operate in more than 75 countries worldwide through 300 institutions. Many bankers forecast that Islamic banking could have control over 50% of savings in Islamic countries within the next decade.

In this regard, according to Iqbal (1997), the Islamic financial system can contribute to the economic development of Islamic countries and can been enhanced due to the mobilization of savings that are rapidly moving from interest-based banks and the development of the capital markets. Greater motivation for using Islamic banks is that its shows that the profitability of Islamic banks can reach rates higher than the fixed rate of interest offered by conventional banks.

Literature on the Islamic banking system has amply demonstrated that the interest-based system has weakened the entire economic system and is a source of great instability. In contrast, the general consensus among Muslims and certain others is that the interest-free banking system tends to enhance stability and it is in fact interest-based debt financing that significantly contributes to economic instability.

The focus of Islamic finance is to allocate a closer link between real economic activities that creates value, job opportunity and economic stability. According to Iqbal (1997), the main difference between Islamic and conventional financial system is expecting to be stable due to the elimination of debt financing and enhanced allocation efficiency and refraining from interest-based activities. In this regard, the chairmen of public relation of Agroinvestbank based in Tajikistan, Boboev (2013), mentioned that the main differences between Islamic and conventional banks is dealing with interest-based transactions, which is prohibited by Islamic law.

Accordingly, Islamic banks do not offer loans to activities that destabilise the economy. Moreover, the Islamic banking system seeks to provide greater economic stability, job creation, poverty reduction and enhancement of the standard of living in the society. Lastly, the Islamic banking system is not solely profit based, but economically seeks the well-being of the society.

213

Such are important factors for the popular adoption of the Islamic banking system by many developing nations.

Therefore, according to Rahimzoda (2013), Tajikistan authority is working on adding Islamic banking laws in the country in order to establish Islamic bank here. This is because of the majority Muslim in the country and that majority is not dealing with current interest-based banking practice which is not allowed in Islamic law. Moreover, the author mentioned that Tajikistan has to adopt Islamic banking sooner or later, and that the positive impact on the Tajikistan economy will be seen, as soon as it is established.

Framework for the Adoption of Islamic Banking
Product Knowledge

According to Noresma (2004), product knowledge is defined as the consumer's knowledge of the Islamic banking products offered by Islamic and conventional banks that operate through the Islamic windows. Examples of these products are *Musharakah*, *Murabahah*, *Mudharabah*, *Ijarah*, *etc*. The study has been done by Ghawashhi at ell (2010) in Malaysia that, willingness of measured organizations for the customer relation management (CRM) adoption is not high; however, telecommunication and financial services in Malaysia are not in the beginning stage in terms of awareness about CRM. Among the three factors examined, technology characteristics did not appear to have any effect on the adoption of CRM for respondents in this study because Malaysian organizations had a relatively good knowledge about CRM technology and its features. So, the author found out that there is no significant relation between product knowledge and adoption of CRM in Malaysia.

However, as a study has been done by Fu at ell (2013), using the theory of reasoned action and the elaboration likelihood model, the study examined the effects of perceived product innovativeness and product knowledge on consumers' intention to purchase and willingness to pay for a consumer technology product., the relationship between subjective norm and purchase intention weakens for consumers who have more product knowledge.

Social Norm (SN)

Social norm or normative pressure, as mentioned by Nysveen *et al.* (2005), refers to the person's perception that most people who are important to him/her should or should not perform the behaviour in question. As the purpose of his study was to investigate the determinants that influence internet-banking acceptance among the customers of Islamic banks, Amin (2007) found that social norm is a significant determinant for acceptance of internet-banking among the bank's customers.

The result of this study is similar to that of Venkatesh and Morris (2000). Venkatesh and Morris (2000) found stronger influence of social norm on behavioural intention. The work of Venkatesh and Morris (2000) was conducted in the context of the use of technology in the workplace. In Malaysia, the study by Ramayah *et al.* (2002a) found that the greater the social norm pressure the higher the intention to use internet-banking. It was found to be the most significant factor that influences intention to use internet-banking. Therefore, social norm basically offers an improvement beyond the general constructs offered by notably perceived usefulness and perceived ease of use. In light of the above, social norm is an important factor that can explain the intention to adopt Islamic banking among a majority Muslim society.

Relative Advantage

According to Rogers (2003), relative advantage requires the adopter to analyse the costs and benefits of using an innovation, which can be expressed economically, socially, or in other ways.

According to Ayinde and Echchabi (2012), in terms of relative advantage the customers do perceive the relative advantage of the Islamic bank compared to the conventional bank. This relative advantage is in terms of knowledge, competence, personnel friendliness, religious customer prospects, products, easy access, and social prestige.

Trust in the Islamic Banking System

Several studies have examined the role of trust in the adoption of innovation and new systems such as Asael and Dennis (2006), and Suh and Han (2002). Many researches argued that the issue of trust is more important in internet-banking because transactions of this nature contain sensitive information and parties involved in the financial transaction are concerned about access to critical files and information transferred via the Internet

According to Al-Majali (2011), the relationship between perceived trust and IBS has established mixed findings. Several past studies such as Liao & Cheung, (2002); Sohail & Shanmugham, (2003); Eriksson, Kerem & Nilsson, (2005); Yu & Lo, (2006); Guerrero, Egea & Gonzalez, (2007), found that the relationship between perceived trust and IBS was significant. On the other hand, Duda, Santhapparaj, Asirvathem and Raman (2007) found that the perceived trust positively affects IBSA but not significantly.

Trust is known as a widely accepted factor in regards with adoption researches and previous scholars indicated that trust is one of the most significant predictors of adoption

(Gholami et al., 2010, Gefen, 2000, George, 2002, Suh and Han, 2003, Liu and Wu, 2007). The current study would intend to investigate trust impact on adaptation of an Islamic bank through other variables have mentioned here.

Awareness

The investigation and understanding of awareness are always significant to guarantee that the financial organization or banking sector remains successful and competitive. There are many different definitions for understanding the idea of awareness. As mentioned by Kotler et al. (2004), the concept of awareness attempts to discover how the customers establish the knowledge of the products or services and to what extent they are missing information about it. According to Walter (1998), the term awareness refers to how far the individual is able to associate the product or brand as an option to satisfying a problem but has little or no information about it. As argued by Sharon (1999), the organizations need to raise the awareness of banking customers as the industry is offering a wide range of customer products beside various alternatives that are made available by banking institutions in securing their competitiveness.

A much easier way to understand awareness is simply to know about the products offered (Aminudin, 1999). As suggested by Shimp (1997), the process of awareness involves informing consumers via advertising, promotion and other marketing communication methods with the company brand, product and services, and informing people about its special features and benefits and showing how it is different in function to competitive brands. In addition, a consumer who receives information from the mass media or through word of mouth also contributes to consumer awareness (Asseal, 1995). Furthermore, the use of mobile devices has been found to be among the more effective and promising means of marketing that resulted in greater public awareness (Pousttchi, 2006; Nysveen et al., 2005; Norris, 2007).

Adoption of the Islamic Banking System

According to Jahayah (2004), intentions is viewed as a function of six factors, which are the person's attitude toward the overall awareness about Islamic banking operations, the person's social norm, the efficient product knowledge, relative advantage and perceived ease of use and accessibility of Islamic Banking service with respect to the behaviour and the adoption of Islamic banking services. In this study, intention is defined as whether Muslim consumers in Tajikistan have the intention of engaging in Islamic banking facilities or otherwise, depending on their attitude and their subjective norms toward Islamic banking facilities. The respondent might have

216

the intention to use Islamic banking facilities but it does not necessarily mean that he or she will actually utilise it.

In the study

The chapter seeks to identify the challenges of the conventional financial banking system in Tajikistan through which to justify the need of the alternative Islamic financial and banking system. The chapter adopts the TID developed by Rogers (2003) to empirically test the adoption and acceptability of the Tajik public towards Islamic Banking and Finance.

The chapter process begins with a comprehensive review of the relevant literature related to the Islamic banking and finance model. This is followed by an introduction to the Islamic banking and finance system and its development. Lastly, an empirical investigation is conducted to test the intention of the Tajik public regarding their perception of the acceptability and adoption of the Islamic banking system. 200 questionnaires were distributed of which 100 were usable. The questionnaires consisted of 6 variables, namely product knowledge (PK), trust (TR), relative advantage (RA), social norm (SN) and awareness (AW). These variables seek to ascertain the readiness to adopt Islamic banking and its products.

However, the respondents are bankers, managers, customers, lecturers and Islamic scholars. According to Polit and Hunger (1999), the population is an aggregate or totality of all the objectives, subjects or members that conform to a set of specifications. The population of the study consists of all people that engage with the banking sector or private business and academicians and Shari'ah scholars in Tajikistan. The population will be selected from the capital city of Tajikistan, Dushanbe due to time constraint and limited resource.

Instruments

This study employed two instruments in generating the survey data from the respondents. The questionnaire covered the quantitative aspects of the study while the interview covered the quantitative aspects of the question.

The writer developed the items in the questionnaire by adopting measures that had been validated by previous research conducted by Ayinde and Echchabi (2012), Aliyu (2011) Ajzen and Fishbein (1980), Thambiah, et al (2010), Ramayah & Dzuljastri (2008), with the items altered to fit the acceptance and intention to use IBS instruments.

The questionnaire was divided into three main sections. Section 1 comprised of demographic information, section 2 were direct measures while section 3 consisted of questions

217

pertaining to Islamic banking. The endogenous variables are attitude, subjective norm, normative belief and behavioural belief while the exogenous variable was behavioural intention.

Attitude was operationalised as an overall expression of positive or negative thoughts (Vogt et al., 2005) toward the intention to use the Islamic banking system. Respondents were asked to rank each item on a 7-point response scale where '1' stands for strongly disagree, '4' undecided, and '7' strongly agree. Intention was operationalised as the extent of approval an individual held for the implementation of Islamic banking system instruments. Behavioural belief was operationalised based on a scale of 7 points response whereby '1' means unlikely probability of using the instruments, '2' not at all likely, '3' somewhat likely, '4' undecided, '5' somewhat likely, '6' likely, '7' strongly likely (Vogt et al., 2005).

Data Analysis

Descriptive analysis, factor analysis, and multiple linear regressions are used in the present chapter the applied software for the current analysis is SPSS version 17.0. To estimate the respondent's feedback, descriptive analysis will be produced for the initial analysis by employing mean, frequency and standard deviation of the collected data. Additionally, in order to gauge the reliability as well as validity of the constructs, factor analysis would be implemented. Multiple linear regressions are used to determine the potential relationship between independent variables of this study (product knowledge, trust relative advantage awareness, and social norm) and the dependent variable of the study (adoption and usage intention of the Islamic banking system). Accordingly, these numerous tests would be able to classify possible factors that have a significant impact on the adoption of Islamic banking as a new innovation.

Data analysis consists of two parts. First is the descriptive analysis, which is based on demographic information of the respondents, and the second measures the perception and adoption of the Islamic banking system based on reliability analysis, factor analysis, Pearson correlation and multiple regression analysis.

Descriptive Analysis

In the descriptive analysis, male respondents comprised 72.3% while female respondents were 27.7%. The age groups were below 20 years (10.9%), 21-30 years (64.4%), 31-40 years (19.8%), 41-50 years (2.0%) and above 51 years (3%). In this survey, 18.8% of the respondents hold certificate/diploma, 11.9% professional, 24.8% bachelor, 37.6% general master and 6.9% PhD degree holders.

Table 1 shows that 40.6% of the respondents were married whereas, 59.4% were single. As regards to the type of employment, 15.8% respondents were from the public sector, 19.8% were from the private sector, 14.9% self-employed and 49.5% were students. In the survey questionnaire, respondents were asked 'what type of baking service currently they are using?' 38.6% respondents replied that they are using public bank services, whereas 52.5% of the respondents are using private banking services. The respondents were also asked about their banking account and based on their response it was observed that 23.8% respondents are using current account, whereas 56.4% and 17.8% respondents are using saving accounts and transfer accounts respectively.

Table 1: Demographic Profile of the Respondents

Description	Percentage
Gender	
Male	72.3
Female	27.7
Age Group	
Below 20 years	10.9
20-30 years	64.4
31-40 years	19.8
41-51 years	2.0
Above 50 years	3.0
Higher Education	
Certificate/Diploma	18.8
Professional	11.9
Bachelor	24.8
Master	37.6
PhD	6.9
Marital Status	
Married	40.6
Single	59.4
Type of Employment	
Public Sector	15.8
Private Sector	19.8
Self Employed	14.9

Students	49.5
Banking Service	
Public bank	38.6
Private bank	52.5
None	6.9
Others	2.0
Banking Account	
Current Account	23.8
Saving Account	56.4
Transferring Account	17.8
Others	2.0

Reliability Analysis

The instruments of this study were tested for reliability by using Cronbach's alpha. According to Hair et al. (2010), Cronbach's alpha refers to the consistency and reliability of the research instruments. A higher Cronbach's alpha value means greater reliability and consistency of research instruments (research items). In this study, all dimensions ranged from 0.793 to 0.909 (see Table 2), exceeding the minimum requirement of 0.70 Cronbach's alpha. Therefore, all the instruments' measures are highly reliable.

Table 2: Reliability analysis

Dimension	No. of item	Cronbach's Alpha
Product Knowledge	04	0.805
Trust	06	0.909
Relative Advantage	05	0.841
Social Norm	05	0.793
Awareness	06	0.885
Adoption	03	0.827

Factor Analysis

The value of factor loading indicates the strength of the relationship between the items and the factor. The minimum requirements for the value of factor loading is 0.3; and according to Sharma (1996), factor loading with a value above 0.4 can be regarded as important, while those above

220

0.5 are considered significant (Sharma, 1996). In this study, varimax, Kaiser-Meyer-Olkin (KMO), and total variance explained used for factor analysis. Based on the varimax rotation, 28 items (statements) constructed into six factors with 70.54% of the total variance explained (see Table 3).

Table 3: Factor analysis of perception and adoption of the Islamic banking system

Variables	Factor loading
Product Knowledge (PK)	
PK1	0.836
PK2	0.735
PK3	0.687
PK4	0.738
Trust (TR)	
TR1	0.750
TR2	0.791
TR3	0.781
TR4	0.810
TR5	0.806
TR6	0.771
Relative Advantage (RA)	
RA1	0.743
RA2	0.708
RA3	0.618
RA4	0.690
RA5	0.634
Social Norm (SN)	
SN1	0.774
SN2	0.773
SN3	0.611
SN4	0.740
Awareness (AW)	
AW1	0.744
AW2	0.665
AW3	0.864
AW4	0.806

AW5	0.655
AW6	0.691
Adoption (AD)	
AD1	0.726
AD2	0.814
AD3	0.648
KMO	*0.812*
Total Variance Explained	*70.54%*

The results of the factor analysis show that the minimum factor loading is 0.61, which is higher than that required. Moreover, KMO value 0.812 indicates all factor loadings results are acceptable for further analysis. The result of factor loadings shows the Eigen values of six factors individually. The highest Eigen value is 9.29, which has 33.18 percent of variance and the lowest Eigen value is 1.27, which has 4.53 percent of the total variance explained.

Pearson Correlation Analysis

The Pearson correlations were estimated to identify the correlations between the two variables. According to Cohen (1988), there are three strengths of coefficient correlation, which are small or weak, medium, and large or strong. Cohen (1988) also mentioned that if the Pearson correlation value (r) ranges from 0.10 to 0.29 or -0.10 to -0.29 then it is considered a small or weak relation, from 0.30 to 0.49 or -0.29 to -0.49 is considered a medium relation and from 0.50 to 1.0 or -0.50 to -1.0 is considered a large or strong relation. However, Field (2005) suggested that the correlation coefficient value should not be above 0.8 to avoid multi collinearity. Based on the Pearson correlation test, the highest correlation coefficient value is 0.589, which is less than 0.8. Thus, there is no multi co linearity problem in this research (see Table 4).

Table 4: Pearson Coefficient Correlation Analysis

	Product Knowledge	Trust	Relative Advantage	Social Norm	Awareness	Adoption
Product Knowledge	1					
Trust	0.351**	1				
Relative Advantage	0.289**	0.533**	1			
Social Norm	0.405**	0.471**	0.419**	1		
Awareness	0.225*	0.283**	0.508**	0.249*	1	
Adoption	0.225*	0.335**	0.570**	0.350**	0.589**	1

**. Correlation is significant at the 0.01 level (2-tailed).

*. Correlation is significant at the 0.05 level (2-tailed).

Regression Analysis

Regression analysis was also carried out between independent variables (product knowledge, trust, relative advantage, social norm and awareness) and adoption as the dependent variable. The R square value as shown in Table 5 was found to be 0.452, which indicates that all the independent variables account for 45.20 percent of the variation in the dependent variable adoption of Islamic banking system.

Table 5: Model Summary of Multiple Regression Analysis

Model	R	R Square	Adjusted R Square	Std. Error of the Estimate
1	.672ᵃ	.452	.422	.73485

a. Predictors: (Constant), Awareness, Product Knowledge, Trust, Social Norm, Relative Advantage

b. Dependent Variable: adoption

Table 6 shows the value of the Standardized Coefficient Beta which contributes to measure each variable of the model. A large value indicates that a unit change in the predictor variable has a large effect on the criterion variable. The t value and p value give a rough indication of the impact of each predictor variable. T-value and p-value suggest that a predictor variable is having a large impact on the criterion. The finding shows that the largest coefficient beta is 0.403, which is for awareness. This means that this variable makes a significant or unique contribution to explaining the dependent variable adoption of Islamic banking system. The coefficient beta for product knowledge = -0.007, trust = 0.002, relative advantage =0.306, and social norm = 0.124. The coefficient betas for product knowledge and trust have the lowest value in the model which indicates the least contribution to the dependent variable.

The p-value in the below Table indicates whether this variable is making a statistically significant unique contribution into the equation. If the p-value is less than 0.05, then the independent variable has significant or positive relationship with the dependent variable. If it is greater than 0.05, then the relationship with the dependent variable is not statistically significant.

Table 6: Coefficients of adoption of the Islamic banking system

Model	Unstandardized Coefficients		Standardized Coefficients	t-value	Sig.
	B	Std. Error	Beta		
(Constant)	1.586	0.543		2.920	0.004
Product Knowledge	-0.006	0.078	-0.007	-0.082	0.935
Trust	0.002	0.075	0.002	0.025	0.980
Relative Advantage	0.297	0.100	0.306	2.967	0.004
Social Norm	0.117	0.089	0.124	1.324	0.189
Awareness	0.375	0.084	0.403	4.481	0.000

Table 6 also shows that two independent variable positive and significantly influence to the adoption Islamic banking system in Tajikistan, and these are relative advantage (p = 0.004) and awareness (p = 0.000). On the other hand, three other independent variables do not have significant influence on the adoption of the Islamic banking system in Tajikistan and these are product knowledge (p = 0.935), trust (p = 0.980), and social norm (p = 0.189).

A similar study conducted by Ashgar (2012), Ayinde and Echchabi (2012), Malek (2011), Thambiah et al (2010), Chikezie et al (2014), Chikezie et al (2014), Jamshidi et at (2012) there is significant relation between awareness and relative advantage with adaptation. On the other hand, similarly, study has been done by Chavoshi, Sim, and Hee (2010), and found there is no significant relation between product knowledge and adoption.

Discussion and conclusion

225

The objective of this chapter is to investigate the challenges of conventional banking practice and adoption of the Islamic banking system in Tajikistan. The findings show that relative advantage and awareness have a significant impact on the adoption of Islamic banking system in Tajikistan.

However, the other three independent variables such as product knowledge, trust and social norm have an insignificant relationship with the adoption of Islamic banking in Tajikistan. In this context, there are direct and indirect reasons for this insignificant relationship with the adoption of Islamic banking in the country. Firstly, no Islamic banking system has been established in Tajikistan. As such, there is little knowledge and social norm regarding Islamic banking. In terms of education, Islamic banking is not taught in universities. The situation is confounded by the fact that little information on Islamic banking is available in the local language.

This chapter revealed that there is a general lack of product knowledge, social norm and trust in the adoption of Islamic banking in Tajikistan. There are a number of major implications for the authorities with regard to the adoption of Islamic banking in order to increase the level of product knowledge, social norm and trust. Informative and effective advertising campaigns about the Islamic banking system need to be designed and promoted in order to reach out to the entire society in Tajikistan. Existing banks needs to promote Islamic banking products and activities. Advertisements through media and internet would be more effective if they are translated into Tajik or Russian languages.

In this context, it is essential for the bank staff themselves to be familiar with their product knowledge about IB schemes. Most importantly, if the Tajikistan government and the relevant authorities aim to introduce Islamic banking, the overall banking culture in Tajikistan has to be changed to the "culture of Islamic banking". The conventional banking system has been operating for decades and is deeply rooted in the minds of the Tajik public. There is therefore a need to change public perception of banking and emphasize the stability and ethicality of Islamic banking to mitigate the years of mistrust and suspicion of conventional banking. To this end, it is extremely important to instil the "culture of Islamic banking" among the Tajik public so that everyone becomes familiar with Islamic banking, irrespective of the geographical boundaries, religious differences, and racial diversity. For this to happen, the various authorities that include the government, the Central Bank of Tajikistan (National Bank of Tajikistan) and the entire banking system, together with the various Islamic bodies and educational organizations have to work hand in-hand.

While this chapter has exposed some interesting results about the awareness, product knowledge, trust and social norm in relation to the adoption of IB, readers should be cautious of some of its limitations. Firstly, the scope of the study covers only the capital city Dushanbe, and generalizing the findings should be within the capital city, and not all parts of Tajikistan. Future studies should attempt to cover the majority cities of Tajikistan. Secondly, this chapter did not make a comparative analysis of the various religions and races of Tajikistan. Although Islam is the main religion of this nation, there are minority religious communities. Thus, it is recommended for future studies to perform a comparative analysis between the Muslim and non-Muslim banking customers, and people of different ethnic groups in Tajikistan, so that more precise results on the adoption and acceptability of Islamic banking in Tajikistan can be determined.

References

Meera, A. (2008), "An Alternative Islamic Global Monetary Order", *The Edge newspaper*, (November 10).

Ayinde, L.O and Echchabi, A. (2012), "Perception and Adoption of Islamic Insurance in Malaysia: An Empirical Study", *World Applied Sciences Journal*, Vol. 20 No. 3, pp. 407-415.

Boboev interviewed by Ozodi on 23/05/2013 retrieved on 6/06/2013 from www.ozodi.org.

Darbone, L. Reva, A. and Zaidi, S. (2010), *Tajikistan Key Priorities for Climate Change Adaptation*, The World Bank Europe and Central Asia Region Poverty Reduction and Economic Management Unit, retrieved from http://econ.worldbank.org.

Cohen, J. (1988), *Statistical power analysis for the behavioral sciences, Second Edition*, Erlbaum, Hillsdale.

Dusuki, A. (2007), "Why do Malaysian Customers Patronize Islamic Banks?" *International Journal of Bank Marketing*, Vol. 25 No. 3, pp. 142-160.

Ergashieva, Z. (2008), *Tajikistan's banking system does not satisfy the needs of country's economy*, Asia-Plus, Dushanbe.

Erol, C. and El-Bdour R. (1989)," Attitude, Behavior and Patronage Factors of Bank Customers Towards Islamic Banks", *International Journal of Bank Marketing*, Vol. 7 No. 6, pp. 31-37.

Erol, C., Kaynak, E. and El-Bdour, R. (1990), "Conventional and Islamic Bank: Patronage Behaviour of Jordanian Customers", *International Journal of Bank Marketing*, Vol. 8 No. 5, pp.25-35.

Field, A. (2005), *Discovering statistics using SPSS, Second edition*, Sage, London.

Gefen, D. (2000), "E-commerce: the role of familiarity and trust", *Omega*, Vol. 28, pp. 725-737.

George, J. F. (2002), "Influences on the intent to make internet purchases", *Internet Research*, Vol. 12, pp. 165-180.

Chavoshi, M., Sim, A.T.H. and Hee, J.M. (2010), "A CRM Adoption Model for Malaysian Telecommunication and Finance Companies", *Journal of Information Systems Research and Innovation*, Vol. xx, pp. 119-125.

Curtis, G.E. (1996), *Kazakstan, Kyrgyzstan, Tajikistan Turkmenistan and Uzbekistan country studies*, Federal Research Division Library of Congress. Available at: www.archive.org/stream/kazakstankyrgyzs00curt_0/kazakstankyrgyzs00curt_0_djvu.txt

Hair, J.F., Black, W.C., Babin, B.J. and Anderson, R.E. (2010), *Multivariate data analysis: A global perspective, 7th edition*, Pearson Prentice Hall, New Jersey.

Noresma, J. (2004), *Factors that Influence Muslim Consumers Preference towards Islamic Banking Products or Facilities: Theory of reasoned action*, Unpublished Thesis, University Sains Malaysia.

Nichol, J. (2014), Central Asia: Regional Developments and Implications for U.S. Interests, Congressional Research Service, U.S.

Kalaithasan, A. and Mohamed, A. (2007), *Prospects for Islamic Banking after the World Economic Crisis*, The National University of Malaysia, Malaysia.

Akramov, K. (2012), "Economic Development, External Shocks, and Food Security in Tajikistan", *IFPRI Discussion Paper 01163*, International Food Policy Research Institute, New Delhi. Available at: http://www.ifpri.org/sites/default/files/publications/ifpridp01163.pdf at 07/10/2012.

Kaynak, E., Kucukemiroglu, O. and Odabasi, Y. (1991), "Commercial Bank Selection in Turkey", *International Journal of Bank Marketing*, Vol. 9 No. 4, pp. 30-39.

Liu, T.C. and Wu, L.W. (2007), "Customer retention and cross-buying in the banking industry: an integration of service attributes satisfaction and trust", *Journal of Financial Services Marketing*, Vol. 12, pp. 132-145.

Falkowski, M. (2009), *Tajikistan faces crisis of statehood,* Center for Eastern Studies, Warsaw, retrieved from http://www.osw.waw.pl.

Makhmedov, Y., Mamurjon, M. and Sukhrob, T. (2012), *Water and energy disputes between Tajikistan and Uzbekistan, and their negative influence on regional co-operation*, Norwegian Institute of International Affairs (NUPI), Norway.

AL-Majali, M. and Kmerah, N. (2011), "Modeling the antecedents of internet banking service adoption (IBSA) in Jordan: A Structural Equation Modeling (SEM) approach", *Journal of Internet Banking and Commerce,* Vol. 16 No. 1, pp. 1-15.

Metawa, S.A. and Almossawi, M. (1998), "Banking behavior of Islamic bank customers: perspectives and implications", *International Journal of Bank Marketing*, Vol. 16 No. 7, pp. 299-313.

Naser, K., Jamal, A. and Al-Khatib, K. (1999), "Islamic banking: a study of customer satisfaction and preferences in Jordan", *International Journal of Bank Marketing*, Vol. 17 No. 3, pp. 135-150.

Niyozov, M.A. (2011), *Money Transaction in Banking System in Tajikistan*, AR-Graft publisher, Tajikistan.

Oke, B.A. (1989), "An Evaluation of the Nigeria Financial System: Problems, Challenges and Prospects", *CBN Economic and Financial Review* Vol. 27 No. 2, pp. xx-xx.

Othman, A. and Owen, L. (2002), "The Multi Dimensionality of Carter Model to Measure Customer Service Quality (SQ) in Islamic Banking Industry: A Study in Kuwait Finance House", *International Journal of Islamic Financial Services*, Vol. 3 No. 4, pp. 124-143.

Honohan, P. (1996), "Diagnosing Banking System Failures in Developing Countries", retrieved from: www.*eircom.net/~phonohan/diagnosing.pdf*.

Rahimzoda, S. (2013), "Without Interest", *The annual meeting of IDB country members*, Tajikistan, Available at: www.ozodi.org/content/article/24995355.html.

Rashidov, A. (2012), "Poor people is Avoiding to deal with banks in Tajikistan", interviewed by Ozodi on 24/4/2012, Available at: www.ozodi.org/content/article/24542251.html.

Wilson, R. (2010), "Why Islamic Banking Is Successful? Islamic Banks Are Unscathed Despite of Financial Crisis?" Available at: www.informatik.uni-frankfurt.de/~osman/islamic-banking.pdf.

Rogers, E.M. (2003), *Diffusion of Innovations, 5th Edition*, The Free Press, NY.

Sallmpur, M. (2012), "Poor people is Avoiding to deal with banks in Tajikistan", interviewed by Ozodi on 24/4/2012, Available at: www.ozodi.org/content/article/24542251.html

Sharma, S. (1996), *Applied Multivariate Techniques*, John Wiley & Sons, New York.

Sohail, S. and Shanmugham, B. (2003), "E-banking and customer preferences in Malaysia: An empirical investigation", *Information Sciences*, Vol. 150, pp. 207-217.

Thambiah, S., Eze, U.C., Tan, K.S., Nathan, R.J. and Lai, K.P. (2010), "Conceptual Framework for the Adoption of Islamic Retail Banking Services in Malaysia", *Journal of Electronic Banking Systems,* Vol. 2010, pp. 1-10.

Vogt, C., Winter, G. and Fried, J. (2004), "Predicting Homeowners' Approval of Fuel Management at the Widland-Urban Interface Using the Theory of Reasoned Action", *Society and Natural Resources*, Vol. 18, pp. 337-354.

Wakhid, S.C. and Efrita, S. (2007), *Adopting Islamic Banks' CARTER Model*, College Science, India, Retrieved from: www.collegescienceinindia.com/oct2008.

Zairani, Z., Rohaya, S. and Hafizi, M.A. (2008), "A Comparative Analysis of Bankers' Perceptions on Islamic Banking", *International Journal of Business and Management,* Vol. 3 No. 4, pp. 157-168.

Zarehan, S. and Abdul-Kadir, H. (2012), "Attitude and Patronage Factors of Bank Customers in Malaysia: Muslim and non-Muslim Views", *Journal of Islamic Economics, Banking and Finance*, Vol. 8 No. 4, pp. 87-100.

Chapter 11

Islamic Insurance in the European Countries: Insights from French Muslims' Perspective

Abdelghani Echchabi
Effat University

Fatiha Echchabi
Independent Researcher

Introduction

On March 2012, *La Compagnie française de conseil et d'investissement (CFCI & associés)* announced its decision to launch the first Islamic life insurance contract in the French market[18]. This initiative is expected to provide French Muslims with an alternative insurance service that is compatible with their religious beliefs. Nevertheless, due to the current situation in France, it is questionable whether French Muslims' behavioural decisions would have remained unaffected. Hence the current study attempts to examine the willingness of the French Muslims in adopting Islamic insurance services, as well as the factors that may influence their decisions.

In this regard, several studies have examined the customers' perception and willingness to buy Islamic insurance (*takaful* thereafter) policies in different contexts. For instance, Bashir, Mail and Abd'Ali (2011) have studied customers' perceptions on *takaful* in Brunei Darussalam. Their results revealed that the most challenging problem facing *takaful* policyholders is the claiming process [4].

Similarly, Aziz, Mat and Zin (2011) examined the perception of the government toward Islamic Motor insurance in Malaysia. Their results showed that the government's servants have a positive perception towards Islamic motor insurance [3].

Likewise, Hamid (2011) investigated service quality perception in *takaful* industry in Malaysia using SERVQUAL model. The findings indicated that there is deficiency in service delivery and this is mainly based on the gaps in the five dimensions of the SERVQUAL model [13].

As it shown above, the studies on *takaful* services perception are still scarce, and also most of them are recent. This indicates that this is a green field that requires further study in order to

---

[18] http://www.lepoint.fr/economie/apres-la-viande-l-assurance-vie-halal-07-03-2012-1438799_28.php retrieved on March 15th, 2012.

enrich this area, and to establish a comprehensive framework to be used in various contexts. Accordingly, the current chapter suggests the Theory of Planned Behaviour (TPB) as a proposed framework that covers all the aspects of the human behaviour i.e. the personal attitude, the social influence, as well as the perceived control over the behaviour.

TPB also called Social Cognition Model (SCM) was introduced in 1985 by Icek Ajzen. It is the extension of TRA with the addition of a third antecedent to behavioural intention i.e. perceived behavioural control (Masrom and Hussein, 2008) [22].

The theory divides the formation of the behaviour into three main sections, namely, external dimensions of the behaviour, internal dimensions of the behaviour, and the final actual part (Masrom and Hussein, 2008) [22]. As shown in Figure 2, volitional human behaviour is immediately predicted by intention to engage in that particular behaviour. Behavioural intention is predicted in turn by three main determinants, namely, attitude towards the behaviour, subjective norm and perceived behavioural control (PBC) (Caperchione, Duncan, Mummery, Steele and Schofield (2008) [6].

The extent to which individuals have a positive (negative) attitude towards a particular behaviour, perceive that significant others support (do not support) them to engage in that behaviour, and believe that they are able (unable) to perform the behaviour, serve as determinant of their willingness (non-willingness) to perform that behaviour (Lee, Cerreto and Lee, 2010) [19].

The attitude towards the behaviour is determined by the sum of accessible behavioural beliefs, which refer to the subjective probability that the behaviour will achieve expected outcomes positively or negatively. Similarly, subjective norm is determined by the sum of normative beliefs which reflect the perceived behavioural expectation or opinions of important referent individuals or groups. On the other hand, perceived behavioural control is determined by the sum of accessible control beliefs which refers to the perceived presence of requisite resources and opportunities to perform a given behaviour (Ajzen, 1991) [1].

For accurate application of TPB, three main requirements should be met. Firstly, intentions and perceptions of behavioural control should be assessed in relation to the particular behaviour in question, and the specified context must be the same as that in which the behaviour occurs. Secondly, intention and perceived behavioural control must remain stable in the interval their assessment and the observation of the behaviour, this is because intervening events may cause changes in intention or perceived behavioural control with the effect that the original measures of these variables no longer permit accurate prediction of behaviour. Thirdly, is the accuracy of the perceived behavioural control, since the theory suggests that PBC should improve, to the extent that it will reflect actual control (Ajzen, 1991) [1].

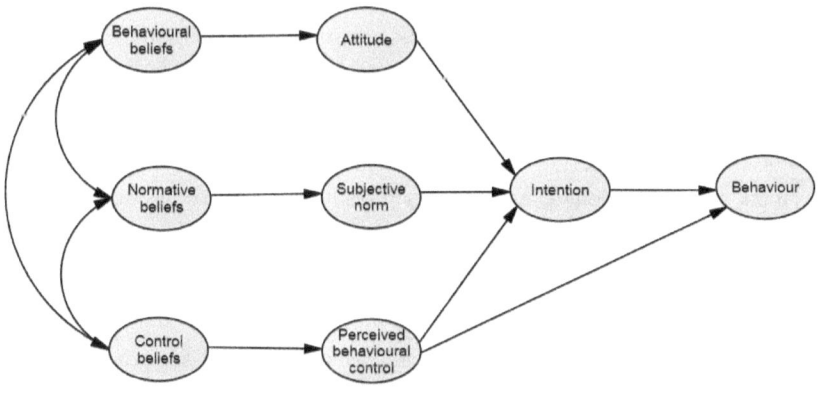

Fig.1: Theory of planned behaviour (TPB)

   PBC refers to the perceived ease or difficulty of performing the behaviour, and it is assumed to reflect past experience as well as anticipated impediments and obstacles (Ajzen, 1991) [1]. According to Ajzen (1991), TPB does not deal directly with the amount of control a person actually has in a given situation; instead, it considers the possible effects of perceived behavioural control on achievement of behavioural goals [1]. PBC has two main antecedents, namely, the control belief, which is the person's perception of his ability to behave, and perceived degree of facilitation, which includes the resources and opportunities the person possesses to execute a given behaviour. The more the person feels he has the ability to perform a behaviour and the more resources and opportunities the person has to execute the behaviour, the higher will be the perceived behavioural control for that specific behaviour (Masrom and Hussein, 2008) [22]. Thus, PBC can be written as follows:

$$PBC = \sum ob_{ij} \, pf_{ij} \quad (1)$$

Where PBC is perceived behavioural control, *cb* is the control belief, and *pf* is the perceived facilitation.

Finally, although there is no perfect relationship between behavioural intention and actual behaviour, intention can be used as a proximal measure of behaviour (Ajzen, 1991) [1]. This observation was one of the most important contributions of the TPB model in comparison with previous models of the attitude-behaviour relationship (Francis, Eccles, Johnston, Walker, Grimshaw, Foy, Kaner, Smith and Bonetti, 2004), and their role in predicting actual performance has been empirically validated [10]. Intentions capture the motivational factors that drive a person to perform a behaviour. In a sense, intention is a measure of effort an individual is ready to exert to accomplish a behaviour. Intentions can only affect the behaviour to the extent that the person's actual behavioural control allows them to (Kanat and Ozkan, 2009) [17].

Behavioural intention is thus influenced by three primary factors, namely, evaluation of the behaviour i.e. attitude toward the behaviour, perceived social pressure to perform or not to perform the behaviour i.e. normative support, and the perceived degree of personal prerogative regarding the behaviour i.e. perceived behavioural control (Dawkins and Frass, 2005) [8]. Thus, behavioural intention under TPB can be expressed as follows:

$$BI = (AB)\ w_1 + (SN)\ w_2 + (PBC)\ w_3\ (2)$$

Where *AB* is the attitude towards the behaviour, *SN* is the subjective norm and *PBC* is the perceived behavioural control. W_1, w_2 and w_3 refer to the weights of these respective variables.

Based on TPB, actual behaviour refers to an observable manifestation of a behaviour, which is performed or not performed with respect to a particular target, in a given situation, at a specific time (Fishbein and Ajzen, 1975) [9]. Actual behaviour is a joint function of intention and perceived behavioural control (Ajzen, 1991) [1], nevertheless, it is suggested that the most important antecedent of volitional behaviour is the intention (Lee, 2008) [20].

Since its development, TPB has been used to study the behavioural intention and actual behavioural with their antecedents in many fields. This includes the internet banking adoption (Shih and Fang, 2004; Yousafzai, Foxall, and Pallister, 2010) [26, 32], information technology usage (Lee, Cerreto and Lee, 2010; Al-harbi, 2010, Wu, Lin and Lin, 2011; Celuch, Goodwin and Taylor, 2007; Siragusa and Dixon, 2009; Ozer and Yilmaz, 2011) [19, 2, 31, 7, 28, 25], perception of government to citizen services (Kanat and Ozkan, 2009) [17], physical activities intention (Caperchione et. al, 2008) [6], union workers participation in employee involvement (Dawkins and Frass, 2005) [8], entrepreneurial intention (Gelderen, Brand, Praag, Bodewes, Poutsma and Gils, 2008) [11], environmental behaviour (Hill, 2008) [14], advertisement (Lee, 2008) [20], food consumption (Tarkiainen and Sundqvist, 2005) [29].

Empirically, the attitude towards behaviours was identified as having a significant positive influence on the behavioural intention. For instance, the findings of Ozer and Yilmaz (2011) revealed that among the three antecedents of behavioural intention, attitude has the highest significant influence on accountants' intention to adopt information technology [25]. In another context, Dawkins and Frass (2005) found that attitude has a high positive significant influence on the union workers' decision to participate in employees' involvement [8].

The above results were also similar to those of Lee (2008), Tarkiainen and Sundqvist (2005), Celuch, et al. (2007), Tohidina and Mosakhani (2010), Wu, Lin and Lin (2011), Lee, Cerreto and Lee (2010), Lu, Hou, Dzwo, Wu, Andrews, Weng, Lin and Lu (2010), Yousafzai et al. (2010), and Shih and Fang (2004) [20, 29, 7, 30, 31, 19, 21, 32, 26]. As far as attitude is concerned, none of the previous studies using TPB found that attitude has insignificant effect on behavioural intention. This suggests that attitude is a major construct in the TPB model.

On the other hand, subjective norm has also been empirically proven to be an important and significant factor in determining the behavioural intention. In this regard, Gelderen et al. (2008) found that subjective norm has a significant positive influence on business students' entrepreneurial intention [11]. Similar results were also obtained by Ozer and Yilmaz (2010), Lu et al. (2010), Lee et al. (2010), Wu et al. (2011), Tohidina and Mosakhani (2010), Dawkins and Frass (2005), Celuch, et al. (2007), Lee (2008), and Tarkiainen and Sundqvist (2005) [25, 21, 19, 31, 30, 8, 7, 20, 29]. Nevertheless, Shih and Fang (2004), Yousafzai et al. (2010), and Caperchione et al. (2008) found that subjective norm has no influence on the behavioural intention [26, 32, 6]. This could be due to the nature and culture of the studied groups in these three cases.

The third antecedent of behavioural intention i.e. perceived behavioural control was also found to be a significant predictor of behavioural intention in the previous studies. In this context, Lee (2008) found that perceived behavioural control has a positive significant influence on the intention to use online video advertising [20]. Similar results were also found by Dawkins and Frass (2005), Ozer and Yilmaz (2010), Yousafzai et al. (2010), Lu et al. (2010), Lee et al. (2010), Wu et al. (2011), Tohidina and Mosakhani (2010), and Lee (2008) [8, 25, 32, 21, 19, 31, 30, 20]. Nevertheless, Shih and Fang (2004) found that perceived behavioural control has insignificant influence on the behavioural intention [26].

With regard to the actual behaviour, Shih and Fang (2004) found that its main predictor in the behavioural intention [26]. The same results were obtained by Wu *et al.* (2011), Tohidina and Mosakhani (2010), and Lee (2008) [31, 30, 20]. Nevertheless, Yousafzai *et al.* (2010) found that both behavioural intention and perceived behaviour control predict actual usage, with intention having more influence on the actual behaviour [32].

Thus, based on the above model, the following hypotheses are posited:

H1: Attitude has a positive influence on the intention to adopt Islamic insurance.

H2: Subjective norm has a positive influence on attitude towards Islamic insurance.

H3: Subjective norm has a positive influence on the intention to adopt Islamic insurance.

H4: Perceived behavioural control has a positive influence on the intention to adopt Islamic insurance.

H5$_O$: French Muslims are willing to shift to Islamic insurance services.

In the Study

The study focuses on the French Muslim population. The target sample size was 100 respondents determined through the previous similar studies in this area (Musara and Fatoki, 2010; Ismail, Mat Desa, and Taupek, 2013; Siddiqi, 2011; Muhamat, Jaafar, and Ali Azizan, 2011, *etc.*) [24, 16, 27, 23]. Out of the distributed questionnaires only 67 were properly and completely filled up and returned. Thus, a response rate of 67 per cent was achieved.

The survey questionnaire was designed to collect information about the perception of the customers towards the attributes of the *takaful* as well as their intention to adopt it in their future transactions. For measuring this information, Likert type scaling was used (1 = Strongly Disagree and 7 = Strongly Agree). Fourteen items were listed in this section and most of them were derived from the previous studies conducted in other countries as highlighted above, as well as from current *takaful* literature with necessary adaptations made for the specific context of the study. The second section of the questionnaire explored information about respondents' profile, i.e. gender, age, marital status, employment status, etc. The questionnaire was made in English and was subsequently translated into French and distributed as such.

The data gathered were subsequently analysed using structural equation modelling and one sample t-test. The choice of this technique was inspired from Hair *et al.* (2010) as well as from similar studies conducted in this area. It is worth mentioning that the analysis was done through AMOS 18 and SPSS 18.

The demographic information indicates that 61.2 per cent of the respondents are male, while 38.8 per cent are female. In terms of age grouping, majority of the respondents are between 20 and 30 years i.e. around 75%, while the remaining 25% are between 31 and 50 years. Overall, around 82 per cent are single while the remaining 18 per cent are married.

Regarding the level of education, around 65 per cent are holding a bachelor's degree, 22% are holding Master's degree, while the remaining 13 per cent are holding a baccalaureate. 78 per cent of the respondents are students, and the remaining 22 per cent are working in the private sector.

Results

Descriptive analysis

Before proceeding to data analysis and hypotheses' testing, it is required to firstly inspect and analyse the overall properties of the data. The initial results in Table 1 show the means and standard deviations for the four constructs of the model. It is shown that the means are all beyond the neutral point of the scale i.e. 4. This initially indicates that the respondents have a tendency to accept Islamic insurance as an alternative to the conventional insurance. Likewise, the results show the positive attitude that the respondents have vis-à-vis Islamic insurance, as well as their perceived control over their decision, and the possible social influence that can affect their decisions. Nevertheless, these are merely initial analyses that will be tested for significance in the following sections.

Table 1: Descriptive statistics

	Intention	Perceived Behavioural Control	Attitude	Subjective Norm
Mean	5.2786	4.6866	5.1851	4.2886
Std. Deviation	1.60134	1.31410	1.56566	1.47698

Validity measures

In applying structural equation modelling, the validity of the model is an important requirement. Validity of the model means that the items measuring a specific construct have a high common variance among each other, the constructs of the model are significantly different from each other, and the interactions between the constructs are justified in the theory. These three conditions represent convergent validity, discriminant validity as well as nomological validity, respectively.

Beside these three types of validity, there is also face validity which is established based on interaction with professionals in the field of study.

According to Hair, Black, Babin and Anderson (2010), convergent validity can be measured through three main instruments i.e. factor loadings of the construct, average variance extracted (AVE) as well as the reliability measures e.g. Cronbach Alpha [12]. In this regard, the Cronbach Alpha should be 0.6 and above, while AVE and the factor loadings should be at least 0.5.

By referring to Table 2 below, it is observed that all the Cronbach Alpha are greater than 0.6, and the AVE values are all above 0.5, likewise, the factor loadings were all greater than 0.5. This indicates that all the thresholds are met, and hence the model achieves convergent validity.

Table 2: Convergent validity measures

Construct	Cronbach Alpha	AVE
Attitude	0.954	0.846
Subjective Norm	0.855	0.783
Perceived Behavioural Control	0.670	0.608
Behavioural Intention	0.913	0.854

The second type of validity if the discriminant validity, it can be measured using several tools. In the current study, it will be done by setting the correlation between two constructs to 1, and then compare the fit indices of the restricted model with the baseline model. Table 3 below shows the Chi square value and the degrees of freedom for both models. The change in the degrees of freedom is 6, while the change in the Chi Square value is 28.416. By comparing the latter with the Chi Square extracted value corresponding to a degree of freedom of 6 and a confidence margin of 0.05, we find a value of 12.59 which is lower than the Chi Square difference. Hence, we can conclude that the model achieves discriminant validity.

In addition, face validity was also ensured by consulting with experts in Islamic insurance and financial services marketing. And finally, the nomological validity was verified by looking at the interaction between constructs.

Table 3: Discriminant validity measures

Elements	Chi square	DF
Baseline model	147.065	71
Restricted model	175.481	77
Change	28.416	6

Finally, the model fit in Table 4 below show a Chi square value of 217.792, an RMSEA value of 0.175, a normed Chi Square value of 3.025, and a CFI value of 0.841. These are acceptable model fits as suggested by Browne and Cudeck (1993), Hu and Bentler (1999) as well as Kim and Forsythe (2010) [5, 15, 18].

Table 4: Model fit indices

Model	NPAR	CMIN	DF	P	CMIN/DF	RMSEA	CFI
Default model	33	217.792	72	.000	3.025	.175	.841
Saturated model	105	.000	0				1.000
Independence model	14	1010.675	91	.000	11.106	.391	.000

Hypotheses' testing

Since the validity of the model is established, the next step is the hypotheses' testing through structural model. It is worth noting that there are five hypotheses, four of them are tested through SEM. The results in Figure 2 and Table 5 indicate that attitude has a significant influence on the intention to adopt Islamic insurance services by Muslims in France. Hence, hypothesis 1 is supported. This is in line with the findings of Ozer and Yilmaz (2011), Dawkins and Frass (2005), Lee (2008), Tarkiainen and Sundqvist (2005), Celuch, et al. (2007), Tohidina and Mosakhani (2010), Wu, Lin and Lin (2011), Lee, Cerreto and Lee (2010), Lu, Hou, Dzwo, Wu, Andrews, Weng, Lin and Lu (2010), Yousafzai et al. (2010), and Shih and Fang (2004) [25, 8, 20, 29, 7, 30, 31, 19, 21, 32, 26].

Likewise, subjective norm was found to have a significant positive influence on the attitude towards Islamic insurance services. Hence, hypothesis 2 is supported as well. However, subjective norm does not have any significant influence on the adoption intention. Thus, hypothesis 3 is rejected. This is in line with the findings of Shih and Fang (2004), Yousafzai et al.

(2010), and Caperchione *et al.* (2008) [26, 32, 6]. Nevertheless, it contradicts with the findings of Gelderen *et al.* (2008), Ozer and Yilmaz (2010), Lu *et al.* (2010), Lee *et al.* (2010), Wu *et al.* (2011), Tohidina and Mosakhani (2010), Dawkins and Frass (2005), Celuch, *et al.* (2007), Lee (2008), and Tarkiainen and Sundqvist (2005) [11, 25, 21, 19, 31, 30, 8, 7, 20, 29]. This suggests that subjective norm might have an influence on customers' adoption of *takaful* in France only through changing their attitude, in the sense that it does not have any direct influence on the behavioural adoption. This indicates that the perception and attitude of French Muslims about *takaful* products and probably other Islamic related products has been influenced by their social environment.

Finally, perceived behavioural control was found to have a significant positive influence on the behavioural intention. Hence, hypothesis 4 is supported. This is similar to the findings of Lee (2008), Dawkins and Frass (2005), Ozer and Yilmaz (2010), Yousafzai *et al.* (2010), Lu *et al.* (2010), Lee *et al.* (2010), Wu *et al.* (2011), Tohidina and Mosakhani (2010), and Lee (2008) [20, 8, 25, 32, 21, 19, 31, 30]. Nevertheless, these findings contradict with those of Shih and Fang (2004) [26]. This could be mainly due to cultural differences between the two population samples.

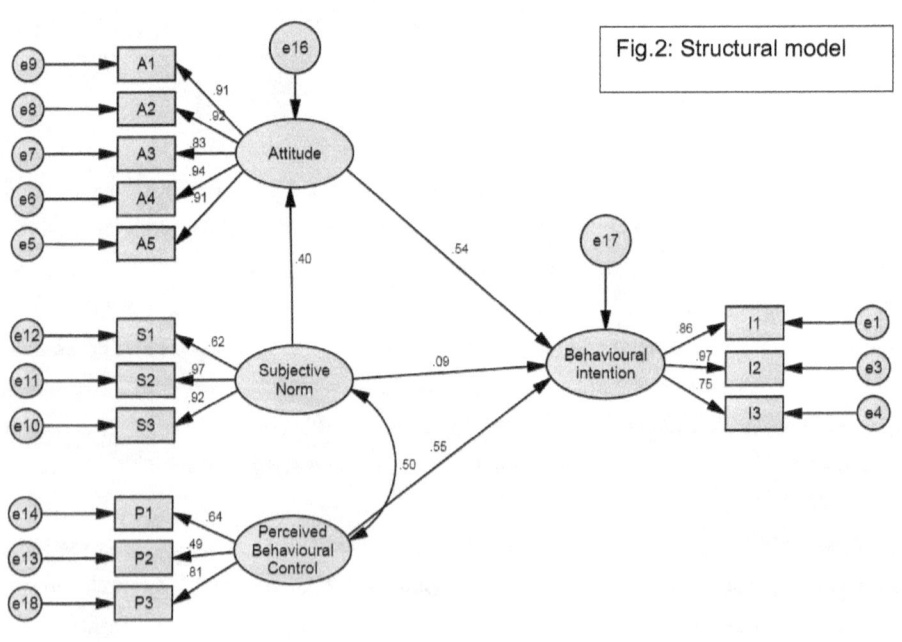

Fig.2: Structural model

Table 5: standardised total effects

	Perceived Behavioural Control	Subjective Norm	Attitude
Attitude	.000	.405	.000
Behavioural intention	.553	.091	.544

T-test

In order to inspect whether the Muslim customers in France are willing to shift to Islamic insurance services, one sample t-test is employed. The results in Table 6 indicate that the mean difference is positive for all the items as well as the intention construct. It is also shown that these mean difference values are all significant, which means that the respondents are willing to shift to Islamic insurance services, depending on the above-mentioned factors. Hence hypothesis 5 is supported.

Table 6: One sample t-test

	Test Value = 4					
			Sig. (2-tailed)	Mean Difference	95% Confidence Interval of the Difference	
	t	df			Lower	Upper
Intention	6.536	66	.000	1.27861	.8880	1.6692
I1	6.367	66	.000	1.373	.94	1.80
I3	5.198	66	.000	1.119	.69	1.55
I2	6.566	66	.000	1.343	.93	1.75

Discussions and conclusions

The main objective of the chapter was to examine the willingness of the Muslim customers in France to shift to the relatively new Islamic insurance services, and the factors that may influence their decision. The results indicated that subjective norm has a strong positive influence on the attitude towards Islamic insurance services. Similarly, attitude and perceived behavioural control were found to have a positive influence on customers' intention to adopt Islamic insurance services. Furthermore, the results indicated that the customers are willing to the Islamic alternative of insurance.

These results have great implications for the body of knowledge, practitioners and policy makers. Specifically, the chapter extends the theory of planned behaviour to a different setting

217

as well as a different field of study. Similarly, the chapter provides great guidance for policy makers and practitioners that should take these considerations into account to establish a strong ground for Islamic insurance services to succeed in France and similar countries.

Nevertheless, the chapter has a number of limitations that should be taken into account in the future studies. Firstly, the sample is relatively limited; hence the results cannot be extended to the whole Muslim population in France. Similarly, the results take into account only Muslim customers while they do not consider the majority Christian portion. Thus, future studies are recommended to select a more representative sample in terms of religion.

The future studies are also recommended to extend the studies in this area, by focusing on similar countries e.g. Canada, Spain, etc. Finally, the future studies are recommended to use a more comprehensive framework such as decomposed theory of planned behaviour (DTPB), mainly due to the uni-dimensional structure in TPB.

References

Ajzen, I. (*1991*), "The theory of planned behavior", *Organizational Behavior and Human Decision Processes*, 50, pp. 179-211.

Al-Harbi, K.A. (2010), "E-learning in the Saudi tertiary education: Potential and challenges", *Applied Computing and Informatics*, 9, pp. 31-46.

Aziz, W.A.B.W.A., Mat, A.B.C. and Zin, E.A.M.E.W. (2011), "A study of contributing factors in Islamic Motor insurance", *Gaziantep University Journal of Social Sciences*, 10, pp. 1-20.

Bashir, M.S., Mail, N.H.H. and Abd'Ali, M.J.A.B. (2011), "Consumers' perceptions on takaful business in Brunei Darussalam", *Proceedings of the International Conference on Management*, pp. 1145-1163.

Browne, M.W. and Cudeck, R. (1993), "Alternative ways of assessing model fit", In K.A. Bollen & J.S. Long (Eds), *Testing Structural Equation Models (136-62)*, Newbury Park, CA: Sage.

Caperchione, C., Duncan, M., Mummery, K., Steele, R. and Schofield, G. (2008), "An examination of the mediating relationship between body mass index and the direct measures of the theory of planned behaviour on physical activity intention", *Psychology, Health and Medicine*, 13, pp. 168-179.

Celuch, K. G., Goodwin, S. and Taylor, S. A. (2007), "Understanding Small Scale Industrial User Internet Purchase and Information Management Intentions: A Test of Two Attitude Models", *Industrial Marketing Management*, 36, pp. 109-120.

Dawkins, C.E., and Frass, J.W. (2005), "Decision of union workers to participate in employee involvement: an application of the theory of planned behavior", *Employee Relations*, 27, pp.511 – 531.

Fishbein, M. and Ajzen, I. (1975), Understanding attitudes and predicting social behavior, Prentice-Hall, New Jersey.

Francis, J.J., Eccles, M.P., Johnston, M., Walker, A., Grimshaw, J., Foy, R., Kaner, E.F.S., Smith, L. and Bonetti, D. (2004), Constructing questionnaires based on the theory of planned behaviour: A manual for health services researchers, Centre for Health Services Research, University of Newcastle, United Kingdom.

Gelderen, M.V., Brand, M., Praag, M.V. Bodewes, W., Poutsma, A. and Gils, A.V. (2008)," Explaining entrepreneurial intentions by means of the theory of planned behavior", Career Development International, 13, pp.538-559.

Hair, J.F., Black, W.C., Babin, B.J. and Anderson, R.E. (2010), Multivariate data analysis, seventh edition, Prentice Hall, Upper saddle river. N. J.

Hamid, F.S. (2011), "Measuring service quality in the takaful industry", SEGi Review, 4, pp. 118-124.

Hill, D.M. (2008), Contextual (Setting/situational) control of pro/anti-environmental behaviour, Unpublished PhD Thesis, University of Arizona, USA.

Hu, L.T. and Bentler, P.M. (1999), "Cutoff criteria for fit indices in covariance structure analysis: conventional criteria versus new alternatives", Structural Equation Modelling, 6, pp. 1-55.

Ismail, I., Mat Desa, N.N. and Taupek, N.N.A. (2013), "Do civil servants accept Islamic banking system in Malaysia?", International Journal of Education and Research, Vol. 1 No. 1, pp. 1-7.

Kanat, I.H., and Özkan, S. (2009), "Exploring citizens' perception of government to citizen services: A model based on theory of planned behaviour (TBP)", Transforming Government: People, Process and Policy, 3, pp.406-419.

Kim, J. and Forsythe, S. (2010), "Factor affecting adoption of product virtualisation technology for online consumer electronics shopping", International Journal for Retail and Distribution Management, 38, pp. 190-204.

Lee, J., Cerreto, F. A., & Lee, J. (2010), "Theory of planned behavior and teachers' decisions regarding use of educational technology", Educational Technology & Society, 13, pp. 152–164.

Lee, J. (2008), Predicting the use of online video advertising: Using the theory of planned behaviour, Unpublished Master Thesis, Michigan State University, USA.

Lu, H.Y., Hou, H.Y., Dzwo, T.H., Wu, W.C., Andrews, J.E., Weng, S.T., Lin, M.C. and Lu, J.Y. (2010), "Factors influencing intentions to take precautions to avoid consuming food containing dairy products: Expanding the theory of planned behavior", British Food Journal, 112, pp.919-933.

Masrom, M., Hussein, R. (2008), *User Acceptance of Information Technology: Understanding Theories and Model*, Venton Publishing, Kuala Lumpur.

Muhamat, A.A., Jaafar, M.N. and Ali Azizan, N.B. (2011), "An empirical study on banks' clients' sensitivity towards the adoption of Arabic terminology amongst Islamic banks", *International Journal of Islamic and Middle Eastern Finance and Management*, Vol. 4 No. 4, pp. 343-354.

Musara, M. and Fatoki, O. (2010), "Has technological innovations resulted in increased efficiency and cost savings for banks' customers?", *African Journal of Business Management*, Vol. 4 No. 9, pp. 1813-1821.

Ozer, G. and Yilmaz, E. (2011), "Comparison of the theory of reasoned action and the theory of planned behaviour: An application on accountants' information technology usage", *African Journal of Business Management*, 5, pp. 50-58.

Shih, Y.Y. and Fang, K. (2004), "The use of a decomposed theory of planned behavior to study Internet banking in Taiwan", *Internet Research*, 14, pp. 213-223.

Siddiqi, K.O. (2011), "Interrelations between service quality attributes, customer satisfaction and customer loyalty in the retail banking sector in Bangladesh", *International Journal of Business and Management*, Vol. 6 No. 3, pp. 12-36.

Siragusa, L, and Dixon, K. (2009), "Theory of planned behaviour: Higher education students' attitudes towards ICT-based learning interactions", *ASCILITE 2009 Auckland: Same Places, Different Spaces, 07/12/2009.* Auckland, New Zealand: The University of Auckland, Auckland University of Technology and Australasian Society for Computers in Learning in Tertiary Education (ASCILITE).

Tarkiainen, A. and Sundqvist, S. (2005), "Subjective norms, attitudes and intentions of Finnish consumers in buying organic food", British Food Journal, 107, pp.808 – 822.

Tohidina, Z. and Mosakhani, M. (2010), "Knowledge sharing behaviour and its predictors", *Industrial management and data systems*, 110, pp. 611-631.

Wu, S., Lin, C.S. and Lin, J. (2011), "An empirical investigation of online users' keyword ads search behaviours", *Online Information Review*, 35, pp. 177-193.

Yousafzai, S. Y., Foxall, G. R. and Pallister, J. G. (2010), "Explaining internet banking behavior: Theory of reasoned action, theory of planned behavior, or technology acceptance model?" *Journal of Applied Social Psychology,* 40, pp. 1172-1202.

Chapter 12

Italian Prospects in Islamic Finance

Paolo Pietro Biancone
University of Turin

Introduction on Islamic Finance in Europe

Literature in the Western world has only recently dealt with Islamic finance in aspects of its tumultuous development in countries where it professes the religion of Islam (Porzio, 2009) and regarding its slow but gradual spread in the Western financial system (Wilson, 2007).

Islamic finance is a phenomenon that cannot be limited to only the Islamic countries, especially given the growing number of Muslims in the West. Muslim communities in non-Islamic contexts are characterized by being highly fragmented in terms of language, socio-economic status and ethnicity, but on a steady rise in terms of income. Older generations of laborers and small shopkeepers have been replaced by a growing number of professionals. This evolvement represents a very significant reality in the international financial environment, especially in regard to the growth rates and the number of people involved. However, there have been very different growth rates from country to country in which it has spread, with specific reference to European countries that do not have a religious Muslim tradition.

Particularly in the UK, where there is a well-established presence of Muslims, Islamists are fueling a growing demand for financial services in line with the Shari'ah. Traditionally well-advanced in the financial sector, the United Kingdom was the first European jurisdiction to amend its tax legislation to allow the execution of financing transactions in line with the procepts of the Shari'ah, avoiding, thus, a legal transaction tax penalty compared to traditional financing, in the case wherein said burden was attributable exclusively to the peculiar financial structure put in place. Besides the United Kingdom, notable attempts of dissemination of Islamic banking have also been made in Germany and Denmark.

France, despite the significant presence of Muslim immigrants, has developed an interest with conscious delay on the Islamic finance phenomenon. Most of the big Western financial institutions, following the model of Citibank, which in 1996 opened its own Islamic subsidiary in Bahrain, are now engaged in this type of activity in the form of branches, or Islamic windows or financial products intended for the Muslim customer. However, the recent development of Islamic finance is attributed to strong support from the French authorities, who have built a proper and welcoming environment.

221

Currently most European Muslims manage their own financial assets through conventional banks, because the leading providers of Islamic financial services are not present in the retail market. The majority is served by large institutions rather than small banks and only a few uses the European branches of Islamic banks. The agreements reached allow the use of credit cards issued by banks of the Islamic world in ATMs of other banks, but this does not fully meet the needs of customers, who often find a limited range of automated services and are penalized with extra charges if they withdraw cash from banks other than their own.

In general, in Italy there are no obstacles to granting authorization to the exercise activities of a bank that establishes in its statute that their banking activities will be carried out according to Islamic norms, but the supervisory authorities must examine, prior, to giving their assessment, the characteristics of each initiative for the corporate purpose of the Islamic bank (Donato, Ferri 2006). Potentially, these features may not be compatible with the Banking Act (Testo Unico Bancario)[19] which art. 14[20] provides for the authorities that are conventionally focused on the function of collecting deposits and lending.

The operative reality in Italy is that many brokers are licensed as banks, yet do not carry out the functions of typical banking, but rather focus on specialization in investment services, since the bank does not only participate in banking activities, but also acts as an intermediary authorized to carry out other financial activities, as long as it is not confidential by law to other categories of intermediaries (such as insurance activities).

Therefore, the specific operating characteristics of Islamic banks are compatible with the Italian financial system (Prof. Claudio Porzio). With regards to the question of the religious motivations that underlie the relationship between Islamic banks and traders, the experience of Banca Popolare Etica in our country and provision of ethical savings products demonstrates the legitimacy and recognition motivated by different financial choices, so that in fact the legislation cannot be applied in a different manner. What has also been debated is the concept of a "joint venture", governed by art. 2549 of the Civil Code, in reference to the operating scheme of certain Islamic financing operations, which could lead to two problems in the relationship between banks and non-financial institutions:

- Interference in the management of the bank by unauthorized persons and banks;
- Risk of dominant position of influence in favor of third parties associated with the transmission of profits or losses.

---

[19] The Banking Act, also known as the TUB ("Consolidated Law on Banking and Credit"), is legislation made in force with a legislative decree of 1993.
[20] TITLE II - Banking, Chapter II-Authorization to banking branches and freedom to provide services.

With reference to the first aspect, the Bank of Italy[21] does not give any decision-making power to the associates or management, since it considers that the joint venture does not constitute a joint management of the subject, but only involves the division of profits and losses in exchange for a contribution that is economically assessable, unless there exist contractual clauses that influence the management decisions of the bank.

Fear of supervisory authorities suggests that the contractual constraints could lead to a dominant position of influence in favor of non-financial associations with violation of the principle of separation. The association agreements on participation, however, must be approved beforehand by the supervisory authority.

The new provisions of the Civil Code in relation to company law have facilitated the construction of Shari'ah compliant contracts, thus broadening the range of instruments for the financing of an enterprise and disciplining the assets for contribution to business with third parties. The total investment in economic participation must be contained within the capital. However, to ensure the performance of Islamic banking activity in Italy, surpassing tho prohibition of interest and the Islamic sector, which contrasts with the general principles of separation between the bank and the Company, and the protection of depositors, the Banking Act should be accordingly modified and adapted.

The rules to protect investors also require adherence by an Islamic bank to the Interbank Guarantee Fund of Deposits for obtaining authorization. Deposit insurance is, next to the supervisory mechanism and the lender of last resort, one of the key components of a safety net aimed at ensuring the stability of the banking system.[22] The Statute of the Interbank Deposit Protection Fund is in accordance with the national legislation transposing the directives on deposit-guarantee schemes, including the protection afforded to depositors claims relating to the funds acquired by the banks with repayment obligation in the form of deposits or in any other form, including bank drafts and comparable securities. The application of different prudential standards lower than those required cannot be assumed even for Islamic banks in Italy. The typical risks of financial intermediation involve the need to apply different forms of prudential supervision to intermediaries and activities for regular management and avoid the repercussions of certain systemic crises.

In addition, the Islamic Bank will have to define the role and responsibility of the *Shari'ah Supervisory Board*. Not having executive power cannot interfere in the management

---

[21] **The Bank of Italy as an independent authority, which carries out supervision, inspection and regulatory activities in relation to the economic and financial operators, authorizes these entities to carry out banking business or activity that involves the collection of deposits from the public and the 'exercise of the credit for their own, when the requirements relate to art. 14 T.U.B.**
[22] **The deposit guarantees that systems are regulated at European level by Directive n.994/19 EC, as amended by Directive 2009/14/EC of 11 March 2009 concerning the coverage limit and the terms of repayment.**

of the bank nor can decisions be made on behalf of the management, only to verify the conformity of transactions with Islamic laws and regulations and the admissibility of the transaction, unless the nature of the relations of the Board with the bank, which may take various forms with members appointed by the shareholders, and with members selected by the Board of Directors are approved by a general Council. The existence of these Councils of the Islamic bank should not interfere with the tasks of officials and internal control audits.

Development Perspectives of Islamic Finance in Italy

Italy is one of the fastest growing markets in Europe. A series of initiatives have been taken by the Italian authorities to study the issues related to an expanded presence of Islamic finance. The Bank of Italy, for example, has hosted a series of conferences on the subject. ABI, the Italian Banking Association was established on a voluntary basis and, besides not having any profit, has set itself the goal of working to promote the activity and promote the interests of the banking and financial system. In its relations with the business world, the ABI has given rise to international meetings to strengthen economic cooperation. With particular attention on the Gulf countries to develop trades, investment, and financing opportunities through, amongst others, the introduction of Shari'ah compliant instruments in Italy. It is currently coordinating a working group on the issue of a sovereign or corporate *sukuk*.

The spread of Islamic finance and compliance with the prohibitions set by the Muslim religion from a theoretical point of view would lead to reduced intermediation activity of Islamic banks, and a redefinition of the paradigm of intermediation, in the sense of understanding the bank first as a partner of a company or business consultant and secondarily as a lender. From an operational point of view, the bank behaves like a conventional bank in terms of costs for companies and returns for depositors, but adopts a different modus operandi to compete in international and local contexts with Western banks. Consequently, its "safe" intermediation operations opens growth perspectives in Italy, taking into account on the one hand the actors who can build a dedicated offer to customers and the Islamic community and other factors that may coordinate the development of this same offer. In Italy as many of 1.3 million people are Muslim,[23] which amounts to 2% of the Italian population, but there is no offer of financial services or products for the Islamic community in Italy.

The birth of the first Italian Islamic bank was expected by 2008 between ABI (Italian Banking Association) and UBA (Union of Arab banks), but the financial crisis has slowed down the development. However, the latest agreement now wants to overcome the limitations of fiscal and financial legislation, as has happened in the UK, where the Institute of Islamic Banking of Britain was activated with only a tax review, always taking into account the degree

---

[23] **On the basis of residence permits issued by Home Office.**

of consistency with the Islamic Shari'ah compliance, which is a dependent variable according to banking projects conceived in optical Islam or born of an economic western entity.

Alongside offering developmental perspectives of Islamic finance in Italy, Italian Islamic banks could also explore the Islamic windows of Italian banks. Opening a window on the Islamic world can be a growth opportunity for those banks that want to become first distributors of products in accordance with the Quran, and second packagers of products of this type. Initiatives dedicated to Islamic finance may also be provided by banks that have launched social banking or banking to welcome initiatives as an international trend. In this context we can also consider the Islamic windows of foreign banks. In fact, there are large banks with international vocations, such as the British HSBC and the OIZ TSB, who have offered full Islamic services extending basic banking services to the needs of customers of Islamic origin. Considering Islamic banks on the basis of European Community legislation, they are free to offer their services to customers in any country of the European Union, by virtue of the investiture obtained by the supervisory authority of the country of origin. In England, considered for its qualification as a portal of Islamic finance as a reference point in the future development of Islamic finance in Italy, Islamic banks are licensed on the basis of certain requirements verified by the FSA. Other subjects may also be involved in the process of construction experience in Islamic Italy, in the opinion of some scholars (MG Starita).

So, besides the ABI-UBA agreement, there are also other Italian banks (UBAE bank, Unicredit bank, Banca Etica and Banca Sella) nearby to offer Islamic products, even if they currently do not have structured products. Notable European Islamic banks are the Islamic Bank of Britain, the European Islamic Investment Bank, and other banks licensed in the UK to retail and wholesale. Another English bank very active in the international arena, and the first to have understood the potential of Islamic finance, is HSBC and its subsidiary HSBC Amanah. These are the people who may be interested in defining an Islamic offer in Italy. Considering now the factors for the takeoff of Islamic finance in Italy, we can say that this, from a systematic point, depends on the following factors;

- regulatory disposition,
- fiscal disposition.

Downstream from conditioning and economic opportunities of the main factors for the intrinsic compatibility of Islamic contracts with Italian law are;

- accounting,
- communication,
- the distribution,
- staff training.

The greater opportunities for Islamic banks in Italy arise from the geographical proximity of Italy to the Middle East and North Africa. Italy is considered a bridge between Europe and the southern shores of the Mediterranean. Based on the trade and good business relationships that bind Italy to the Islamic countries, we can usefully analyze the activity of the Bank UBAE Union of Arab Banks and European banks, which act as a link between the countries of North Africa and Europe. UBAE Bank has developed unique capabilities to assist trade between countries of the Arab world and with international trade. They have become highly regarded as so-called expertise in trade finance or financial assistance for the acquisition of raw materials or the early liquidation of the receivables associated with the foreign market. The relational capital of UBAE Bank is a good starting point for the establishment of the first Islamic Bank in Italy.

The opportunities for Islamic windows in the Italian bank scene may be summarized as follows: the banking needs of the Islamic community in Italy of the first generation with access to these facilities are based on financial needs related to remittances, savings and some investment. The second generation will have more refined financial needs as they trigger entrepreneurial activities that require bespoke services. In some regions of the north this is already happening. Basic banking services should be offered to attract the interest of the emigrants and enable initiatives to promote financial integration of communities of immigrants in Italy. Particular opportunities exist for European Islamic banks to exploit the success of the Islamic finance in Britain. The Islamic Bank of Britain is only one of the five authorized that specializes in retail. Its eight branches are a benchmark for other Islamic banks.

Sharia compliant for Small and Medium Enterprises

Small and Medium Enterprises (SMEs) contribute heavily to the economic growth worldwide as they had a major share in capital accumulation and also creation of the employment opportunities. SMEs compose 99.9% of the total Italian enterprises.

A detailed chapter aims to explore the eligibility of the Italian SMEs as a Sharia compliant to get introduced to the Islamic financial system and verify the possibility of financing them through Islamic financial instruments.

Testing for Shari'ah compliant had required to apply the Shari'ah screening methodology. Screening is composed of qualitative and quantitative screening criteria where the companies get screening for their permissibility of passing both of them. Using a databank Aida, a set of hypotheses had been imposed according to the most rigid criteria of most popular worldwide used indices of Shari'ah compliant screening processes to verify the eligibility of the Italian SMEs and in specific the unlisted ones.

Starting by the first phase which is the qualitative criteria screening that should exclude all enterprises that has any non Halal activities or Haram activities like: alcohol, pork

226

related products, pornography, tobacco, gambling, interest bearing financial services (i.e. conventional banks and insurance companies), weapons and defense, biological human and animal genetic engineering (ex: cloning), media and advertising companies with exception to news channels, newspapers, and sports.

The second phase is the quantitative screening where the financial ratios of the companies are tested for not exceeding specific threshold. The three main aspects that should be tested are the leverage level (debt level ratio), interest ratio, and the liquidity ratio (cash and Account receivables), and finally the portion of revenue that is generated from non halal activities.

Hypothesis for the tested companies:

- Companies should be Italian and owned by one or more individuals or families.
- Unlisted companies only.
- Starting qualitative screening through the type of industry of the companies to exclude all Haram (non-Halal) activities that are considered not permitted according to Shari'ah.
- The quantitative screening starts with the financial variable index for verifying the liquidity ratio. As it is testing a new assumption for the unlisted companies so there is no available market capitalization. As a result, the formula was set to measure relatively to the shareholders equity (24 months). The formula is:
  Total Accounts Receivables / Total Shareholders' Equity
  With threshold: < 33%
- The second financial variable index is for verifying the Interest ratio. The formula is:
  Cash & Interest-Bearing Securities / Total Shareholders' Equity
  With the imposition of threshold: < 33%
- The third financial variable index is for verifying the debt level ratio. The formula is:
  Total Debts / Total Shareholders' Equity
  With the imposition of threshold: < 33%
- The fourth and last financial variable index is for verifying the non permissible income ratio. The eighth filter was set to impose the formula and limit it to the accepted threshold. The formula is:
  Non-Permissible Income / Total Revenue
  With the Imposition of threshold. < 5%
- Finally, the exclusion of all inactive companies and to limit the pool to legally active companies

Outcome Results:

The exclusion of the Non-Halal i.e. Haram activities which are prohibited according to Sharia had only excluded few company's despite of imposing many impermissible activities ensuring that all prohibitions are totally covered. The sample had resulted of exclusion of few numbers of companies.

This gives a strong message regarding the business activities of the Italian SMEs are not having a problem with the qualitative criteria of Shari'ah compliance and there is a great pool and a sufficient market share to start with.

Moving to the screening for financial ratios where a fall down of the number of companies as the financial and accounting structure of the Italian SMEs are not fitting so much with the Shari'ah requirements. There were a lot of companies that were excluded in the quantitative criteria screening i.e. starting from 16,271 companies to get 454 companies passing the screening which is considered a very high percent of exclusion.

The problems in the financial structure can be summarized in: first it is based on liquid current assets (accounts receivables) which are not highly appreciated in the Islamic financial system, second point is the debt level which reflects the financial risk (total debts/market capitalization) where Sharia appreciate low levels. More than half of the total companies that gone through the debt level filter had been excluded. This conveys that the 52% of the Italian SMEs is financed through debt. This reflects high financial risk.

Reviewing the other two ratios which are the interest ratio and the non permissible income ratio, it was found that the companies which were excluded because of the interest ratio imposition were not huge as the other two financial ratios. The interest ratio is to look for the cash and interest-bearing securities portion in the company but since our pool is SMEs and providing the exclusion of the high level of debt and accounts receivables so the portion of the interest ratio was not so high and had almost met the threshold.

The last ratio was for the non permissible income. Since the sample was done excluding totally all non-Halal activities then it was evident that the non-Halal in the financial statements of the remaining companies would be sorted out in the interest of the financial income coming from conventional sources.

In analyzing the outcomes of the empirical data after having displayed all the used hypothesis it was found many facts that helped to understand the nature of that companies and the problem that mostly shared of excluding them. The majority of companies that had passed the screening are from the Real Estate sector followed by the Management & Consultancy Services sector.

The Training Project

Economic relations between Italy and the Middle Eastern countries are facilitated by geographical contiguity. Italy is the ideal partner in the effort of both Arab and Islamic countries (such as Iran, Turkey and others) to expand their production base, on account of Italian specialization of low and medium intensity production of capital and the flexibility of the national production system, favored by the high density of small and medium enterprises.

The training project, proposed by us, to bring Islamic finance into our country is a profitable opportunity to further enhance our knowledge and share it with our financial community and academia. The aim of the course is to provide a complete picture of Islamic finance, the analysis of the founding principles and the potential for development of the sector with reference to the Italian market, and the more technical aspects relating to individual financial instruments at the disposal of Islamic Banking. This can be achieved in addition to gaining knowledge on the mechanisms that regulate the commercial and financial processes from a perspective of interaction between the market and Western finance institutions and those of the Islamic culture.

There are a growing number of established international financial centers, such as London, Tokyo, Hong Kong and Singapore, all of which have started projects of integration between Islamic finance and other financial systems. The evolution of Islamic finance has aimed at strengthening its development. With this endeavor, two important institutions, namely the IFSB founded in 2002 and the AAOIFI founded in 1990, have both become points of reference to ensure uniformity of architecture and ensure the financial stability of the Islamic system.

Our mission is to start a training, education, research and professional consultation center and promote the dissemination of Islamic finance at national and international levels, spurring the possible integration of our banking system and the alternative that will undoubtedly deliver significant benefits to the Italian economy. The Center also serves as a bridge in order to examine best practices in banking and finance from proffers studies that compare traditional practices with those in the Islamic world.

The School of Management and Economics (former Faculty of Business and Economics) is part of the University of Turin (Italy), founded in 1404. The faculty celebrated its first centenary in 2006, it was renamed School of Management and Economics in 2012 and divided into two departments: The Department of Management, and the Department of Economic and Social Sciences, Mathematics and Statistics. It now has 70,000 students, a staff of more than 220 full, associate and assistant professors and offers a wide range of Italian and English taught programs both at undergraduate and graduate levels.

The Department of Management is assembling a Bachelor's degree and a Master's degree course in English, intended to train both Italian and international students interested in learning study issues related to Islamic finance.

Development projector of Retail Products

The migrants are included in the economic and social Italian structure to such an extent that they represent a very significant segment of the market. Therefore, the present project aims to create alternative financing and investment routes that are immediately usable within the legal and fiscal Italian system, for Islamic investors and the community of immigrants from the southern shores of the Mediterranean and resident in Italy.

Development, in the medium term, of Shari'ah compliant finance in Italy not only responds to the need for investment, but also the need to save by the Islamic community in our country. In particular, the progressive sophistication of financial needs related to the presence of the second generation of immigrants and the gradual development of business activities, requires an assessment of the potential of the Italian market in offering Shari'ah compliant retail financial products.

The articulation of the retail offer could be targeted to meet the basic financial needs (liquidity, investment, financing for home purchases and capital goods for the development of productive activities), but the structuring of the supply and the choice of which business model to adopt must be determined in order to best exploit profitability perspectives for the bank, customers' convenience and operational complexity. With this aim, this chapter propose to carry out compatibility studies of Islamic products and collaborate with micro-credit banks, cooperative credit and the big banks from which the traditional products will be emulated and adapted into Islamic products.

Until now, the supply / demand focus has been on money transfer services (remittances, payment instruments) prevalently provided by the postal channel and skilled operators, and it is this particular phase of the Islamic community's financial markets that is an interesting segment for banks, and therefore the development of a Shari'ah compliant commercial option is being carefully evaluated.

Currently in Italy the needs of Muslim residents are being fulfilled by the experience of the staff in the multiethnic project "Agenzia Tu", within the banking group UniCredit. The specific objective of this project is to meet the needs of foreign citizens who are struggling to gain access to bank services, such as consumer credit or home loans. It is in this way that the initiative is aimed at UniCredit Bank, which is dedicated to new players of the economic and labor market.

Thus, the role of our project is to facilitate the process of social integration, giving the Muslim community the opportunity to choose financial products and unconventional investments. This will address a real financial need that is otherwise often exacerbated by the inability to resort to conventional finance products. Worth noting is that Muslim residents' (amounting to approximately 1.3 million individuals) savings are estimated at over 500 million per year (excluding savings for remittances to their countries of origin).

So, we have a situation in favor of the development of Islamic finance. In the short term, however, we must address some of the issues already settled by other large EU countries, such as the lack of specific regulations and the need for changes to the Tax Code so as to not affect the transactions of Islamic finance. Then there are cultural factors and difficult to dispel myths, such as the belief that Islamic finance is only for Muslims, that it is a primitive financing method, that it is riskier and more expensive than conventional finance, which is governed only by Shari'ah principles, and the mentality that the conventional system does not need replacing.

Development project of an Investment Fund for SMEs Financed by Islamic Investors

The overview of the implementation of the model of Islamic finance outlined so far is necessary in order to assess the ways in which Italy can further open up to the Islamic investment funds' market. The objective is to contribute and to increase the flow of Arab capital and strengthen bilateral economic relations.

The current Islamic investment fund seems to be the instrument with the lowest degree of discretion among those proposed in a western market. To measure the performance of Shari'ah compliant investments, we have created some indices that summarize the performance of a basket of securities that, by their nature, may be subject to investment by funds. We mention the main *Islamic Dow Jones market* index on the square in New York and the *FTSE Global Islamic Index* on the London market.

The Islamic indexes currently cover equities of companies in 46 countries. There are two Italian titles in the lists of titles compatible with Islamic finance: ENI and ENEL. To be included in these indices and overcome the difficult examination of Shari'ah compatibility allows access to a huge Islamic market, as well as providing an opening and the capacity for a dialogue with a different culture. A certification recognized by Islamists is not the prerogative of only large corporations. *A certification by a recognized Islamic body of an Italian company listed or not listed would make a great "business card" for companies that want to present themselves on the Islamic Middle Eastern markets or observant Muslims who would like to invest in Italy.*

Almost all Islamic funds on the market are equity funds, since the purchase of bonds that generate interest would itself be impossible. They are therefore usually risky instruments targeted at experienced investors with a time horizon extending over the long term. Which market in Italy? Also keeping in account that the majority of immigrants of Islamic faith in Italy come from North Africa, while the area of greatest spread of Islamic banks is in Asia. These immigrants often have contacts with western banks in their countries and so it is logical to assume that even here can be integrated into ordinary system. Furthermore, the social class of Muslims in Italy is not very well-off and have limited remittances to their countries of origin rather than using traditional banking services (except perhaps for their mortgage) or investment. Other potential investors could be subscribers of "ethical funds", which are also not Islamic, or large investors in the Middle-East, to Islamic specialist funds such as Italian companies.

The only product currently located is an investment fund proposed by BNL BNP Paribas: BNP Paribas Islamic Fund - Equity Optimizer. It is an equity fund originally founded in France and Bahrain, subsequently brought to Italy by BNP (a French bank also present in our country through the branches of BNL). The fund selects, via the process of an annual review, 30 actions from the component securities of the Dow Jones Islamic Market Titans 100 Index,[24] each with a weight of 3.33% on the entire portfolio. The selection is made according to the highest rate of return on equity and respects Islamic principles. The establishment of the fund and the investment process are validated by the Shari'ah Supervisory Committee. Investment activities are addressed in order to comply with the directives relating to the criteria of the Islamic Shari'ah, so it is not permissible that the fund pays or receives interest, although it is permissible to receive dividends. If this happens, the amount of dividend income will be donated to charities.

The UK remains the hub of Islamic finance and Switzerland, the cradle of international banks, is willing to participate in Islamic finance in the future, at least in terms of collection, but Italy certainly has a prime location at least from the point of view of geography, potentially establishing itself as a protagonist on the world stage of the situation in the Mediterranean. The current political and economic situation, however, could represent an opportunity to regain lost ground. While Islamic banks are located in Switzerland, the UBS has recently opened a branch in Bahrain, the Noriba, in accordance with the Shari'ah. Italy can be regarded in the same sense, and attract investments by institutions or sovereign funds belonging to Islamic States and use these investments as a means of financing for small and medium Italian enterprises.

Statistical analysis, theory and empirical tests have amply demonstrated the importance of small and medium-sized enterprises that compose the industrial structure of our country of approximately 4.5 million.[25] Today, employment in large manufacturing firms appears to accommodate 16.3% of the total workforce, compared to 83.7% of small and

---

[24] **Dow Jones Islamic Market TM Europe Index.**
[25] **We refer to the statistical studies in the periodical publications by ISTAT (General Census of industry and services) in addition to the data contained in the Annual Reports of the Bank of Italy.**

medium businesses. In fact, in the Italian experience, the industrial districts are the spontaneous response to an economic system peripherally packed with great potential.

For an Italian company to be included in an Islamic index and overcome the difficult question of "Shari'ah compatibility", as well as potentially accessing a huge market such as the Islamic population, could provide an opening opportunity for dialogue with a different culture, and an additional card for observant investors who would like to invest in Italy.

Conclusions

The opportunity to attract foreign capital to sustain economic progress, on the one hand, and the intensity of trade and financial links with the southern shores of the Mediterranean, on the other, make it increasingly important that our country and its financial system are well equipped with the knowledge and tools needed to interact with operating systems' statements that comply with the Shari'ah principles.

The positive aspects arising from the combination of "greater liquidity funding from the Muslim community and a strong message of social integration" on the basis of establishments in London, Berlin, Paris, and Amsterdam should originate from Italy as the source dispersing then into the European banking scene. In the end, to summarize, we can say that the project aims to identify what could be a unique opportunity and promote it in order to intrigue the young people through training courses on Islamic finance and attract foreign capital and funds in terms of retail and investment.

The Islamic finance to work and generate the aimed opportunities it should have all the structure in which it would work with i.e. Shari'ah complaint investments and business activities. The Shari'ah complaint would be needed in several aspects like attracting Arab sovereign funds, Retail banking services for Muslim clients, Sukuk in the stock exchange, and for financing and investment opportunities for SMEs.

Islamic finance would be of a great opportunity to the Italian SMEs. In an empirical chapter it was observed how Italian companies are considered to a great extent eligible for Sharia complaint from a qualitative criterion screening prospective and this is a very encouraging outcome. The real problem facing the Italian SMEs to be a Sharia compliant is the quantitative criteria screening. The real challenge for the SMEs is to have some changes in their financial structure.

Also, the opportunity to attract investment remains of utmost Importance. As the authors suggest, it is legitimate to think "Islamic finance could be an effective means to attract Islamic investment in Italy". This is not a game of little consequence, considering that, according to the estimates of the United Kingdom Islamic Finance Secretariat, the volume of activity in Britain was 509 billion dollars in 2006 and reached 1.290 billion by the end of 2011. In this framework, therefore, the goal is to bring out the fact that Italy can meet the restrictive requirements, such as to represent investment opportunities for financial institutions (sovereign wealth funds, banks, asset management companies and others) looking for good opportunities.

REFERENCES

Biancone, P.P. (2012), *Il bilancio della Banca Islamica e la rappresentazione dei principali contratti finanziari*, FrancoAngeli, Italy.

Cabanel, P., Di Motoli, P., Hasan, R., Losano, M.G., Moya, M., Gian Rusconi, E., Zagrebelsky, V. and Furstenberg, N.Z. (2013), "L'Islam in Occidente",*Quaderni Laici*, Vol. 8, pp. 23-86.

Abul A'la, M.S. (1999), *Economic system of Islam*, In Khurshid Ahmad, 4th edition, Islamic Publications, Lahore, pp. 5-10.

Visco, I. (2013), "The European Challenge Rome", *Opening address by Governor for the IFSB Forum*, 9 April, pp. 1-5.

Guide to the Dow Jones Islamic Market Indices, retrieved online on: http://www.djindexes.com/mdsidx/downloads/rulebooks/Dow_Jones_Islamic_Market_I ndexes_Rulebook.pdf

Osservatorio sulla finanzia Islamica, retrieved online on: http://www.m2a.unito.it/osservatorio-finanza-islamica/

Gomel, G., Cicogna, A., De Falco, D., Penna, M.V.D., Sarzana, L.D.B.D., Di Maria, a., Di Natale, P., Freni, A., Masciantonio, S., Oddo, G. And Vadalà, E. (2010), *Finanza Islamica e sistemi finanziari convenzionali, tendenze di mercato, profile di supervision e implicaizoni per le attività di Banca centrale*, No. 73.

European Central Bank (2013), *Islamic Finance in Europe*, occasional paper series No. 146, European Central Bank.

Wilson, R. (2007), *Islamic finance in Europe*, European University Institute, San Domenico di Fiesole, RSCAS Policy Papers No 07/02, retrieved on: www.ieu.it/RSCAS/WP-Texts/07_02.pdf.

Zambon, S. (2011), "The Managerialisation of Financial Reporting: An Introduction to a Destabilising Accounting Change", *Financial Reporting, Special Issue*.

The Banker (2011), *Top 500 Islamic financial institutions*, The Banker.

Porzio C. (2009), *Banca e finanza islamica*, Bancaria Editrice, Rome.

Akhtar S. (2008), *Financial Globalization and the Islamic finance services industry*, IFSB, Kuala Lumpur.

Gafoor A. (1996), *Interest-free Commercial Banking*, A.S Noordeen, Kuala Lumpur.

Chapter 13

Islamic Finance in Russia

Renat BEKKIN

Södertörn University

Islamic banking

In 1916, a book "*Zakah*" written by a Muslim scholar Musa Bigeev in old Tatar language was published in Petrograd[26]. The author of this book was the first scholar (not only in the Russian Empire but also worldwide) who described a concept of Islamic bank and gave this financial institution a title 'Islamic bank'. It was only 80 years later, however, that the first bank that marked itself an 'Islamic bank' appeared in Russia.

Badr-Forte Bank

The first Islamic financial institution in Russia was a bank called *Badr-Forte Bank*. The bank was set up in Moscow in 1991 and started Islamic banking operations in 1997. Although its name did not contain the word 'Islamic' or any other reference to its specific (Islamic) nature, the bank's charter (which according to Russian laws is subject to registration in the Central Bank of Russia) stated, that the bank may "act according to Russian and international laws by applying Islamic modes of financing which do not contradict the banking laws of Russia". *Badr-Forte Bank*'s Islamic nature was attested by its membership in the IDB's General Council of Islamic Banks.

Absent specific rules for Islamic banks, the bank had to work in the conventional regulatory environment balancing between the Islamic principles of banking and the requirements of Russian banking legislation. Due to the specifics of Russian laws (prohibition for banks to engage in trade operations and mandatory deposit insurance scheme to name the most important ones) contrary to the very principles of Islamic banking *Badr-Forte Bank* had to compromise in some respects. Instead of classic deposit-taking and trade financing and investment activities, the bank had to focus on foreign trade operations (cross-border money transfers, guarantees and letters of credit). Its retail Islamic banking offering was limited to current accounts and money transfers supplemented by Islamic mortgages that the bank launched shortly before its closure in 2006.

---

[26] *Bigeev, M* (1916). *Zakah*. Petrograd. The facsimile of this book and its translation into Russian were published by T.H. Habibullin and I.A. Zaripov: *Bigeev, M* (2013). *Zakah*. Nabereznye Chelny.

During the decade of its existence (1997-2006) the bank had no branches and was not widely known to the general Muslim public, even in Moscow where the bank's headquarters were located, let alone in the area.

In December 2006, the Central Bank of Russia revoked the banking license of *Badr-Forte* on the grounds of money-laundering and gross violation of the procedural requirements for reporting suspicious transactions. There have been a few attempts to recover the license, but they were in vain.

It is interesting to note that the Muslim community both in Moscow and in other regions of Russia met *Badr-Forte Bank*'s closure indifferently. Some people even expressed their joy that a 'Shia bank' was at last closed[27]. Some criticized the bank for not having social responsibility programmes for the benefit of the Muslim community in Russia.

Non-banking institutions providing Islamic financial services in Russia

At present, there are no Islamic banks in Russia. However, a few non-banking institutions offer Islamic financial products. They are based in and primarily target two Russian republics with large Muslim communities: Republic of Tatarstan and Republic of Dagestan and to a lesser extent Republic of Bashkortostan.

The pioneer in this field, *Yumart Finance*, was founded in Kazan in 2010. It was established in the form of a partnership in commendam by asset management company *Yumart Finance* and investment company *Eriadna*. In September 2011, *Yumart Finance* merged into *Amal Finance House*, the other player in the market of Islamic financial services in Tatarstan at that time. The partnership provided a range of Shariah-compliant products based on *murabaha* and *ijara* contracts for both corporate and retail clients, including financing of car purchase (*murabaha*), consumer financing (*murabaha*), mortgages (*ijara wa iqtina'*), as well as working capital financing (*murabaha*) and leasing of cars and equipment (*ijara*). A number of retail deposit plans were also available.

It is not feasible to analyze the results of *Yumart Finance*'s performance due to lack of available data and rather short period during which it operated. After the merger with *Amal Finance House*, the latter became one of the leaders in the market for Islamic financial services in Russia (and the only such company in Tatarstan)[28].

Amal Finance House is a group of companies operating under the umbrella brand "*Amal Finance House*". The group comprises a management company, an investment

---

[27] The CEO of the bank Adalet Dzhabiyev is a Shia Muslim. Later in 2008, he founded an investment company Al-Shams Capital.

[28] Some staff from *Yumart Finance* moved into *Amal Finance House* (see: The First Merger in the Islamic Financial Market in Russia (2011). Available at: <www.muslimeco.ru/eng/onews/166/>).

company, a leasing company, a trading house and a bank. The latter, a Kazan branch of *Bulgar Bank* (a mid-size Tatarstan bank licensed by the Central Bank of Russia) is a key element of this group. It is a dedicated branch of *Bulgar Bank*, which has a separate correspondent account in the Central Bank of Russia. All payments and cash management are performed through this branch.

Amal Finance House offers a broad range of financing and savings services using *murabaha, ijara, mudaraba* and *musharaka* contracts.

Another initiative to create an Islamic financial services provider in the Volga-Urals region took place in Nizny Novgorod at about the same time. In March 2011, *Vostok Capital*, a branch of *Ellipse Bank* in Nizhny Novgorod started its Shariah-compliant operations. In other words, *Vostok Capital* became an Islamic "window" of a conventional *Ellipse Bank* (similar to the Kazan branch of *Bulgar Bank*, *Vostok Capital* opened a separate correspondent account in the Central Bank of Russia in order to secure that its money does not commingle with that of the head office of *Ellipse Bank*).

According to the information provided by *Vostok Capital*, it offered the following services for corporate entities and individual entrepreneurs: cash management, asset financing using *ijara* and *murabaha* contracts, FX operations, and operations with precious metals (purchase and sell of coins and bars of precious metals). More or less the same range of services was available to retail clients. In comparison to *Amal Finance House*, Vostok Capital provided a more limited scope of financial services. In particular, it did not have investment accounts.

Until recently, *Amal Finance House* and *Vostok Capital* shared the market for Islamic financial services in the Volga-Urals region. *Amal Finance House* with headquarters in Kazan had a branch in Niznekamsk (Tatarstan), a representative office in Ufa (Republic of Bashkortostan) and two representatives in Moscow and Izhevsk (Republic of Udmurtia). *Vostok Capital* with head office in Nizny Novgorod had an office in Ufa. In the end of 2013, *Ellipse Bank* faced financial problems. According to the bailout plan carried out by the Central Bank of Russia, the bank was acquired by the state corporation Agency for Deposit Insurance and Commercial Bank Russian Capital that now jointly control it. After the change in the management, which inevitably followed the change of control in the bank, the Islamic financial services project on the basis of *Vostok Capital* was closed.

Accordingly, *Amal Finance House* became a single player in this market in the Volga-Urals region. This, however, did not put it in a much more advantageous position. The main problem it faces is the lack of clientele[29]. Despite aggressive marketing (especially in Kazan),

---

[29] This problem has been repeatedly pointed out by the representatives of *Amal Finance House*. However, the company does not disclose the number of clients (at least in public sources).

very few Muslims are ready to bring their money to the company as investors or take Islamic loans. *Amal Finance House*'s representatives explain this by poor financial literacy of potential Muslims clients[30]. However, in our opinion, this explanation is not convincing. As far as Shari'ah-compliant financing is concerned, what matters more is unreasonably high cost of financing which may be almost twice as big as the cost of a loan provided by a conventional bank. Whether or not you are a financially sophisticated client, you will feel this difference well. The same problem was at *Yumart Finance*.

That said, for a long time neither *Amal*'s website nor its management in public speeches explained why their financing was so expensive. Some years ago, we had a discussion with the company's representative on this subject and he said speaking about *Yumart Finance* that the company had to borrow from conventional banks due to lack of own funds and client money. Consequently, the price that clients taking financing from *Yumart Finance* had to pay in return included the cost of this conventional *riba*-based funding. Taking into account lack of transparency typical of other companies offering Islamic financial services in Russia, one may not exclude they use or have used such source of funding too. Only in June 2014, the CEO of *Amal Finance House* published an article where he tried to explain why the price that a client borrowing from *Amal Finance House* has to pay was so high. One of the reasons for that, he wrote, were high fees of *Amal*'s Shari'ah advisors[31].

There is, unfortunately, lack of transparency in what concerns Shari'ah advisors of *Amal Finance House* too. For instance, their website does not contain any information on the company's Shari'ah advisors other than their names and insignia (it is noteworthy that neither in-house Shari'ah controller (Gazinur Safiullin) nor a person engaged in external Shari'ah audit (Bulat Mulyukov) has any academic books by which we could judge their qualifications)[32]. We could not find there any information about how decisions are taken by the company's Shari'ah supervision bodies, what principles govern decision-making, what the procedure is. Neither does the company publish *fatwas* made by the company's Shari'ah supervision bodies concerning transactions executed by *Amal Finance House*. Obviously, none of the above does a credit to *Amal Finance House* in terms of information transparency of their business. Moreover, we could not find on the company's website any information about charitable activities of *Amal Finance House*. As we remember, at one time, *Badr Forte Bank* was criticized for lack of social responsibility programmes.

---

[30] Islamic finance projects in Russia (2011). Ed. M. Kalimullina. Moscow. P. 28.
[31] *Nizameev, R.* (2014). Islamic Finance: Too Expensive? Available at: <www.islamnews.ru/news-146531.html>
[32] Bulat Mulyukov has earlier served as a Shariah advisor in *Yumart Finance*. This figure is advertised as the only Shariah expert in Islamic finance in Russia. This is based on the fact that he was a listener of a short-term course in Shariah supervision organised by AAOIFI in Bahrein.

Other financial institutions that launched Islamic financial products in Russia some time later adopted the model used by *Yumart Finance* and *Amal Finance House*. In particular, we are talking about two companies, *La Riba Finance* and *Finance House Masraf*, which were founded in 2011 and 2013 in Dagestan. The former took as the example *Amal Finance House*'s model and the latter that of *Yumart Finance*.

Partnership in commendam *La Riba Finance* was established in the end of 2011 by the Dagestan bank *Express Bank*, a regional leader among the banks in Dagestan in terms of the number of clients. Not being capable of offering Islamic financing products on its own[33], Express Bank grew this business via *La Riba Finance* which it actively supported.

In January 2013, however, the Central Bank of Russia revoked the bank's license accusing *Express Bank* of fraudulent reporting about the bank's assets hiding the loss of own funds (capital) as well as resistance to the Central Bank's officers carrying out inspection and commission of supervisory actions at the bank. It is interesting that *La Riba Finance* continued to work even without support of *Express Bank*.

The range of services offered by *La Riba Finance* is, largely, not much different from those that were offered by *Yumart Finance* or *Amal Finance House*. This includes corporate and consumer financing, real estate financing and financing for the purchase of vehicles. For investors (limited partners in the partnership in commendam), there are three types of deposits. One of them is a charitable contribution "Insan" which allows transfer of accrued income on a monthly basis as a donation (*sadaqa* or *zakah*) to the Charity Fund "Insan" to help all the needy Muslims. Among other services provided by *La Riba Finance* is free of charge calculation of amount of *zakah*, including allocation of this amount with subsequent reporting to the client if the client orders so. *La Riba Finance* also provides consulting services in all questions of conducting business. Unfortunately, we could not find the company's financial statements on its website; hence, we cannot say how successful its business model is.

As concerns Shari'ah supervision, in Dagestan the functions of a Shari'ah supervisory body in all Islamic financial companies are performed by the canonic department of the Spiritual Board of Muslims of Dagestan. The company's website does not contain any further information about Shari'ah supervision at *La Riba Finance*. There are neither names of the members of Shari'ah supervision bodies nor any *fatwas* issued by them.

There is very little information about another company offering Islamic financial products in Dagestan, *Masraf Finance House*. The website of this company, which was

---

[33] The only exception was an interest-free *halal* debit card which Express Bank launched in 2008 on its own. The bank made a huge advertising campaign for this card, however, the card found its first holder only in 2011. (see Islamic finance projects in Russia (2011). Ed. M. Kalimullina. Moscow. P. 35.)

founded in 2013, looks like a business card and gives only very basic information about the company. Some former employees from *Amal Finance House*'s office in Kazan work there.

Such is the current state of the Islamic banking services market in Russia. Both *Amal Finance House* and *La Riba Finance* plan to grow customer base, including through entering other regions of Russia with large Muslim population. So far, despite aggressive marketing campaign, the demand for Islamic financial services is still very low in all regions where they are available (Tatarstan, Dagestan and Bashkortostan). The main reasons for limited demand are risks for investors[34] and cost of financing for borrowers. As regards non-guaranteed return of invested money, this is a well-known linchpin of Islamic banking in comparison to conventional banking. In the context of Tatarstan, where at every step there are advertisements of quasi-banking institutions inviting people to put their money on deposit with a yield of over 100% per annum, offer of non-guaranteed profit on deposits by a non-transparent structure that refers to its devotion to Islam and a non-existent authority of its Shari'ah supervisory bodies is hardly appealing.

The lack of own funds and client money can push an Islamic financial institution to borrow from conventional financial institutions. Given the lack of transparency of the institutions under consideration, it is not feasible to check this fact.

Therefore, the question to use or not to use Islamic financial services offered by *Amal Finance House* and similar structures should be answered by Muslims according to their faith. By faith, we mean not whether or not they believe in Allah but rather whether or not they believe the words that are pronounced by the representatives of these financial institutions.

Islamic insurance (*Takaful*)

The lack of reliable information is a big challenge for writer of Islamic finance in Russia generally and Islamic insurance in particular. Information contained on the Internet is often inaccurate or misleading. Journalists writing abstract articles on Islamic finance and newly-baked 'experts' often do not bother to double-check data found on the Internet and obtained from third-hand. As a result, unreliable information roams from one work to another about particular companies or banks which allegedly offered or are offering Shari'ah-compliant financial services.

The examples do not need to go far. Back in 2002, the media reported that insurance company *NASCO* in Tatarstan offered its customers a service for the accumulation of funds for the *hajj* in accordance with the principles of Shari'ah[35]. Subsequently, the company made

---

[34] Principal amount of investment on investment accounts in *Amal Finance House* and investments made by limited partners into the capital of the partnership in commendam *La Riba Finance* are not protected.
[35]See, for example: *Kashapov, R.* (2002). "For Muslim pilgrims", in *Time and money*, № 179 (24735); "Insurance according to the Quran". (2005), in *Insurance case*, № 1, P. 8; *etc.*

a clarification: they were talking about the programme *Idel-Hajj* started in 2001. This programme has been marked a joint project of the Spiritual Board of Muslims of the Republic of Tatarstan (DUM RT), insurance company *NASCO* and *Tatfondbank*[36]. The programme, according to its promoters, was aimed primarily at the accumulation of funds for the *hajj* and *umrah*. In addition, it was contemplated that the programme would also help to "invest money in different directions of Shari'ah-compliant business, including small and medium-size businesses of the younger generation"[37].

However, in practice it turned out that there are no such accumulative insurance services, consistent with the principles of Shari'ah neither in *NASCO*, nor in the *Idel-Hajj*, but voiced in the media information was nothing more than a marketing ploy. Situation did not change after the *Idel-Hajj* became an independent company, one of the leading Russian *hajj* operators[38]. Nevertheless, to this day you can find articles and even monographs, which featured "pioneer experience" of *NASCO* in development of Islamic insurance[39]. Such virtual projects periodically arise in our days. They can be obtained from the works of not very conscientious authors who do not bother to double check the information found on the Internet[40].

Another Tatarstan company called *Itil* also did nor manage to go very far in the development of *takaful*. Originally, it intended to develop a division within the company operating in accordance with Islamic principles of insurance. In the autumn of 2004, the company set up a dedicated department of Islamic insurance. However, in early 2005 the project was put on hold. The company decided to look for a co-investor from the Gulf. The company's management began negotiations on cooperation in the project with an Islamic insurance and reinsurance company *Dubai Islamic Insurance & Reinsurance Company*

---

[36] *Kashapov, R.* (2002). "For Muslim pilgrims", in *Time and money*, № 179 (24735).

[37] *Gataullin, R.* (2004). "On the possibility of creating a free economic zone of 'Halal' standard", in *Islamic financial relations and prospects for their implementation in the Russian Muslim community*, Moscow: Moscow Islamic University. P. 31.

[38] The author of these lines for six months as a client unsuccessfully sought from employees of *Idel-Hajj* to send him the relevant documents for the contract by the funding program. However, each time under various pretexts sending of documents postponed to a later date, citing to the absence of the director at the time or a problem with the printer, etc. Subsequently, in November 2004, during a seminar "Islamic economic model: perspectives of realization in the Muslim and non-Muslim communities" the representative of DUM RT - Deputy Chairman Mufti *Waliullah Yakupov* in conversation with the author confirmed that the loyalty program *Idel-Hajj* based on Islamic financing methods" still does not work.

[39] See, for example: Islamic financial and credit institutions in foreign countries' economies. (2011). Ed. V.G. Timiryasov. Kazan, Pp. 166-167.

[40] For example, some *S.P. Fukina* writes about insurance company *Takaful*, which until July 2012 allegedly provided in accordance with Shariah "services for insurance against accidents and illnesses, health insurance, insurance of land transport, corporate property insurance, except for vehicles and agricultural insurance, property insurance of citizens, except for vehicles and liability insurance of vehicle owners" (*Fukina, S.P.* (2014). "Specifics of Islamic insurance and prospects for its introduction into the insurance market in Russia", in *Vestnik of Astrakhan Government Technical University of Economics*, № 1, Pp. 113-114).

(*Aman*), but both sides failed to reach an agreement. Shortly thereafter, the *takaful* project on the basis of *Itil* was aborted.

In the mid-2000s, representatives of various Russian insurance companies studied the possibility of introducing some Islamic insurance services into the domestic market. However, this interest did not go beyond a mere curiosity about exotic insurance system. Companies valued the project related risks (including political, associated with so-called "Islamic factor") and preferred to wait and see.

One of these companies was *Renaissance Insurance*. The company's interest in Islamic insurance was due to the fact that there were many pilgrims on their way to *hajj* and *umrah* among its existing clients. Desire to attract the maximum number of pilgrims and create more comfortable conditions of insurance for existing customers were the main rationale for *Renaissance Insurance* 's decision to start a *takaful* project.

The documentation for a variety of insurance products (compulsory third party car insurance and hull insurance, insurance of corporate and private property, cargo insurance, *etc.*) was subject to an expert analysis carried out by the Shari'ah advisor (R.I. Bekkin) that *Renaissance Insurance* engaged in the project. Necessary modifications and additions to the documentation made it possible to proceed with the development of Islamic insurance products.

However, the main question remained unresolved for a long time: how would the funds of policyholders paid in the form of installments for Islamic insurance products be invested? At that time in Russia there were no banks offering Shari'ah compliant bank accounts. An agreement was reached with one of the Russian banks to open a special purpose account for the funds of the project "*Takaful*" where the funds are not to be mixed with money received from the sale of non-Islamic insurance policies. The bank was supposed to allocate a manager in order to administer this account.

The decision was not perfect in terms of Islamic law. However, in the absence of Shari'ah-compliant banking services in the country, the company had only two solutions in the arsenal: to try to ensure the terms for placement of funds in a conventional bank which are as much as possible permissible from the point of view of Islamic law or suspend the project. After consultation with the Shari'ah advisor, the company decided to proceed with the first option.

The form of organisation of Islamic insurance business in the company has been another lynchpin of the project. The management of *Renaissance Insurance* declared that it is not ready (at least before the start of sales of Islamic insurance policies) to create an independent structure in the form of a separate company or Islamic insurance "window" within the insurer.

According to the business plan, the company was supposed to go to market with a line of Islamic insurance products in summer 2009, but the launch of the final phase of the project (start of Islamic insurance policy sales) was postponed several times. By late autumn 2009, it was announced that shareholders had decided to put the project on hold with a "non-priority" mark.

While *Renaissance Insurance* was working on the *takaful* project there were reports in the media in November 2009 about the intention of the Russian logistics investment group *Safinat* to develop Islamic insurance in Russia[41]. It was stated that in the early 2010 it would commence sales of Islamic insurance policies. The project consultant was a Kuwaiti insurer specialising in Islamic insurance, *First Takaful Insurance Company*. It was announced that two offices of the new Islamic insurance company would soon be opened in Moscow and Kazan.

However, despite strong statements, this project has never been implemented. The question remains unanswered: whether in fact experts of *Safinat* and *First Takaful Insurance Company* made real steps to design appropriate Islamic insurance products or it was nothing more than a declaration of intention – like the one that took place in the company *NASCO*.

One more Islamic insurance project developed by another major Russian insurance company *ROSNO* followed approximately the same scenario. Amendments were made to the *ROSNO* documentation for insurance products (third party liability insurance, motor insurance, insurance of corporate and private property, cargo insurance) to make them Shari'ah-complaint. As in the case of *Renaissance Insurance*, financial model in *ROSNO* was based on the *wakalah* (agency model). *ROSNO* project was suspended at the same stage as that carried out by *Renaissance Insurance*.

Experience of participation in Islamic insurance projects at different Russian companies allowed the author of these lines to conclude that the most likely success scenario for Islamic insurance in Russia is its implementation within a small company. Despite large financial opportunities that major insurers can boast of; it is much easier for a small company to develop and carry through such a risky project as Islamic insurance. The stakes are high, but the payoff in case of success is high too.

Experience of *Evro-Polis* insurance company proved that these expectations were correct. On 1 June 2012, the company started sales of Islamic insurance policies for people traveling abroad. The idea of Islamic insurance in Russia was finally put into practice.

---

[41]See, for example: *Grishina T., Kiseleva E.* (2009). "Insurance learns the ropes of Shariah", in Kommersant (Kazan), № 209 (4264), 10 November. Available at: <URL: http://www.kommersant.ru/doc/1272108>; "*Safinat*" and "Alliance Capital" signed an agreement on the establishment of Russia's first *takaful* company (2009). 09 November. Available at: <http://lenta.ru/news2/2009/11/09/safinat/>

Evro-Polis no longer faced the problem of allocation of insurance funds as acute as its predecessors did. By the time the work on the project commenced, three financial institutions have been offering Islamic banking services in Russia: *Vostok Capital* (Islamic banking "window" of *Elipse Bank*), *Amal Finance House* and *Yumart Finance*. These financial institutions were present at that time in Kazan, Nizhny Novgorod, Ufa and Moscow. Not accidentally, *Evro-Polis* began to develop Islamic insurance in two of the mentioned cities (Kazan and Ufa): firstly, because the company also had offices there, secondly, because there were financial institutions offering the set of Islamic banking services that the company needed.

Evro-Polis opened special Islamic current accounts in Islamic "windows" of *Ellipse Bank* and *Bulgar Bank* in order to hold insurance premium received from clients (policyholders). In the absence of suitable Shariah-compliant instruments on the Russian market, the company had to keep the funds on current accounts without investing them.

For *takaful* operations in *Evro-Polis*, a combination of *wakala* (agency) and *waqf* model[42] was chosen. This model allows each policyholder to participate in charitable activities with part of the insurance premium and according to the Shari'ah advisor of the company (R.I Bekkin), meets the essence of the Islamic concept of insurance, as well as the goals and objectives of the company – without breach of the Russian laws.

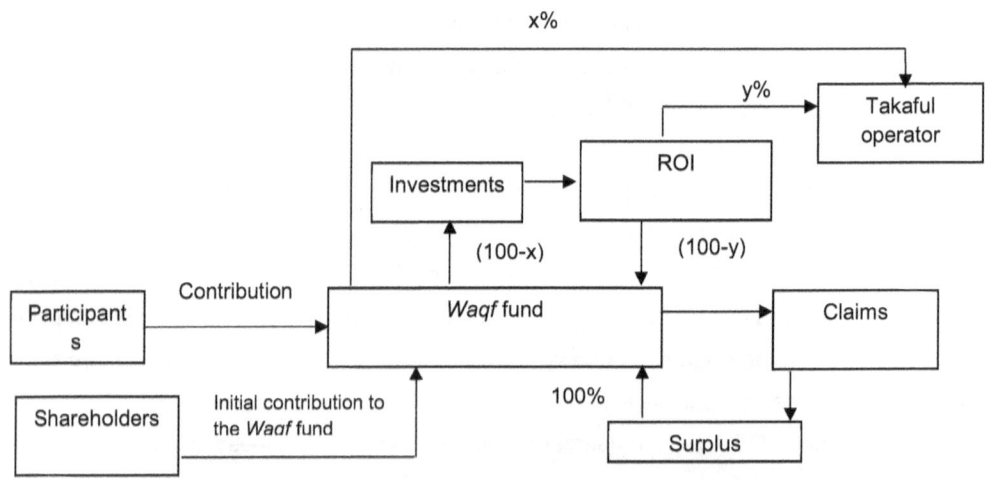

Fig. 1. Agency (*wakala*) model + *waqf* used in *Evro-Polis* company

---

[42] *Waqf* is a property alienated for charity. When certain property is made *waqf* (or, according to some Muslim theologians, when the intention to create *waqf* is announced), it no longer belongs to the founder of *waqf* (*waqif*), nor is it transferred into the ownership of those who manage *waqf* in the interests of the *waqf* beneficiaries (receivers of *waqf*-created profits) designated by the *waqif*. It is prohibited to use *waqf* property for purposes other than those designated by the *waqif*.

Shari'ah supervision in the company was implemented by a single Shariah advisor (R.I. Bekkin). The fact that there was no Shari'ah Board in the structure of the company, comprising at least three people (in accordance with the standards of the AAOIFI – the Accounting and Auditing Organisation for Islamic Financial Institutions) is not an exclusive feature of *Evro-Polis*. This practice can be observed in other structures that offer Islamic financial services in Russia. This is due to, primarily, the lack of qualified personnel in Russia and the reluctance of market participants to attract foreign specialists because of their high fees. The institute of an individual Shari'ah advisor exists in Pakistan. More important is the fact that the company has attracted as a Shari'ah advisor a secular scholar who is an expert in Islamic law and Islamic finance, while in other Russian Islamic financial institutions the function of Shari'ah control and supervision was monopolised by representatives of the Muslim clergy.

However, the *Evro-Polis* Islamic insurance project was inherent in a number of drawbacks. Some of them were caused by the inability to fully implement the concept of *takaful* under the Russian laws, the others by the internal difficulties of the company. Thus, absence of a separate division in the form of an Islamic insurance "window" or a separate company significantly influenced the development of sales of Islamic insurance products at *Evro-Polis*. The idea of transforming the Kazan branch of *Evro-Polis* into a separate Islamic insurance company was discussed, but the question has not been resolved. Pretty soon, the shareholders of the company lost interest in Islamic insurance, and in the beginning of summer 2013 the project was actually abandoned.

With regard to implementation of the *takaful* concept in the form of a mutual insurance society, this approach is the most correct in terms of Shari'ah, but it is not popular with Russian businessmen. Among the reasons for not wanting to develop Islamic insurance based on a mutual insurance company are existing legal restrictions for mutual insurance companies related to the amount of capital and the size of the customer base.

We expect that in the next few years major insurers should come up with more initiatives to create Islamic insurance "windows". *Takaful* has a better chance of success in Russia than Islamic banking[43], taking into account the fact that the insurer has the ability to provide a flexible tariff policy. If we take *Evro-Polis* as an example, the price of Islamic insurance policies there was no different from conventional insurance policies of the same type. Moreover, the company provided a discount if the client proved that the insurance policy of competitors in the conventional insurance was cheaper.

---

[43] As was noted elsewhere in this book, the main problem of Russian Islamic financial institutions is the lack of own capital. This forces them to resort to borrowing in the interbank market. Therefore, the cost of financing in an Islamic bank may at times by two times exceed the cost of a conventional bank loan. As a result, customers (including Muslims) do not show much interest in the services of Islamic banking and quasi-banking institutions.

Waqfs

At the dawn of Islamic finance, when there were no Islamic banks at all, some of the scholars were writing that it would be enough to create an effective mechanism of collecting and distributing *zakah* and to restore *waqfs* in order to set up a fair economic system in the Muslim world. However, even today only a handful of countries have put in place working *zakah* systems and efficient *waqfs*. Even in the countries with developed Islamic banking, investment and insurance systems *zakah* and *waqfs* do not play a key role in economic development.

Russia can be viewed as one of the countries with historically developed *waqf* usage, which was seemingly lost during the Soviet era.

In the middle of June 2004, Kazan hosted the 7th All-Russia Seminar of the Heads of Spiritual Administrations of the Muslims called «*Waqf* and Its Prospects in Russia Today». According to the imams who spoke at the event, today, *waqf* is the only chance for Russia's Muslim religious organisations to preserve their financial independence. Judging by what was said at the seminar and by the information presented at previous similar seminars, the Muslim spiritual leaders do not always clearly understand the purpose of *waqf*.

Sometimes *waqf* is confused with other Islamic institutions: *gyshar* ('*ushr* is the more correct name, that is, tithe, or a tenth part of the yield), *zakah*, as well as the revenues produced by some religious rituals: *khatemlar* (gatherings that pray for the dead) and *janaza* (burial rites).

Quite often *waqf* is treated as a fund for financing of operational expenditures of mosques and Muslim clergymen. It is hard to start a constructive dialogue if those who want to develop the *waqf* system have vague ideas about it.

Significantly, similar problems also existed in Russia before the 1917 October Revolution: one of the first officially registered *waqfs* bequeathed in 1830 to the First Main Mosque of Kazan by merchant Gabdulla Yunusov did not specify the rules of its management and control over the revenue it produced. This was by far not the only example of misunderstanding the *waqf* institution in the Volga region: the heirs of a rich industrialist, Utiamyshev refused to fulfill his will under which part of his money was intended for *waqf*, arguing that there was no specific procedure for executing the will[44].

Prominent Tatar enlightener of the 19th century, Shigabuddin Mardjani (1818-1889), rejected the interpretation of *waqf* exploited by rich merchants to control the economic life of the community (*mahallya*). It was mainly thanks to his efforts that the question regarding the direct purpose of *waqf* which corresponded to Shari'ah was raised and a system of collective self-administration in individual Muslim parishes established. The number of embezzlements in the charity sphere decreased along with, first, the power of the patrons in the Yunusov

---

[44] *Salikhov, R.* (2005). '*Kak vozrodit blagotvoritel'nost?*', in *Tatarskiy mir*, No. 1 (54), February 2005. P. 3.

246

brothers' *mahallya* and then of other Tatar merchants who had been dominating their communities. Thus, approximately since the mid-nineteenth century in the Volga region *waqf* started being used for its main social purpose, that of an institute for protecting economic interests of Muslim communities and their individual representatives.

The legal procedure for transforming property into *waqf* was adopted in the late 19th century. Under the procedure, a founder of *waqf* (*waqif*) applied in writing to the assembly of parishioners representing the community. He was required to give a detailed description of the property designated for *waqf*, state its value, beneficiaries and terms and conditions for its management. The community empowered the mosque leaders to apply to the governor with a request to seek permission to establish *waqf* from the Ministry of the Interior Affairs of Russian Empire. The latter's permission was sent to the Orenburg Mohammedan Spiritual Assembly[45] which, in turn, approved the permission and informed the parishioners of the ministry's decision. After a dedicatory inscription was made on the property transferred to *waqf*, creation of *waqf* was attested by a notary. The community was responsible for annual reporting about *waqf* management and bookkeeping[46].

It should be said that in the pre-revolutionary Russia, so-called cash *waqf* was rather very popular: the *waqif* allotted a certain sum, the interest on which was used by the mosques, Muslim clergy, students of religious schools (*shakirds*) and other beneficiaries for which the *waqf* was intended. In this way, while one of the provisions of Islamic law was strictly observed, another, much more important provision[47], the ban on usury (*riba*), repeatedly formulated in the Quran, was violated: "Those who devour usury will not stand except as stands one whom Satan by his touch has driven to madness. That is because they say: 'Trade is like usury', but Allah hath permitted trade and forbidden usury" (2:275).

This interpretation of *waqf*, which does not fit the classical pattern, was not restricted to Russia alone. At one time, outstanding Muslim theologian Mehmed Birgevi sharply criticized the practice of donating cash for religious purposes which served as one of the cornerstones of financial transactions in the Ottoman Empire. This money was normally loaned under

---

[45] Orenburg Mohammedan Spiritual Assembly was set up by the Katherine the Great to manage various affairs of Muslims of the Russian Empire.

[46] "*Waqf*" (2004), in "Islam na evropeyskom Vostoke: Entsiklopedicheskiy slovar", Ed. by R.A. Nabiev, Kazan, P. 49.

[47] It seems that in Russia today the Muslim clergy does not object to usury operations when administering *waqf*. The draft amendments to the Law on the Freedom of Conscience and Religious Associations offered by the SAM RT and related to *waqf* property said, in part: «*Waqf* can include any property, be it a plot of land, building, structure, or other real estate, the right to use any securities, as well as jewelry, books, and other movable property in the Republic of Tatarstan and outside it» (Dokumental'nye materialy o deiatel'nosti Dukhovnogo upravlenia musul'man Respubliki Tatarstan v period s 14.02.1998 po 14.02.1999 (1999), Kazan. P. 20). The fact that all types of securities are related to property that can be transferred to *waqf* violates the Quaranic ban on usury.

interest, which contradicted the Islamic ban on usury. At the same time, religious and secular institutions used only profits created by this money[48].

In the Volga region, a large number of Muslim parishes were financed by the interest from bank deposits. After the 1917 October Revolution, *waqfs* were abolished in various regions of Russia, although this happened over time. *Waqf* institutions existed for longest in the North-Eastern Caucasus. Only ten years after the revolution, in 1927, a decree nationalising the *waqf* property was issued by the local authorities of the Dagestan Autonomous Socialist Soviet Republic.

The *waqf* issue is repeatedly discussed in present-day Tatarstan at the highest level. In the mid-1990s, at one of the first meetings, members of the Muslim clergy and then republic's president, Mintimer Shaimiev, discussed the possibility of setting up a *waqf* system badly needed for the construction and maintenance of mosques and madrasahs, and for public activities. The president formed a special commission to study the issue in depth. Specialists were sent to Turkey to gain experience. A few years later, a united congress of the republic's Muslims created the post of Chairman of *Waqfs*, in the rank of first deputy mufti, and a W*aqf* Department under the *mufti*. The very concept of *waqf* was first introduced into the republic's legislation by the Law of Tatarstan on the Freedom of Conscience and Religious Associations.

The provision on the *waqf* property and its inalienability, contained in this law, was just a declaration of intentions rather than a legal norm that was spelling out existing practices. However, even this provision over time has raised questions on its compliance with federal legislation, and the law was subsequently amended. Nevertheless, the provision on *waqf* property, although nonexistent in practice, was retained.

The members of the State Council of Tatarstan have insisted that all efforts to provide a legal framework for non-existent *waqfs* are useless unless necessary changes are made in federal laws. In June 2008, they came up with an initiative to include the notion of '*waqf* property' into Russian legislation. Earlier that year, the Chairman of the Muslim Religious Board of the Republic of Tatarstan, Gusman Ishakov, proposed the same measures. There has been no reaction from the federal authorities so far.

The issue of spelling out the notion of *waqf* in federal legislation is also important in terms of restoring Muslim ownership of the *waqf* property, nationalised after the 1917 October Revolution. For example, in the Republic of Crimea, when local Tatars argue for restoring their ownership of the lands confiscated during the Soviet rule, they refer among other things to the existence of *waqf* property in the tsarist times in Russia. As was mentioned before, work is done by Tatarstan historians and law scholars on finding previously existing *waqfs* in the Volga

---

[48] *Kemper, M.* (2004). "Musul'manskaia etika i 'dukh kapitalizma'' in *Islamskie finansy v sovremennom mire: ekonomicheskie i pravovye aspekty*, P. 41.

region. However, even if the notion of *waqf* is introduced in federal legislation, it will not guarantee the Muslims that their *waqf* property, confiscated after the revolution, would be returned, since the major part of documentation concerning those *waqfs* was lost.

In terms of setting up new *waqfs*, even without the notion of '*waqf* property' spelled out in the Russian federal legislation, those willing to do so can use many other legal mechanisms at their disposal. For example, in order to set up the aforementioned cash *waqf* there is no need to create any institutional structure.

There are two forms of cash *waqfs*. In the first case, cash turned into *waqf* is given to the beneficiary as an interest-free loan. This form raises no objections on the side of Islamic law scholars. In the other form, which is questionable from the Shari'ah perspective, money is provided as a loan with an interest rate, where the interest is transferred to the beneficiary. The modern world provides plenty of other ways to use cash *waqf* in compliance with Shari'ah rules. One example is transferring shares that have been approved by Islamic scholars into *waqf*. The shareholder might decide that all of the dividends on shares or part of them will be used for charity purposes.

As for real estate as the subject for *waqf*, in 2004 the State Duma (the lower chamber of Russia's parliament) passed amendments to the Land Code, which transferred, free of charge, land under the buildings and other facilities used for religious and charity purposes to the religious organisations that owned them. Those religious organisations that did not own the buildings in which they function would receive the land under them free of charge for the entire period they continue using the buildings. These amendments were intended to favour the Russian Orthodox Church, but other faiths benefited from them as well.

Therefore, from a legal point of view, there are no problems with instituting *waqfs* in Russia or, to be correct, institutions close to *waqfs*. Neither were there such problems in the previous legislation, which was vaguer about *waqf* property. As concerns *waqfs* in their classical interpretation in the Muslim law, they cannot be set up in modern Russia – except for the mentioned cash *waqf* (first from).

Those who propose using a trust management agreement (chapter 53 of the Civil Code) in order to set up a *waqf* forget that this type of agreement in contrast to *waqf* is limited in time and cannot be concluded for a period over five years (art. 1016, point 2 of the Civil Code). Moreover, current legislation does not allow an individual who does not have a status of an entrepreneur or a non-commercial organisation to be the manager of the trust (art. 1015, point 1 of the Civil Code).

Naturally, this situation requires appropriate amendments to the legislation. Certainly, it would be naive to talk about introducing provisions of Islamic law on *waqf* property into Russian legislation. And the problem is not even in the political complications. A more serious obstacle lies in the loss of Islamic legal culture in Russia. The institution of *waqf* lost its former social and cultural meaning. For example, in Dagestan Muslim schools and higher educational establishments are now mainly functioning on personal donations (*sadaqa*) and incomes derived from leasing out property and trade rather than on *waqf*-created incomes. The same is true of the Volga region where the *waqf* culture was lost even earlier than in Dagestan. Moreover, many faithful, including well-to-do Muslims, believe that *waqf* is too complicated to be effectively controlled. Whereas in Dagestan, the Muslim communities (*jamaats*) are strong enough to control the use of *waqfs*, in Tatarstan and other regions, embezzlement cannot be excluded. This explains why the faithful who want to engage in charity find it much easier to hand the money to those who need it in the form of *sadaqa* or, rarely, in the form of *zakah*, rather than to deal with an institution unknown to the contemporary Russian legislation.

In view of the above, *waqf* today and tomorrow is a different phenomenon that has little in common with the classical *waqf* of the Islamic law. It seems that in the context of the lost Islamic legal culture in Russia as a whole (and Dagestan in particular), most *waqf*-related issues should be regulated by Russian legislation and adats, while Islamic law will no longer affect this institution in the old way.

Does all of the above mean that *waqf* in contemporary Russia has no prospects? Not at all. We believe that Russia losing its *waqf* culture, which existed before the revolution, is positive rather than negative. Contemporary Tatar historians often recall the experience of using *waqfs* in the Volga region in mid-19th century. However, the fact that a substantial part of these *waqfs* functioned in violation of a fundamental Islamic law on the prohibition of usury is omitted. A large part of *waqfs* in the Volga region were the results of usurious operations. That means that Russian Muslims, instead of restoring *waqfs* that are questionable from the point of view of Shari'ah, have a chance to set up new *waqfs*, capable of coping with the challenges of the 21st century, one of which is the demand of Islamic SMEs for financing. The process of creating new characteristics for the *waqf* institute is inevitable. In contrast to *zakah*, *waqf* is open to a wider interpretation within specific provisions of the Quran and Sunnah on charity.

Waqf in modern Russia is usually associated with religious *waqfs*, not the philanthropic ones. This is explained by the fact that the problem of *waqfs* is mostly raised by Muslim clerics and people associated with them.

One of the leading contemporary *waqf* specialists, Monzer Kahf, divides *waqfs* into the following categories: philanthropic, religious (mosques, graves of the religious leaders, gravestones etc.) and private. At the same time, a *waqf* in any of the three groups can be direct or secondary. In the first case, *waqfs* directly perform their charitable, religious or social role: e.g. a well transferred into *waqf* is a free source of water for everybody. In the case of the secondary *waqf*, material objects or revenue from them are initially invested in various spheres and only afterwards are the revenues from these investments donated for charity purposes. An example of secondary *waqf* is cash *waqf*.

In modern Russia, direct *waqfs* are practically ignored while they are in fact an example of non-targeted help to the impoverished. For example, a *waqf* in the form of a public library, given the high prices of books, may practically be the only source for the poor to raise their social status by increasing their knowledge. As we know, revenues from *waqfs* as well as from *zakah* and *sadaqa* can be transferred gratis to those who are not capable of providing for themselves (children, disabled etc.), as well as to those who are in temporary need of resources, including resources for implementing specific projects. As for the *waqfs* that have their primary goal as receiving revenues, there is no need to reinvent the wheel. The experience of Western states, where *waqf* and quasi-*waqf* enterprises effectively function, can be borrowed. The managing organisation, specialising in managing *waqf* property, plays the role of a collective *mutawalli*.

Although the main goal of the Russian *ummah* lies in developing charity *waqfs*, the philanthropic enterprises that want to provide various services and not generate revenue should not be left unnoticed. It is hard to deny the importance for Muslim people of a *waqf* in the form of a public library, where besides access to books the visitors can enjoy free access to the Internet, including access to scientific and other articles on various aspects of Muslim faith.

The institute of *waqf* can prove to be effective in the sphere of helping Muslim migrants in Russia to adapt. It is common knowledge that there are large numbers of migrants from Central Asia working in the country: according to the Russian Migration Service, about five million citizens of Uzbekistan, Kirgizstan and Tajikistan temporarily live and work in Russia. Most do not speak proper Russian, do not know basic information about the country, its laws etc. It is the migrants from former Soviet republics who are most actively involved in developing SMEs. Increasing their knowledge will undoubtedly facilitate an increase in the effectiveness of their businesses.

To help Muslims from other countries adapt to the Russian environment it is necessary to set up a non-governmental centre, where migrants can study the Russian language, Russian legislation, and even master a new profession. It is even possible to pay stipends to needy Muslim students from the funds of this quasi-*waqf*. The centre can be set up either by one legal entity or by a number of individuals.

The real support to SMEs belonging to Muslims in Russia is provided by their fellow believers. This way, given the high rent prices for commercial real estate, some owners or renters of the buildings provide them gratis. Specifically, there are known cases when publishers, specialising in Islamic literature, were given offices to sell books and other printed matters for free. Moreover, these premises can be used for an extended period of time. Statistics on this kind of activity are hard to find since businessmen try not to make it public. In other words, help for SMEs does not have to take the form of cash, but can also be a substantial decrease in their expenses. In this respect, information and consultancy services financed through a *waqf* or quasi-*waqf* can also be priceless. As for the financing of Muslim religious boards and mosques, at present the most effective sources of their financing in Russia are *sadaqa* and partly *zakah*, not *waqf*.

Islamic taxes

It is not accidental that the Muslim Religious Boards in Russia promote federal legislative amendments regarding *waqf* and almost ignore the issue of *zakah* while the latter could be a part of a federal religious tax like for example 'church tax' in Germany.

The lack of interest in *zakah* among Muslim clergymen is logical. As distinct from *waqf*, *zakah* is not a universal instrument designed to cover the expenses of religious organisations. Most theologians, for example, are convinced that the money received as a purifying tax should not be used to build mosques in places where there are enough of them. They believe that the state (obviously, the Muslim state) should shoulder these expenses. In a non-Muslim state, likewise, it is undesirable to spend the larger part of *zakah* on the same things[49]. *Zakah* can be used, however, to fund education, publishing, and other activities designed to promote religious knowledge among Muslims.

As for the culture of *zakah* in Russia, it was lost during Soviet rule, just like the culture of *waqf*. However, during the first years of the Soviet rule *zakah* was collected in places with predominantly Muslim population (the Volga region, the North Caucasus, Central Asia) and was used to buy tools for collective farms[50]. Yet, during the following years *zakah* was not collected in the areas of compact settlement of Muslims. It was replaced by irregular *sadaqa* paid by devout Muslims on the days of religious holidays.

In Russia, only a few Muslims have realised that they ought to pay *zakah*. Prominent Muslim theologian from the Volga region Utyz Imyani (1754-1834) believed with good reason that monetary donations for charities should hardly be encouraged: they create too great temptations for those who collect them. Imams, after all, are common people who might borrow more from the alms than they really needed. The Quran mentions the tax collectors («those employed to administer the (funds)») among those for whom *zakah* is intended: "Alms are for the poor and the needy, and those employed to administer the (funds): for those whose

---

[49] "Lecture delivered by Dr. Ashraf al-Amawi" (2001), in "*Ekonomicheskoe i finansovoe upravlenie musul'manskimi religioznymi organizatsiiami: realii i perspektivy*", Moscow, P. 76.

[50] *Bobrovnikov, V.O.* (2004). «Islamskiy renessans», in *NG-Religii*, No. 10 (140), 2 June.

hearts have been (recently) reconciled (to Truth); for those in bondage and in debt; in the Cause of Allah; and for the wayfarer, (thus is it) ordained by Allah" (9:60).

Sooner or later the Russian Muslims would inevitably come across the issue of *zakah* since – unlike *waqf* – it is one of the five pillars of Islam. In some regions of Russia, the Islamic clergymen are trying to use other religious taxes, although their original meaning is not always certain in the Shari'ah. In some districts of Tatarstan, imams ask collective farm chairs to donate potatoes for the students of Muslim religious establishments[51]. This should be described as the collection of *sadaqa*, a charitable donation paid once in a while, not *ushr* (tithe) called *gyshar* (gyshyr) in Tatarstan.

Another matter if *zakah* paid by Muslim businessmen in the form of an interest-free loan given to those collective farms or individual farmers under the condition that they should provide the needy with food instead of paying back the principal of the loan – in other words, to provide those who belong to at least one of the eight categories of *zakah* recipients.

The *zakah* culture has been very slow to strike root in Russia because the local Muslims know next to nothing about it. The above example shows that most of the believers do not distinguish between *zakah* and other Islamic charities. So far, the clergy has failed to deal with this ignorance. Several years ago, a Russian anthropologist, Ahmed Yarlykapov, did some books in the North Caucasus. He described this situation: the imam of a mosque in Maykop (capital of the Republic of Adygea, Russia) set up two boxes – one for *zakah*, the other for *sadaqa* – only to remove them after a while because the believers could not distinguish between them[52].

However, confusion of *zakah* and *sadaqa* is half the trouble. In Moscow, regular payments of Muslims that cover administrative expenses of local communities are often called *zakah*. It is obvious that the leaders of those communities deliberately seek to sacralise the membership dues collected for the community's needs and attach a 'special' status to them. From the author's point of view, such tricks are rather improper. The believers see that the money paid as '*zakah*' does not go to those categories that were indicated in the Quran, and consequently they lose trust in *zakah* as an institution that contributes to effective redistribution of wealth in society for the benefit of its needy members.

Abuses are inevitable while redistributing the part of the purifying tax that is supposed to go to the collectors of *zakah*. Often their share goes up to 30 per cent of the redistributed *zakah*.

In recent years in Russia, paying such Muslim tax as *zakah al-fitr* has been observed. Some Muslim peoples of Russia, for example, Adygs and Kabardin, distribute *zakah al-fitr* even before the end of fasting. At the same time, paying *zakah al-fitr* is regulated not only by

[51] *Zalialetdinov, M.* (2004). «*Razvitie sistemy waqufov v Rossii*», in "Islamskie finansovye otnoshenia i perspektivy ikh osushchestvlenia v rossiyskom musul'manskom soobshchestve", P. 69.
[52] Yarlykapov, A.A. (2004). «*Religioznoe povedenie*», in "Islam i pravo v Rossii", Issue 3, Moscow, P. 58.

Shari'ah, but by local customs as well. Yarlykapov described a case, when one of the women in *aul* (village) Hatukai in Adygeya while calculating *zakah al-fitr* included not just her children among those for whom she should pay the tax, but her cows as well, saying that they are also living creatures and she should pay alms for them too. In another *aul* in the region, Koshehabl, *zakah al-fitr* was distributed mostly among relatives and close friends of the payer[53].

Unfortunately, it is the local superstitions and prejudices rather than conscious necessity to follow one of the five pillars of Islam that form the basis of paying irregular alms by many Muslims in Russia. For example, in the North Caucasus they pay *sadaqa* for deceased relatives if the payer saw them in dreams.

Given that there is no centralised *zakah* system in Russia, some regional Muslim religious administration assumed the function of collection and distribution of the purifying tax. At the same time, in most mosques the clergy and believers continue to confuse *sadaqa* and *zakah*.

The Republic of Karelia probably has the most positive record of collection and distribution of *zakah* in today's Russia with direct participation of the local Muslim religious authorities. There, the collection and distribution of *zakah* is the responsibility of the regional Muslim religious board, which has communities in major cities of Karelia.

The success of the Karelian community in collecting and distributing *zakah* is largely explained by its small population. The community members know each other as well as those who can pay *zakah* and those who are in need. Consequently, the Muslim Religious Board of Karelia fulfills a rather technical task of collecting and distributing the purifying tax. It is also important that the mufti of Karelia, Wisam Ali Bardwil, places emphasis on the necessity to pay *zakah* in his sermons, publications and public speeches.

As to official Muslim organisations on a federal level, the majority of Muslims believe that their capacity to collect and distribute *zakah* is much less than of Muslim boards on a regional level. One of the most transparent systems for the collection and distribution of *zakah* was created in Tatarstan. Briefly, it looks as follows. Information on the allocation of funds collected as *zakah* is published on the website of the *Zakah* Committee of the DUM RT. However, here still there is an issue with unaccounted money which was collected via boxes located in public places such as department stores. The lack of knowledge of the concept of *zakah* among Russian imams also does not strengthen the confidence of Muslims to this purificatory alms.

Today, it is too early to talk about establishment of a centralised all-Russia *zakah* collection and distribution system under the aegis of the Russian Mufti Council or some other

[53] Yarlykapov A.A. (2006). *"Narodny islam i musul'manskaya molodezh' Central'nogo i Severo-Zapadnogo Kavkaza"*, in 'Etnographicheskoe obozrenie'. No. 2.

Muslim co-ordination structures given the absence of a Muslim religious board that would be common for all Muslims. The first step on this path should be improvement of the database of those who receive the purifying tax.

Given the imperfect system of *zakah* collection and distribution under the aegis of the Muslim religious boards in Russia, it is often misinterpreted by both officials collecting *zakah* and *zakah* payers. For example, instead of paying *zakah* to a dedicated fund or *zakah* officials, some payers tend to give money (including in the form of non-interest loans) to small and medium-size enterprises (SMEs), usually to those that are owned or run by businessmen originating from the same ethnic community.

To collect and distribute *zakah* in Russia it is not necessary to amend the legislation. Yet it is necessary to provide tax remissions for regular payers of *zakah*. Otherwise, *zakah* is bound to be irregular charity payments – in other words, it will merge with *sadaqa*. However, there is nothing wrong in the development of an Islamic charity based on *sadaqa*. The main condition here is the same as in the case of *zakah*: the payers should be provided with a transparent system of collecting and distributing of their money. *Sadaqa* has several advantages over zakah in Russia; one being that it does not need intermediaries in the form of bodies responsible for the collection and distribution of collected funds. The only thing needed is technical support to ensure that those who lack the funds and those who can grant them, find each other. A good example is the Islamic charitable project named Sadaka.ru. The purpose of this project, according to its website, is to unite Muslims to help brothers and sisters in faith who are in difficult life situations. There is a special form on the website, which anyone in need of financial assistance can fill out. Those who want to help can directly contact the needy through the information displayed on the site. The website organisers themselves do not accept any funds to their accounts.

The disadvantages of such projects should include the fact that not all those in need have access to the Internet, and that in such a situation the deception by the applicant in the section 'need help' is quite possible. So far, these projects have been effective in large cities with high levels of Internet users and with large numbers of wealthy Muslims. Despite this, there is hope that the future of Islamic charity is for projects such as Sadaka.ru, which enables benefactors and those in need to find each other directly, without any difficulties. It is possible that such innovation will be popular among payers of *zakah*, who do not trust the existing structures responsible for the collection and distribution of *zakah*; fortunately, there is a technical opportunity to calculate purification tax using online *zakah*-calculators.

As to compact Muslim communities in small towns and rural areas, the most effective form of Islamic charity remains traditional *sadaqa* – and sometimes *zakah*. The effectiveness of collection and distribution of the latter will be directly dependent on the competence of the local spiritual leaders of the Muslim community in the issue of *zakah*, as well as their honesty in such matters.

However, an independent entity in the form of a *zakah*-foundation is not the solution. Such independent foundations, not under the wing of the official Muslim structures, will attract increased attention from security services. By way of example, in 2009 a fund called "Solidarity" was set up and in five years became the leading *zakah* collection fund in terms amount of *zakah* collected (from 2009 to 2013 it managed to collect 39 million rubles as *zakah*). The founders of the fund explain this success by the fact that they try to be as much as possible transparent in bother *zakah* collection and allocation.

"Halal" UIF

In January 2008, BCS Management Company launched "*Halal*" unit investment fund ("*Halal*" UIF). The fund includes shares of the companies which activity does not contradict Shariah.

As of 15 January 2008, the cost of net assets of the UIF reached 10.9 million rubles. It is worth noting that "*Halal*" UIF was launched not at the most appropriate time. The beginning of 2008 was marked by the fall of stock exchange indexes. Private investors rushed to the asset managing companies to buy investment fund units hoping to receive high profits when they would grow in value. However, in the spring of 2008 it became already clear that the stock market entered into period of volatility during which a private investor can hardly hope to profit from investment. The fall of the stock markets in the end of summer of that year made investments into unit investment funds highly loss making.

However, even during the first half of 2008 when the quotations of "*Halal*" UIF were supposed to be growing along with the stock market there was not much interest in it, even in Tatarstan despite a heavy advertising campaign there.

During the next six years, quotations of "*Halal*" UIF were volatile along with the Russian stock market generally. Deepening of the crisis on the stock market did not contribute to the success of "*Halal*" UIF. In September 2014, BCS announced about liquidation of the fund.

Conclusion

What conclusions can we draw from this short Russian experience in the field of Islamic finance? One can think that this experience is negative. However, we do not share this view. If we take England for example, the first attempts to start Islamic financial business there in the 1980s, also failed. However, the lessons were learnt, and the next attempts appeared to be successful (Islamic Bank of Britain and others). We hope that this experience will be the basis for the next projects in this field. We think that businessmen, starting the new projects, will take into account the mistakes, made by their less successful colleagues, and eventually will succeed.

To someone the contents of this chapter may seem too pessimistic. This impression is not entirely correct. Despite the fact that Islamic finance is often positioned as an alternative to conventional financial system, Islamic finance and Muslims do not live on a separate planet. They are a part of the society in which they live no matter whether it is a Muslim or a non-Muslim country. Accordingly, the situation with the ethics of business existing in a given country cannot help influencing Islamic finance. Russia is still in the stage of transition from wild capitalism with all the ensuing consequences. Therefore, there is nothing surprising in the fact that the outcome of Islamic finance projects in Russia is a reflection of the principles and concepts prevailing in the society. Where in the absence of the national idea the idea of enrichment has become the main ideal.

As for the future, we expect that new Islamic financial institutions will continue to appear, but their market share is so small to seriously talk about their impact on the financial system of the country and Russian *ummah*.

References

Bigeev, M (1916), *Zakah*. Petrograd. The facsimile of this book and its translation into Russian were published by T.H. Habibullin and I.A. Zaripov: *Bigeev, M.* (2013). *Zakah*. Nabereznye Chelny.

Islamic finance projects in Russia (2011), Ed. M. Kalimullina. Moscow. pp. 28. Nizameev, R. (2014). Islamic Finance: Too Expensive? retrieved at: www.islamnews.ru/news-146531.html

Kashapov, R. (2002), "For Muslim pilgrims", in *Time and money*, № 179 (24735); "Insurance according to the Quran", (2005), in *Insurance case*, No. 1, pp. 8

Gataullin, R. (2004), "On the possibility of creating a free economic zone of 'Halal' standard", in *Islamic financial relations and prospects for their implementation in the Russian Muslim community*, Moscow: Moscow Islamic University. pp. 31.

Islamic financial and credit institutions in foreign countries' economies. (2011). Ed. V.G. Timiryasov. Kazan, pp. 166-167.

Fukina, S.P. (2014), "Specifics of Islamic insurance and prospects for its introduction into the insurance market in Russia", in *Vestnik of Astrakhan Government Technical University of Economics*, No.1, Pp. 113-114.

Grishina T., Kiseleva E. (2009). "Insurance learns the ropes of Shariah", in *Kommersant* (Kazan), No. 209 (4264), 10 November. retrieved at: <URL: http://www.kommersant.ru/doc/1272108>

Salikhov, R. (2005), "*Kak vozrodit blagotvoritel'nost?*", in *Tatarskiy mir*, No. 1 (54), February 2005. pp. 3.

Waqf, (2004), in "Islam na evropeyskom Vostoke: Entsiklopedicheskiy slovar", Ed. by R.A. Nabiev, Kazan, pp. 49.

Kemper, M. (2004). "Musul'manskaia etika i 'dukh kapitalizma" in *Islamskie finansy v sovremennom mire: ekonomicheskie i pravovye aspekty*, pp. 41.

Ashraf al-Amawi" (2001), in *"Ekonomicheskoe i finansovoe upravlenie musul'manskimi religioznymi organizatsiiami: realii i perspektivy"*, Moscow, pp. 76.

Bobrovnikov, V.O. (2004). "Islamskiy renessans", in *NG-Religii*, No. 10 (140), 2 June.

Zalialetdinov, M. (2004). «*Razvitie sistemy waqufov v Rossii*», in "Islamskie finansovye otnoshenia i perspektivy ikh osushchestvlenia v rossiyskom musul'manskom soobshchestve", pp. 69.

Yarlykapov, A.A. (2004), *"Religioznoe povedenie"*, in "Islam i pravo v Rossii", Issue 3, Moscow, pp. 58.

Yarlykapov A.A. (2006), *"Narodny islam i musul'manskaya molodezh' Central'nogo i Severo-Zapadnogo Kavkaza"*, in 'Etnographicheskoe obozrenie'. No. 2.

Chapter 14

Current State and Future Prospects of Islamic Banking in Morocco: An Empirical Investigation

Hassanuddeen Abd. Aziz & Abdelghani Echchabi
Effat University

Abdullah Mohammed Ayedh & Osman Sayid Hassan Musse
Universiti Sains Islam Malaysia

Dhekra Azouzi
El-Manar University

Chaabane Oussama Houssem Eddine
International Islamic University Malaysia

Introduction

Islamic banking refers to "banking in consonance with the ethos and value system of Islam and governed, in addition to the conventional good governance and risk management rules, by the principles laid down by Islamic law (*shari'ah*). Interest free banking is a narrow concept denoting a number of banking instruments or operations, which avoid interest. Islamic banking, the more general term is expected not only to avoid interest-based transactions, prohibited in *shari'ah*, but also to avoid unethical practices and participate actively in achieving the goals and objectives of an Islamic economy" (Said, Ahmad and Javaid, 2009).

The industry has witnessed a tremendous growth since the early attempt by Ahmad El-Naggar to launch the first Islamic bank in Mit Ghamr in Egypt in 1963. Currently the Islamic banking assets are estimated at over USD1.7 trillion, with an average annual growth rate of 17.6 per cent. The number of Islamic banks customers is currently estimated at 38 million globally[54]. Islamic banking is currently been practiced in more than 75 countries. The Islamic banking and finance industry are becoming an important component in the economic and social development of these countries, but particularly in the MENA region, whereby it is considered an adequate substitute that caters the financial needs of the people without conflicting with their social and religious values (Ali, 2012).

---

[54] **World Islamic Banking Competitiveness Report 2013-2014**

This argument has been supported by empirical studies across countries. For instance, Echchabi, Olorogun and Azouzi (2014) examined the prospects of Islamic insurance services in Tunisia in light of the Jasmine revolution, and they found that that the Tunisian customers are willing to switch to Islamic insurance services, mainly due to their compatibility to their social and religious values as well as to their financial needs and past experiences. Furthermore, many studies revealed the importance of the religious factor in opting for Islamic banking services in the region (Metawa and Al-Mosawi, 1998; Erol and ElBdour, 1989; Naser, Jamal and El-Khatib, 1999; Bley and Kuehn, 2004).

In the specific case of Morocco, Islamic banking has been in practice since 2007. However, it has been progressing at a slow pace over the past few years, mainly due to political and regulatory issues. This situation started to slightly change after the Moroccan Party of Justice and Development (PJD) won the 2011 elections, whereby, many regulatory issues were eased and much effort has been deployed to solve the remaining legal problems. This becomes crucial at this juncture, since the country inspires to become a regional Islamic banking and finance hub.

In line with the above argument, the objective of this study is two-fold, firstly to scrutinise the history and current practice of Islamic banking in Morocco, and secondly to examine the perception of the Moroccan customers about Islamic banking products, and the factors that influence their patronisation behaviour. It is noteworthy that empirical studies on Islamic banking in Morocco are still scarce. One of the few studies in this context is Echchabi and Aziz (2012a) where emphasis was on the religious dimension and its impact on the selection of Islamic banking products. The results revealed that religiosity is a significant factor in customers' selection and adoption of Islamic banking services, furthermore, the findings showed that the Moroccan customers are generally willing to adopt Islamic banking services. This study has focused only on the religious aspect, while other potential factors were marginalised.

On the other hand, the study by Echchabi and Aziz (2012b) was more comprehensive in terms of theoretical framework as it was based on the decomposed theory of planned behaviour (DTPB). The findings revealed that uncertainty, relative advantage, compatibility, awareness and social influence have significant impact on the adoption of Islamic banking services. Nevertheless, this study focused on a relatively smaller sample size i.e. 200 respondents. Hence, further studies with larger sample size are required. On this basis, and in line with the theory of innovation diffusion (Rogers, 2003), the following model is established to achieve the aforementioned objective.

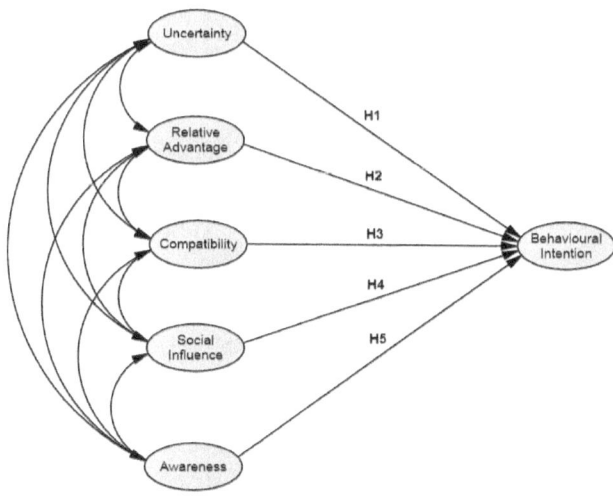

Figure 1:
Theoretical Model

Uncertainty refers to "the degree to which a number of alternatives are perceived with respect to the occurrence of an event and the corresponding probabilities of these events" (Thambiah, Ismail, Ahmed and Khin, 2013; Rogers, 2003). Uncertainty is measured in this study by reference to the Islamic banking services aspect related to the profits and losses uncertainties and the ambiguity in calculating various fees, dividend payments, etc.

Relative advantage is defined as "the degree to which an innovation is perceived as being better than the idea it supersedes" (Thambiah et al., 2013; Rogers, 2003). In this study, relative advantage is measured in terms of economic benefit, efficiency in service providing, knowledge and timeliness of the banks' staff, and social prestige.

Compatibility refers to "the degree to which an innovation is perceived as being coherent with the current values, past experiences, and the needs of potential adopters" (Thambiah et al., 2013; Rogers, 2003). Compatibility in this study is measured by the compatibility of the banking services to the social and religious values, lifestyle, financial needs, and the previous banking services used.

Social influence is defined by Sayid, Echchabi and Aziz (2012) as the degree to which the individuals' decision is influenced by his/her environment. It generally refers to a number of referent groups such as family, work colleagues, media, etc.

Awareness refers to the extent to which the individual is aware of the existence of the innovation (product or service) and at the same time the extent of his/her knowledge of its preliminary features. The combination of these two dimensions is necessary in the study of

Islamic banking in Morocco due to the restricted commercialisation and marketing approach authorised by the government.

Based on the model in Figure 1, uncertainty is assumed to have a negative influence on the behavioural intention, while relative advantage, compatibility, social influence and awareness have positive influence on the behavioural intention. In line with the above model, the following hypotheses are posited and are tested in the following sections:

H1: Uncertainty has a negative influence on the usage of Islamic banking services in Morocco.

H2: Relative advantage has a positive influence on the usage of Islamic banking services in Morocco.

H3: Compatibility has a positive influence on the usage of Islamic banking services in Morocco.

H4: Social influence has a positive influence on the usage of Islamic banking services in Morocco.

H5: Awareness has a positive influence on the usage of Islamic banking services in Morocco.

Islamic banking in Morocco

Islamic banking in Morocco is a result of repetitive trials and persistent efforts by many parties, including potential customers, finance and economic associations, financial institutions, political parties, etc. These attempts started since mid-1980s; however, the first concrete and significant step toward the introduction of Islamic banking in Morocco was in 2007, by issuing recommendation number 33/G/2007 (applicable since October 1st, 2007) approving the commercialisation of three main Islamic banking instruments, namely, *murabahah*, *musharakah and ijarah*, while *salam* and *istisnaa* are still in the process of study by Bank Al Maghrib (BAM thereafter). These products are assumed to be marketed only by certified financial institutions, and through specialised subsidiaries. It is noteworthy that the terms definition, standards and other features of these instruments were established in collaboration with GPBM (Professional Group of the Moroccan Banks) and by referring to the AAOIFI (Accounting and Auditing Organization for Islamic Financial Institutions) standards.

In this regard, *Ijarah* is defined by BAM as "any contract, under which a financial institution shall put a movable or immovable determined, identified and owned asset in the disposition of a customer on rental basis for a purpose authorized by law". According to BAM, *Ijarah* cannot be used for intangible assets as well as rights of natural resources exploitation. In this context, *ijarah* as stipulated by BAM include both operating *ijarah* as well as *ijarah wa iqtinaa*.

On the other hand, *musharakah* is defined by BAM as "any contract for the acquisition of holdings by a financial institution in the capital of an existing company or a company in the process of creation, in order to make a profit". This includes both fixed (standard) *musharakah* and *musharakah mutanaqisah* (diminishing partnership). The loss sharing ratio is based on the capital contribution of each party, while the profit-sharing ratio is agreed upon by the *musharakah* parties (partners).

Finally, *murabahah* refers to "any contract whereby a financial institution acquires a movable or immovable asset, at the request of a client, to sell it to him at a cost plus an agreed fee in advance". It is worth noting that the payment by the client can be made either in one or multiple annuities depending on the agreement with the bank.

Currently, there are four main banks offering these services, namely, AttijariWafa Bank, Banque Populaire, BMCE, and BMCI (Cherkaoui, 2014). These banks have merely offered financing services based on *Murabahah*, while *ijarah* has been less prioritised, and none has offered services based on *musharakah*. Nevertheless, the group AttijariWafa Bank took a step forward by creating a subsidiary specialised in Islamic banking services, by the name Dar Assafaa in 2010. It is noteworthy that the BAM resolution does not allow the usage of any religious associations (e.g. Islamic, *shari'ah*, etc.) in the commercialisation and marketing of these services. Hence, presently, Dar Assafaa is said to be specialised in "alternative financial services".

Dar Assafaa offers four main alternative financial services, based on *murabahah*, namely, Safaa Immo for housing financing, Safaa Auto for vehicle financing, Safaa Conso for the purchase of various products and services, and Safaa Tajhiz for home equipment and furniture. Dae Assafaa is operating in eight cities i.e. Agadir, Casablanca, Fes, Marrakech, Meknes, Oujda, Rabat and Tangier.

Though Islamic banking has been authorised and been operating in Morocco since 2007, it is considered as operating under-potential as it failed to attract the Moroccan customers, that are obviously majority Muslims. This might be due to several reasons. Firstly, the relatively higher price of those services and the over-taxation (double taxation), which the government still attempts to solve. Secondly, the restrictions by BAM prohibiting the use of any religious associations to this product, and also not disallowing the *shari'ah* scholars to be involved in the process of verifying and confirming the conformity of these products to *shari'ah* rules. This may have made the Moroccan customers unable to appreciate the difference between these alternative services and the conventional banking services. Thirdly, the absence of specialised training programs for banks' personnel, especially the banks offering these services, resulting in their inability to efficiently promote these services to the customers. Lastly is the slowness and complexity of the commercial codes and laws establishment or reform. This is caused by the slowness of the system itself, as well as the in-depth involvement of the dominating financial institutions and business players and their influence in the decision-making process. It is needless to mention that the regulatory framework of Islamic banking practice and related legal aspects are necessary for the development of the industry in any context. Thus, the authorities are highly required to take a step forward to develop the regulatory process of the Islamic banking practice in the country.

However, since the Moroccan Party of Justice and Development (PJD) won the 2011 election, many measures (e.g. banking operations, securitisation, Islamic insurance, etc.) have been scrutinised to ensure a better progress of the Islamic banking industry in Morocco (Cherkaoui, 2014) using a pragmatic approach coherent with the sociocultural context of the country and the international experiences. It is expected that in the next few years, a number of local and foreign banks will be granted the authorisation to operate as full-fledged Islamic banks, especially at this stage where the country inspires to become a regional hub for Islamic banking.

In the Study

The study focuses on the Moroccan context. The target sample size was 400 respondents from most of the Moroccan regions. Out of the distributed questionnaires only 348 were properly and completely filled up and returned. Thus, a response rate of over 87 per cent was achieved, which is an acceptable rate (Dusuki and Abdullah, 2007).

The survey questionnaire was designed to collect information about the perception of the customers towards the attributes of the Islamic banking services as well as their intention to adopt them in their future transactions. For measuring this information, Likert type scaling was used (1 = Strongly Disagree and 7 = Strongly Agree). 34 items were listed in this section and most of them were derived from the previous cross-country studies (Thambiah et al., 2013; Sayid, Echchabi and Aziz, 2012; Echchabi, Olorogun and Azouzi, 2014; Sarea and Hanefah, 2013), as well as from current Islamic banking and finance literature with necessary adaptations made for the specific context of the study. The second section of the questionnaire explored information about respondents' profile, i.e. gender, age, marital status, employment status, etc. The questionnaire was initially prepared in English and was subsequently translated into French and distributed as such. The corresponding pilot test was also conducted prior to the final data collection.

The data were subsequently analysed using linear regression. The choice of this technique was inspired by Hair, Black, Babin and Anderson (2010) as well as from similar studies conducted in this area. It is worth mentioning that the analysis was done through SPSS 18.

The respondents' profile shows that about 69 per cent of the respondents are male while 31 per cent of them are female. Furthermore, about 44 per cent of the respondents are between 31 and 40 years old, 28 per cent are between 20 and 30 years old, 16 per cent are between 41 and 50 years old, and 12 per cent are above 50 years old. In addition, about 43 per cent of the respondents are holding Bachelor's degree, 37 per cent are holding a

Certificate/Diploma, and 20 per cent are holding Master's degree. Similarly, 55 per cent of the respondents are holding positions in the private sector, 20 per cent are students, 15 per cent are holding positions with the public sector and about 10 per cent are self-employed.

Results

Reliability

Prior to the hypotheses' testing, it is important to address the reliability of the constructs. There are usually multiple measures of reliability used in the previous studies. However, the most common measure is the Cronbach Alpha. The value of the latter should be at least 0.6 to be acceptable (Juul, Van Rensburg and Steyn, 2012; Yee, San and Khoon, 2011; Nordin, Abu Talib, Yaacob and Sabran, 2010). The reliability values in Table 1 are largely above 0.6. Hence, the survey constructs are reliable and further analyses can be conducted.

Table 1: Reliability Measures

Constructs	Cronbach Alpha
Uncertainty	.866
Relative advantage	.764
Compatibility	.784
Social influence	.903
Awareness	.828
Behavioural intention	.689

Linear Regression

The linear regression results in Table 2 indicate that uncertainty does not have a significant influence on the intention to adopt Islamic banking services in Morocco. Hence, hypothesis 1 is rejected. This contradicts the findings of Echchabi and Aziz (2012b). This could be mainly due to the unawareness and/or misconception about Islamic banking services and which is caused mainly by the restrictions applied by the government regarding the marketing of the Islamic banking services in Morocco since their introduction.

On the other hand, relative advantage has a significant positive influence on the intention to adopt Islamic banking services in Morocco. Hence, hypothesis 2 is supported. This is in line with the findings of Echchabi and Aziz (2012b). The relative advantage of Islamic banks is perceived and measured via the economic benefit, banks' staff knowledge and efficiency in providing services, and the social prestige offered by these services. Thus, these dimensions have to be emphasised by the financial institutions offering Islamic financial services.

Similarly, compatibility has a significant positive influence on the intention to adopt Islamic banking services in Morocco. Hence, hypothesis 3 is supported. This is in line with the findings of Echchabi and Aziz (2012b). Thus, much emphasis on the marketing and management strategies should be on the social and religious values, the specific financial needs of the customers and their past experience in terms of banking services, and the traditional aspects of the Moroccan culture.

In addition, social influence was found to have positive significant influence on the intention to adopt Islamic banking services in Morocco. Hence, hypothesis 4 is supported. This is in line with the findings of Echchabi and Aziz (2012b). In this regard, the institutions offering Islamic banking services in Morocco should be using group/collective marketing, focusing on spouse, parents, peers, siblings and media influence.

Finally, awareness was found to have no significant effect on the intention to adopt Islamic banking services. Hence, hypothesis 5 is rejected. This contradicts the findings of Echchabi and Aziz (2012b). This might be mainly due to the restrictions applied by the government authorities, and which does not permit the market players to provide full information about these services to the Moroccan customers and the international investors.

Table 2: Multiple Regression Output

Model	Unstandardized Coefficients		Standardized Coefficients	t	Sig.
	B	Std. Error	Beta		
(Constant)	1.650	.368		4.480	.000
Uncertainty	-.029	.058	-.026	-.501	.617
Relative Advantage	.148	.072	.142	2.052	.041
Compatibility	.404	.069	.409	5.861	.000
Social influence	.116	.046	.150	2.539	.012
Awareness	.077	.045	.092	1.693	.092

Discussions and conclusion

The main purpose of the chapter was to review the current state of Islamic banking practice and current issues in Morocco, and to examine the factors that influence the Moroccan customers to adopt Islamic banking services. The results indicate that the relative advantage, compatibility, and social influence are the main factors that influence the adoption of Islamic banking services in Morocco. Furthermore, it is revealed that the government ambitions to become a regional Islamic banking and finance hub is faced by legal and regulatory issues that are still persistent after six years of implementation.

These findings have significant implications for the theory, for the policy makers and regulators as well as for the practitioners. Particularly, the chapter is an extension of the theory of innovations diffusion to a different setting and to a different area that has been under-studied empirically. Hence the chapter proves the applicability of this theory in this new context. Similarly, the current chapter provides insights to the practitioners and policymakers on the important dimensions to be emphasised to promote the Islamic banking industry in Morocco and similar countries. Particularly, much emphasis should be on the relative advantage of Islamic banking compared to the conventional banking system. Similarly, emphasis should be on the compatibility of the Islamic banking services with the religious and cultural values, as well as compatibility with the past banking instruments used by the customers. Moreover, the marketing strategy of the banks should focus on group strategies, focusing on parents influence, peers and siblings, as well as social and classic media.

On the other hand, the policy makers and regulators are highly required to promote Islamic banking services in Morocco through various means. Firstly, they are required to permit *shari'ah* scholars and *shari'ah* supervisory boards to be involved in the process of certification and compliance aspects. Secondly, they are required to permit the Islamic banks to operate independently, without an association to the long existing conventional banks, in order for the potential customers to appreciate the distinct features of Islamic banking and its superiority to the conventional banking system especially in terms of religious compliance. Thirdly, the corresponding authorities are required to efficiently establish a number of regulatory and fiscal policies and regulations to ensure competitiveness and smoothness of the Islamic banking system in a potential dual banking system, eventually dominated by the long existing conventional banking system.

The current chapter has a number of limitations that should be taken into account in the future studies in this area. The current study as well as the past studies have analysed the Moroccan context of Islamic banking merely from the customers perspective. In this regard, a clearer view of the Islamic banking industry in Morocco should be studied, by examining the position of BAM, local and foreign banks, *shari'ah* scholars, etc. on the aforementioned issues. Furthermore, the future studies are also recommended to extend these findings to other contexts and preferably using other models as well, and applying mixed methods.

References

Ali, S.S. (2012), *Islamic banking in the MENA region*, Islamic Research and Training Institute, Jeddah, Saudi Arabia.

Bley, J. and Kuehn, K. (2004), "Conventional versus Islamic finance: Student knowledge and perception in the United Arab Emirates", *International Journal of Islamic Financial Services,* Vol. 5 No. 4, pp. 1-13.

Cherkaoui, A. (2014), "L'expérience marocaine en matière de la commercialisation des produits bancaires alternatifs", *Seminar on Islamic Banking: Between the Current Challenges and Future Prospects* (pp. 813-839), Islamic International Foundation for Economics and Finance, Fes.

Dusuki, A. W. and Abdullah, N. I. (2007), "Why do Malaysian customers patronise Islamic banks?", *International Journal of Bank Marketing,* Vol. 25 No. 3, pp. 142-160.

Echchabi, A. and Abd. Aziz, H. (2012b), "Empirical investigation of customers' perception and adoption towards Islamic banking services in Morocco", *Middle-East Journal of Scientific Research,* Vol. 12 No. 6, pp. 849-858.

Echchabi, A. and Aziz, H. A. (2012a), "The relationship between religiosity and customers' adoption of Islamic banking services in Morocco", *International Journal of Contemporary Business Studies,* Vol. 3 No. 5, pp. 25-31.

Echchabi, A., Olorogun, L. A. and Azouzi, D. (2014), "Islamic insurance prospects in Tunisia in the wake of the Jasmine revolution: A survey from customers' perspective", *Journal of Islamic Accounting and Business Research,* Vol. 5 No. 1, pp. 15-28.

Erol, C. and El-Bdour, R. (1989), "Attitude, behaviour and patronage factors of bank customers towards Islamic banks", *International Journal of Bank Marketing,* Vol. 7 No. 6, pp. 31-37.

Hair, J. F., Black, W. C., Babin, B. J. and Anderson, R. E. (2010), *Multivariate Data Analysis (7th Edition),* Prentice Hall, Upper Saddle River.

Juul, L., Van Rensburg, J. and Steyn, P. (2012), "Validation of the King's Health questionnaire for South Africa in English, Afrikaans and IsiXhosa", *South African Journal of Obstetrics and Gynaecology,* Vol. 18 No. 3, pp. 82-84.

Metawa, A. and Al-Mossawi, M. (1998), " Banking behaviour of Islamic bank customers: Perspectives and implications ", *International Journal of Bank Marketing,* Vol. 16 No. 7, pp. 299-313.

Naser, K., Jamal, A. and Al-Khatib, K. (1999), "Islamic banking: A study of customer satisfactionand preferences in Jordan", *International Journal of Bank Marketing, Vol.* 17 No. 3, pp. 135-151.

Nordin, N. M., Abu Talib, M., Yaacob, S. N. and Sabran, M. S. (2010), "A study on selected demographic characteristics and mental health of young adults in public higher learning institutions in Malaysia", *Global Journal of Health Science,* Vol. 2 No. 2, pp. 104-110.

Rogers, E. M. (2003), *Diffusion of Innovations, 5th Edition,* Free Press, New York.

Said, P., Ahmad, I. and Javaid, F. (2009), *Handbook of Islamic banking products and services,* State Bank of Pakistan, Karachi, Pakistan.

Sarea, A. M. and Hanefah, M. M. (2013), "Adoption of AAOIFI accounting standards by Islamic banks of Bahrain", *Journal of Financial Reporting and Accounting,* Vol. 11 No. 2, pp. 131-142.

Sayid, O., Echchabi, A. and Aziz, H. A. (2012), " Investigating mobile money acceptance in Somalia: An empirical study ", *Pakistan Journal of Commerce and Social Sciences,* Vol. 6 No. 2, pp. 269-281.

Thambiah, S., Ismail, H., Ahmed, E. M. and Khin, A. A. (2013), " Islamic retail banking adoption in Malaysia: The moderating effect of religion and region", *The International Journal of Applied Economics and Finance*, Vol. 7 No. 1, pp. 37-48.

Yee, C. J., San, N. C. and Khoon, C. H. (2011), "Consumers' perceived quality, perceived value and perceived risk towards purchase decision on automobile", *American Journal of Economics and Business Administration*, Vol. 3 No. 1, pp. 47-57.

Chapter 15

An Exploratory Study of the Economic Viability of and Opportunities for Islamic Banking in Nigeria

Ahmad Bello Dogarawa, PhD

Department of Accounting, Ahmadu Bello University, Zaria, Nigeria

Introduction

Islamic banking is becoming systemically important in some countries and in many others, too big to be ignored. Within a span of less than five decades from its inception in a modern form in 1963, Islamic banking has increasingly become an integral part of the global financial system that is catering for the specific need of not only the Muslim community but also non-Muslims who want to pursue their economic activities devoid of interest. Since from the late 1990s, Islamic banking has been gaining international recognition as a viable and competitive form of financial intermediation that offers a wide range of financial products and services not only in Muslim countries but also in the secular world.

The unmatched support Islamic banking has been enjoying from International Monetary Fund (IMF) and World Bank since the late 1980s through early 1990s has continued to position the hitherto infant industry more strategically and competitively in global financial system. Today, Islamic banking industry is being represented by over 250 Islamic financial institutions that operate in about 75 countries of the world that include Bahrain, Sudan, Egypt, UAE, Saudi Arabia, Malaysia, Brunei and Pakistan, USA, UK, Canada, Switzerland, South Africa and Australia, and with international banks such as Standard Chartered; Citibank; HSBC; ABN Amro; UBS; American Express; BNP Paribas; Bank of America; Commerzbank; Barclays; Deutche Bank; ANZ Grindlays; Golman Schs; Royal Bank of Canada; Pictet & Cie; Flemings; Merrill Lynch and Kleinwort Benson taking the lead in provision diversified interest-free financial products (Ahmad, 2004).

In view of the potential economic viability of Islamic banking and the prospects of it serving as an alternative source and use of finance for tens of millions of financially excluded Muslim and non-Muslim Nigerians, Central Bank of Nigeria (CBN) released a revised framework for the regulation and supervision of Non-Interest Financial Institutions (NIFIs) in June 2011 after four decades of unsuccessful effort to establish Islamic banks in Nigeria by largely Muslims who constitute about 55% of the over 150 million population. One of the matters arising from the release of the framework is whether Islamic banking is of any relevance to the Nigerian economy and whether or not its economic potentials and opportunities, if any, justify the effort of introducing it over the years.

This chapter explores the economic viability of and opportunities for Islamic banking in Nigeria. The chapter is both descriptive and exploratory with presentation based on review of theoretical and empirical literature. The chapter is justified in view of the fact that it will contribute to placing policy makers in particular and other stakeholders in general on a sound footing to appreciate the economic potentials and viability of Islamic banking and the opportunities it portends in the Nigeria's banking environment. The chapter will also add to the pool of available literature on the subject matter.

Conceptual Issues in Islamic Banking

CBN (2011:1) on the one hand defines Islamic banking as "a system of banking whereby banks or other financial institutions transact banking business, engage in trading, investment and commercial activities as well as provide financial products and services in accordance with *Shari'ah* principles and rules of Islamic commercial jurisprudence. The General Secretariat of the Organisation of Islamic Conference (OIC) on the other hand, defined an Islamic bank as "a financial institution whose status, rules and procedures expressly state its commitment to the principle of Islamic *Shari'ah* and to the banning of the receipt and payment of interest on any of its operations" (Hassan, 1999:60). An Islamic bank is therefore a financial intermediary and trustee of other people's money like any conventional bank with the possible difference that the payoff to all its depositors is a share in profit and loss in one form or the other and its operations are conducted based on the principles of Islamic *Shari'ah* (Dar and Presley, 2000; Ahmad, 2008).

IB is based on some unique principles that distinguish it from conventional banking. The principles derive from the axiom of justice and are in harmony with the reality and nature of human beings. The system, which is founded strictly based on the principles of *Shari'ah*, absolutely prohibits receipt or payment of any predetermined, guaranteed rate of return thereby closing the gate to the concepts of interest and usury in all financial dealings (Dogarawa, 2011a). It also rules out the use of debt-based instruments and reprehends speculative behaviour in business. It further promotes risk-sharing, encourages entrepreneurship and insists on the sanctity of contracts (Iqbal, 1997).

Prohibition of interest and usury, known as *riba* in Islamic terminology Is the main demarcating line between Islamic and conventional banking systems in addition to the fact that the latter is based on mundane and manmade laws while the former is based on divine guidance. Iqbal, Askari and Mirakhor (2009) posit that the prohibition is based on arguments of social justice, equality, and property rights. They argue that social justice demands that borrowers and lenders share equitably rewards as well as losses accruable from use of funds

271

and that the process of wealth accumulation and distribution in the economy be fair and representative of true productivity.

Under the Shari'ah-compliant system therefore, it is forbidden to charge, pay or receive interest. Jain (1929) cited in Visser & Mcintosh (1998) traces back the practice of interest to approximately 4000 years and throughout its succeeding history, it has been variously condemned and prohibited by religious institutions that include Judaism, Christianity and Islam on the one hand and on the other hand, Western philosophers such as Plato, Aristotle, Catos, Cicero, Seneca and Plutarch, and ancient politicians and modern socio-economic reformers mainly on moral, ethical, religious and legal grounds (Birnie, 1958 cited in Visser & Mcintosh, 1998).

Criticism of interest in Judaism is found in many biblical references that include Exodus 22:24-25; Leviticus 25:36-38; Deuteronomy 23:19-21; Ezekiel 18:8, 13:7, 22:12; Proverbs 28:8; Psalms 15:5; and Nehemiah 5:7. Chapra (2004) adds that one of the various *talmudic* extensions of these biblical references even compares money-lender to a murderer who the *Mishnah* disqualifies from giving evidence in a court of law. In Christianity, provisions of the Old Testament with regards interest were sustained and a New Testament reference, Luke 6:35, was added to reemphasise the prohibition. In Islam, the provision of Qur'an, 2:279 declares that those who take interest are at war with the Almighty Allah and His Prophet (peace and blessing of Allah be upon him). Other Qur'anic references on the prohibition of interest are 30:39; 4:161; 3:131; and 2:275-278. In addition, Prophet Muhammad (peace and blessing of Allah be upon him) stated that: (i) interest is one of the seven destructive things; (ii) the giver of, the receiver of, the scribe and the witness to interest are cursed; (iii) eating a *dirham* from interest knowingly is worse than committing adultery/fornication 36 times; (iv) interest is of 73 gates the least of which is similar to marrying one's mother (Dogarawa, 2010). Chapra (2004) points out that while the Qur'an and Hadith prohibit interest in an unequivocal term, no distinction was made between interest and usury, and even a small gift is not allowed as a condition for a loan.

Profit-making from speculation/gambling (*mayseer*) activities is not permissible if the intention behind the transaction is not to realise a gain from some productive effort but to rely on a chance or engage in transactions that ensure *ex ante* profits (Hussien, 2010). For example, making an equity investment in a company that engage in an Islamically permissible business activity in order to realise future dividends and capital gains on the investment for instance will be allowed provided the intention is not to make quick profit by speculating the expected share price movement over a very short period of time but based on a careful assessment of the company's past results and future prospects. Under prohibition on speculation, transactions such as Options, Futures, Swaps and forward contracts that insure profit ex ante are not allowed for Islamic banks.

Certainty of key terms is a key requirement for any transaction under the IBF. Transactions involving high level of uncertainty where for example, clear description of the assets being sold, the sale price and the time of delivery of the assets to the purchaser are not know are not permissible in Islam. In the case of leasing, the transaction will not be permissible if the clarity of the leased assets or lease duration or the rent payable under the lease is not determined (Hussien, 2010). Islamic banks are therefore not allowed to engage in contracts in which there is uncertainty about the subject matter, price, or both such as hedging and derivatives. The import of this prohibition is to minimize possibilities of misunderstanding and conflicts between contracting parties (Imam and Kpodar, 2010).

In addition to the above prohibitions, it is essential for Islamic banks to ensure the sanctity of every transaction they are going into. This necessary code of conduct for Islamic banks entails that they deal in only *halal* (legally permissible) activities. Financial institutions under IB mechanism are not allowed to lend to individuals or invest in companies involved in activities considered to have a negative impact on society (for example, gambling, pornography, cinema, etc.) or that are illegal under *Shari'ah* such as financing construction of a plant to make alcoholic beverages or tobacco and pork business (Imam & Kpodar, 2010).

Effort to Establish Islamic Banking in Nigeria

Over the years, efforts have been made by several institutions to provide Islamic financial products and services. The first recorded effort to provide Islamic banking services was made by Muslim Bank West Africa Limited in Lagos around 1961. The effort was however short-lived as the bank was directed to close down in 1962 by the then Minister of Finance (Orisankoko, 2010). The existence of the Muslim Bank has remained a subject of controversy in Nigeria. However, Orisankoko (2010) cited two court cases contained in Ajayi (1999) in both of which Muslim Bank West Africa was mentioned as defendant to prove that the bank really existed and even operated in Lagos between 1961 and 1962. Literature on Islamic banking in Nigeria was almost completely silent about propagation efforts in the 1970s.

In late 1980s, a number of conferences and seminars were organised by University based Islamic centres and various Islamic groups to create awareness among Nigerians particularly Muslims on the evils of interest/usury and the need for adopting interest-free banking on the one hand, and on the other hand, to make the Government see reason why Muslims should be given the opportunity to conduct their financial activities in line with the provisions of *Shari'ah*. The effort yielded positive results. In addition to Reading material in form of textbooks, books of reading, conference proceedings, leaflets and pamphlets arising from the conferences and seminars were made available in both English and some local languages to enlighten people about Islamic banking and its *modus operandi* and why Muslims in particular and Nigerians in general deserve to have it. Having created enough awareness among the people, different groups started calling on government to officially recognise Islamic banking and facilitate its emergence.

The year 1991 appeared to be a new dawn for Islamic banking effort in Nigeria. The then military administration headed by General Ibrahim Badamasi Babangida (retired) issued the Bank and Other Financial Institutions Decree (as amended). The Decree was seen as the first singular effort by the Government of Nigeria to recognise and facilitate the emergence of Islamic banking in Nigeria. Under the heading 'General and Supplementary', section 39(1) of the Decree provides: "except with the written consent of the Governor, no bank shall, as from the commencement of this Decree, be registered or incorporated with a name which includes the words "Central" "Federal," "Federation," "National", "Nigeria", "Reserve", "State", "Christian", "Islamic", "Moslem", "Qur'anic", "Biblical". Further, under the heading 'Display of interest rates', section 23(1) provides:

> Every bank shall display at its offices its lending and deposit interest rates and shall render to the Bank information on such rates as may be specified, from time to time, by the Bank; provided that the provisions of this subsection shall not apply to profit and loss sharing banks.

The fore mentioned sections were seen to have recognised Islamic banking in Nigeria and provided the foundation for the establishment of PLS banks. Orisankoko (2010) documents that based on these provisions, two banks were said to have been licensed in 1992 to carryout banking business using PLS modes but none could commence operation. In the early 2000s, Habib Bank Nigeria Limited created an Islamic banking window for provision of Shari'ah-compliant financial products based on the provisions of these sections. The bank enjoyed a lot of patronage from both Muslims and non-Muslims in Nigeria though the Islamic banking window was short-lived. Around the same period, few microfinance banks especially in the North and South-West parts of the country had tried to blend some of their products to look like Shari'ah-compliant but without much success.

In April 2003, JAIZ International Bank, now JAIZ Bank was registered to carry out banking operations in line with the Islamic Shari'ah. Although a lot has been done by various stakeholders to actualize the dream, the bank could not see light of the day until recently when CBN granted Approval in Principle (AiP) for it to operate as a regional interest-free bank. The bank, which was originally billed to commence operation in September 2011 with offices in Abuja, Kaduna and Kano, could not start banking business as at the middle of October 2011. An international bank, Stanbic IBTC was also granted license to operate a window of Islamic banking around the same time (Dogarawa, 2011c).

Highlights of the NIFIs Framework

According to CBN (2011:1), the framework was developed in recognition of the increasing number of requests from persons, banks and other financial institutions wishing to offer Shari'ah compliant products and services in Nigeria. The framework whose objective is to provide minimum standards for non-interest banking operation in Nigeria is issued pursuant to Section 33 (1) (b) of the CBN Act 2007 and Sections 23(1); 32(1); 52; 55(2); 59(1)(a); 61 of BOFIA 1991 (as amended). To support the framework, two additional guidelines, Guidelines on Shari'ah Governance for Non-Interest Financial Institutions (NIFIs) in Nigeria; and Guidelines on Non-Interest Window and Branch Operations of Conventional Banks and Other Financial Institutions were also released. The apex bank requires that the framework be read along with the two supporting documents for better understanding.

The requirement to read the framework along with the other two documents implies that CBN provides for three types of non-interest banking arrangements in Nigeria: full-pledged, subsidiary and window. This is not far from the reality of the country's conventional financial system. Under the window arrangement, conventional banks wishing to offer interest-free financial products are expected to separate both the funds and accounts of the two different types of banking activities. According to Sole (2007), such requirement necessitates banks to establish different capital funds, accounts and reporting systems for each type of activity and as such where a conventional bank opens an interest-free window, it will in reality mean that the bank is establishing a separate entity from the rest of its activities. Although the arrangement is popular in many countries, experts have proved that in practice, non-interest banking window is often abused and compromised as many conventional banks find it difficult to satisfy the requirement of maintaining a separate account for their non-interest banking activities. In Nigeria, where banks are well known for unprofessional activities, there is fear that the provision for window arrangement would be grossly abused.

CBN (2011:2) defined NIFIs in the framework to mean: (i) full-fledged non-interest deposit money bank or subsidiary; (ii) full-fledged non-interest microfinance bank or subsidiary; (iii) non-interest branch of a conventional bank or financial institution; (iv) non-interest window of a conventional bank or financial institution; (v) a development finance institution registered with the CBN to offer noninterest financial services either full-fledged or as a subsidiary; (vi) a primary mortgage institution registered with the CBN to offer noninterest financial services either full-fledged or as a subsidiary; and (vii) a finance company registered with the CBN to provide non-interest financial services, either full-fledged or as a subsidiary. According to the document, interest-based banks and other financial institutions operating in Nigeria may offer or sell Shari'ah-compliant products and services through subsidiaries, windows or branches only.

CBN's definition of NIFIs in the framework shows that the framework is not confined to Deposit Money Banks (DMBs) but is also meant for non DMBs. Based on the definition; micro-finance banks, development finance institution, primary mortgage institutions and finance companies are all covered by the framework. Any of these financial institutions may offer non-interest financial products and services either full-pledged or as a subsidiary. This provision undoubtedly expands the scope of the framework and poses bigger supervisory and regulatory challenges to CBN and other supervisory agencies. The implication is that the authorities will have to do a lot to be able to regulate and supervise NIBs in view of the array of non-interest financial activities the latter may likely venture into.

The guideline further stipulates that a CBN Shari'ah council (CSC) shall be formed to advise the apex bank on Shari'ah matters for effective regulation and supervision of NIFIs in Nigeria. This clearly indicates the resolve of the apex bank to ensure that all regulatory and supervisory guidelines are strictly *Shari'ah*-compliant on the one hand, and on the other hand, NIBs operate within the confines of the *Shari'ah*. Under the IBF system, the regulatory authority is expected to play a dual role: to provide prudential supervision especially in the areas of moral hazard considerations, safeguarding the interests of demand depositors and systematic considerations; and to ensure that banks offering interest-free financial products are strictly complying with *Shari'ah* in their operations and reporting procedure. Therefore, contrary to the fear expressed by some naive persons that the CBN under the present administration is trying to Islamise the country's financial system and preach animosity among Nigerians by deciding to form the CSC, *Shari'ah* council/*Shari'ah* advisory board for NIBs and the regulatory authority has always been part of non-interest banking so much that Sole (2007) considers it as a critical success factor for the implementation of non-interest banking into a conventional system.

On audit, accounting and disclosure requirements, the framework obliges NIFIs to comply with relevant provisions of the general financial institutions disclosure requirements contained in CAMA 1990 (as amended) and BOFIA 1991 (as amended) and in addition, to comply with the relevant standards issued by IBF standard setting organisations such as Accounting and Auditing Organisation for Islamic Financial Institutions (AAOIFI); Islamic Financial Services Board (IFSB); and to report and disclose accounting information based on relevant standards issued by Nigerian Accounting Standards Board (NASB). Moreover, the guidelines required all NIFIs to comply with the Generally Accepted Accounting Principles (GAAP) codified in local standards issued by the NASB and the International Financial Reporting Standards (IFRS)/International Accounting Standards (IAS).

The requirement for banks desiring to provide Islamic financial services to comply with relevant standards issued by AAOIFI and IFSB no doubt poses a great challenge of manpower development to the industry. At the moment, there is dearth of knowledge about the reporting procedure of interest-free banking and very little is known about AAOIFI and IFSB in Nigeria. In fact, there is hardly a report or communiqué of conference or workshop on interest-free banking in Nigeria without the lack of human competencies especially in accounting and audit requirements being mentioned.

Viability of and Opportunities for Islamic Banking in Nigeria

The introduction of Islamic banking in Nigeria is timely and very important. This is because the system has proven globally to be a viable financial intermediation channel in supporting economic growth. It also has a significant untapped business potential in the country. Dogarawa (2010) posits that its introduction is a response to the needs and aspirations of Muslim community that has been struggling for it for over four decades. The system is expected to, among other things act as a vehicle for mobilising funds that have been outside the interest-based banking system for productive purposes, in particular for Muslim communities; serve as a means of achieving financial inclusion; attract investment especially from Middle East; provide opportunity for manpower development, capacity building and expertise exchange; generate additional employment; promote quality service and healthy competition; and fulfil the demands of not only the teeming Muslim but also non-Muslim population. Specifically, Dogarawa (2011b) discusses the economic viability of Islamic banking in Nigeria as briefly presented hereunder.

Vehicle of Funds Mobilisation

Islamic banking has the potential to act as a vehicle for mobilising funds that have been outside the interest-based banking system for productive purposes. Writers have shown that over the years, many people in Nigeria, particularly Muslims, have been avoiding interest-based banks for no reason other than interest. This category of potential bank customers has been found to be keeping money at home or in the shop rather than operating bank account in spite of the risk associated with that. Findings of some of the books have indicated that such people are ready to take their funds into the banking system once an alternative is provided. Accordingly, Joseph (2011) observes that the practice of Islamic banking will no doubt help mobilize savings and provide more investible funds to the financial system in view of lots of idle funds in the economy, interest-free banking practice will help mobilize for business purpose.

Means of Achieving Financial Inclusion

The challenge of persistent poverty that has been bedeviling Nigeria since the 1980s has necessitated the need for Government to join the league of countries struggling to reduce the gap between the have and have-nots through financial inclusion. A 2008 World Bank document defines financial inclusion as "an absence of price or non-price barriers in the use of financial services." The essence of inclusive finance is to ensure that a variety of suitable financial services is made available to every individual at an affordable price and to enable them know about and access the services (Dogarawa, 2011c).

Sanusi (2011) cited in Dogarawa (2011c) explains that 70% of Nigeria's population is living below the poverty line and 46.3% are financially excluded. He notes that as at September 2010, the 24 Deposit Money Banks (DMBs) operating in Nigeria have a total of 5,789 branches and when added to the 816 microfinance banks, Nigeria has a total of 6,605 bank branches with each branch serving an average number of 22,710 people.

In order to achieve financial inclusion and create appropriate financial institutions to serve the economically active poor and low-income households, CBN launched the Microfinance Policy, Regulatory and Supervisory Framework for Nigeria (MPRSFN) in 2005 to provides for the establishment of more viable and vibrant microfinance banks that will cater for unbankable section of Nigerians and promote financial inclusion. As at 31st January 2009, CBN confirms that a total of 846 microfinance (MF) banks were licensed to provide micro-finance services in Nigeria (Lemo, 2009). Of this number, only 170 are in the Muslim dominated Northern part of the country (Bashir, 2009).

Kano state, the commercial centre of the North with its population of about 10 million, 95% of which is Muslim, had only six (6) MF banks (Lemo, 2009) and the highest number of economically active poor, while Yobe State, with its population of 2.3 million of which 90% is Muslim has only one (1) MF bank. Earlier in 2008, the immediate past CBN Governor revealed that in Jigawa, Kebbi, Kogi, Bauchi, Kwara, Yobe, Zamfara, Gombe, Sokoto and Adamawa, an average of 75% of the population was living below poverty line and that the incidence of poverty in the three Northern regions was very high compared to the three southern regions with 71% in North-West, 72% in North-East and 67% in North-Central as against 43% in South-West, 23% in South-East and 35% in South-South (Dogarawa, 2009).

A number of reasons have been discerned as responsible for this serious gap despite concerted effort made by CBN to sensitise the people and create awareness on the important economic role of microfinance in the Northern region. In February 2009, CBN organised Microfinance Forum in Kano and Jigawa states to find out the causes of low patronage and/or participation in microfinance by the Muslim dominated Northern region. The outcome of the open discussion indicates that despite its recorded success, conventional interest-based microfinance had been rejected in most Muslim communities, principally due to its non-compliance with the Islamic principles, particularly the issue of paying and receipt of interest (*riba*), which is forbidden under the *Shari'ah*. Coincidentally, Sodiq (2010) later documents evidence showing that rejection of conventional MFIs is also a phenomenon in the South-West Muslim dominated part of the country due to religious belief.

Islamic banking is expected to help arouse the interest of bankable Muslims who hitherto show lukewarm attitude toward the system to actively participate in banking. It is also expected to avail unbankable members of the society the opportunity to be part of Government's effort to achieve financial inclusion.

Investment Drive

Joseph (2011) posits that with the license to set up Islamic banking given to Stanbic IBTC Bank Plc, an International bank operating in Nigeria, the country stands the chance to attract foreign capital through Nigeria-based International banks that will engage in non-interest banking and from new international financial institutions which formerly have no investment in Nigeria but see interest-free banking as attractive or consistent with their line of business. Islamic banking in Nigeria has the potential to create a window for and attract such idle funds.

In addition, the aftermath of September 11, 2001, which has in no small measure affected investors from particularly Middle East who had substantial part of their investments indiscriminately trapped in view of USA's effort to fight terrorism and block the flow of suspected funds for the financing of terrorist activities even after clean bill of safety had been given to many of such funds has made many of the victims who had investment In USA-based *Sharl'ah*-compliant Institutions to withdraw their funds and reinvest them elsewhere. Many of the victims have already taken such funds to Asia and some African countries and are willing to invest more funds in interest-free and/or *halal* (Islamically permissible) businesses. With the NIFI framework, Nigeria is likely to attract such funds for Islamic financial and non-financial businesses.

Exchange of Expertise

Islamic Development Bank (IDB) has always been conscious of the poverty incidence in its member countries and particularly in Sub-Saharan African member countries and of its obligations to play its role to help the countries in their fight against poverty. Having this in mind, IDB has launched several programmes to assist member countries in a number of areas (Khan, 2007). Introduction of Islamic banking will avail Nigeria (a member of IDB) the opportunity to benefit from IDB programmes in at least three ways: (i) support for establishment of a network of institutions that would perform *Shari'ah* compatible charity activities such as *Zakah* and *Waqf* that Islamic banks can use to discharge part of their social responsibility role, (ii) support for Islamic financial institutions with expertise through the technical assistance and training programmes of Islamic Research and Training Institute (IRTI), a specialised unit of the IDB; and (iii) extension of assistance to students and provision of scholarships in the disciplines of IBF and Islamic Economics.

Each of the fore mentioned benefits has a multiplier positive economic effect on the Nigerian economy. First, it will strengthen world's effort to incorporate faith-based institutions in the fight against poverty. Second, it will provide platform for manpower development and capacity enhancement. Third, it will provide more opportunity for people to study and specialise in different branches of Islamic economics. Finally, it will help widen the horizon of finance practitioners to understand the other side of economics.

Employment Generation

Unemployment is a serious phenomenon in Nigeria that is constantly increasing. Tens of thousands of University graduates and other holders of post-secondary school certificates are on a daily basis roaming street in search of job. Banks, given the notion of their fat pay-packages, are considered point of first call to many such unemployed youth. Islamic banking is expected to provide employment opportunity for many of the educated unemployed. Existing conventional banks that may wish to open window or subsidiary of Islamic banking will have to recruit new staff that will complement their existing workforce or even specialise in Islamic financial products and services. New entrants that will be licensed to operate mainly Islamic banking on their part will need staff members from cashiers to managers, cleaners to security guards, marketers, and Information Technology (IT) staff. This will definitely contribute to tackling unemployment problem in the country.

Promotion of Quality Service and Healthy Competition

Two aspects of banking activities that customers in Nigeria complain about are poor service delivery to customers and cut-throat and unhealthy competition among banks. As an alternative to conventional banking, Islamic banking is expected to serve as a competitor that will promote quality service delivery and healthy competition. It is also expected to break the ring of monopoly that conventional banks are enjoying in Nigeria, which in turn will prevent banks from charging prohibitive interest rates as well as hidden charges.

Conclusion

The recent framework for the regulation and supervision of NIFIs released by CBN has opened a new chapter on whether or not Islamic banking is economically viable and of any relevance to Nigerian economy. The framework also raises a number of regulatory and operational challenges to CBN and bank operators respectively. Islamic banking no doubt presents a number of viable economic benefits and opportunities to the Nigerian economy. To actualise the economic potentials of IB in Nigeria and justify the struggle for its implementation over the years, CBN and bank operators respectively need to address the regulatory and operational challenges that usually follow the introduction of Islamic banking into an existing conventional financial system.

References

Ahmad, S. (2004), "Islamic Banking and Finance in the Contemporary World", www.biharanjuman.org/Dissertation_XLRI-Islamic_Finance_Shakeel_Ahmad.doc

Ahmad, W. (2008), "Islamic Banking in the UK: Opportunities and Challenges", *M.Sc. Accounting and Finance Thesis*, Kingston University, London, at: http://ssrn.com/abstract=1349170.

Ajayi, O.A. (1999), *Law and Practice of Banking*, Andy-P Corporate Bureau, Ibadan.

Bashir, T. (2009), "The Microfinance Business and its Relevance in Nigeria", *One-Day Microfinance Investors' Forum,* Central Bank of Nigeria, Kano State.

Birnie, A. (1958), *The History and Ethics of Interest*, William Hodge & Co., London.

Central Bank of Nigeria (1999), *Banks and Other Financial Institutions (Amendment) Decree*, CBN Press, Lagos.

Central Bank of Nigeria (2011), "Framework for the Regulation and Supervision of Institutions offering Non-Interest Financial Services in Nigeria", FPR/DIR/CIR/GEN/01/010, retrieved online at: http://www.cgap.org/gm/document-1.9.49950/Framework%20for%20the%20Regulation%20and%20Supervision%20of%20Institutions%20Offering%20NonInterest%20Financial%20Services%20in%20Nigeria.pdf.

Chapra, M.U. (2004), "The Case against Interest: Is it Compelling? *International Conference on Islamic Banking and Finance*, in Brunei, 5-7 January.

Dar, H.A. and Presley, J. R. (2000), "Lack of Profit and Loss Sharing in Islamic Banking: Management and Control Imbalances", *International Journal of Islamic Finance*, Vol. 2 No. 2, pp. 3-18.

Dogarawa, A.B. (2009), *Islamic Microfinance as a Means of Poverty Reduction*, Central Bank of Nigeria, Kano.

Dogarawa, A.B. (2010), "Interest-free Banking in Nigeria: The Role of Professional Accounting Bodies under the Current CBN Reform", *Annual Convention of the Institute of Chartered Accountants of Nigeria*, Sheraton Hotels and Towers, Abuja

Dogarawa, A.B. (2011a), "Global Financial Crisis and the Search for New Financial Architecture: Can Islamic Finance Provide Alternative?" *1st African Accounting and Finance Conference*, Accra, Ghana, September 7–9.

Dogarawa, A.B. (2011b), "Economic Potentials of Islamic Banking in Nigeria and the Challenges of Introducing it into the Conventional Financial System", *5th Brainstorming Session on Islamic Banking in Nigeria and International Relations*, Nigerian Institute of International Affairs, Lagos, October 6.

Dogarawa, A. B. (2011c), "Financial Inclusion in Nigeria and the Prospects and Challenges of Islamic Microfinance Banks", *2nd International Conference on Inclusive Islamic Financial Sector Development*, Khartoum, Sudan, October 9-11.

Hassan, M.K. (1999), "Islamic Banking in Theory and Practice: The Experience of Bangladesh", *Managerial Finance*, Vol. 25 No. 5, pp. 60–113.

Hussien, A. (2010), "Global Financial Crisis and Islamic Finance", MPRA Paper No. 22167, retrieved on: http://mpra.ub.uni-muenchen.de/22167/1/MPRA_paper_22167.pdf

Imam, P. and Kpodar, K. (2010), "Islamic Banking: How Has it Diffused? IMF Working Paper, WP/10/195, retrieved on: http://www.imf.org/external/pubs/ft/wp/2010/wp10195.pdf

Iqbal, Z. (1997), "Islamic Financial Systems", *Journal of Finance and Development*, Vol. 34 No. 2, pp. 42–45.

Iqbal, Z., Askari, H. and Mirakhor, A. (2009), *Globalization and Islamic Finance: Convergence, Prospects and Challenges*, John Wiley and Sons, Singapore.

Jain, L.C. (1929), *Indigenous Banking in India*, MacMillian & Co., London.

Joseph, O.O. (2011), "Is Islamic Banking Evil? *Vanguard Online Community*, available at: http://community.vanguardngr.com/forum/topics/is-islamic-banking-evil?page=1&commentId=4565467%3AComment%3A309637&x=1#4565467Comment309637

Khan, M.F. (2007), "Integrating Faith-based Institutions (Zakah and Awqaf) in Poverty Reductions Strategies (PRS)", available at: http://ctool.gdnet.org/conf_docs/Khan_paper_BRP_wk.doc.

Lemo, T. (2009), "Opening Remarks", *One-Day Microfinance Investors' Forum*, Central Bank of Nigeria, Kano State.

Orisankoko, A.S. (2010), "The Propagation of Non-Interest Banking in Nigeria: An Appraisal of the Ideological Risk", available at: http://lawlib.wlu.edu/lexopus/works/850-1.pdf

Sanusi, L.S. (2011), "Financial Inclusion Would Boost Economic Growth", *Opening Remarks at the 5th Annual Microfinance and Entrepreneurship Awards*, available at: http://www.vanguardngr.com/2011/01/financial-inclusion-would-boost-economic-growth-sanu/

Sodiq, O.O. (2010), "Islamic Microfinance and Poverty Alleviation at Grassroots in South-Western Nigeria: A Case of Al-Hayat Relief Foundation", available at: http://ssrn.com/abstract=1673162

Sole, J. (2007), "Introducing Islamic Banks into Conventional Banking Systems", International Monetary Fund Working Paper, WP/07/175.

Visser, W.A.M. and Mcintosh, A. (1998), "A Short Review of the Historical Critique of Usury", *Accounting, Business and Financial History*, Vol. 8 No. 2, pp. 175-189.

www.ingramcontent.com/pod-product-compliance
Lightning Source LLC
Chambersburg PA
CBHW030618220526
45463CB00004B/1330